Skin Flutes & Velvet Gloves

A Collection of

Facts and Fancies,

Legends and Oddities

About the Body's

Private Parts

SKIN FLUTES
&
VELVET GLOVES

Dr. Terri Hamilton

ST. MARTIN'S PRESS
NEW YORK

www.stmartins.com

Illustrations by Jamison Gish

Library of Congress Cataloging-in-Publication Data
Hamilton, Terri.
Skin flutes & velvet gloves : a collection of facts and fancies,
legends and oddities about the body's private parts/
Terri Hamilton.—1st U.S. ed.
p.   cm.
ISBN 0-312-26951-X
1. Generative organs—Folklore.   2. Penis—Folklore.
3. Vagina—Folklore.   I. Title.
GR489.5 .H35 2001
398'.353—dc21   2001019170

First Edition: April 2002

10   9   8   7   6   5   4   3   2   1

CONTENTS

THANKS

As she has been throughout my life, my sister Neva Cheatwood was beside me through every phase of this project—so much so that I almost feel guilty claiming sole authorship. From planting the original seed, to getting on the wrong train with me to deliver the final manuscript, it is not melodramatic to say that without her, this book would not be. In spite of a slight three-thousand-mile geographical inconvenience, she selflessly donned the hats of an entire office staff, variously assuming the roles of agent-finder, publicist, word processing expert, format designer, copyeditor, and wordsmith (thanks for all the worms, Roxanne), not to mention cheerleader, financial backer, and late-night woe listener. There are no words to adequately express the depth of my love and gratitude to and for my sister. I am blessed . . . and I know it.

The extraordinary illustrations are the work of Jamison Gish, a wonderfully gifted artist destined to become a household name.

I am deeply grateful to this remarkable young man, who generously—and unflinchingly—etched these drawings while completing his senior year of high school.

A serendipitous encounter brought the multi-talented Nasreen McMullen into my life, and with her the cover I had dreamed of (along with a wonderful photo, dazzling business cards, and a fabulous Web site!). A simple thank-you is woefully inadequate, but rest assured I will be singing her praises for years to come.

The gods were smiling on me when Blanche Schlessinger became my agent. She walked me from doubtful uncertainty to enthusiastic optimism, and was unwavering in her belief that this project would find the right home and the right "clothes." Thank you, Blanche, for your wise counsel, professional diligence, "above and beyond" endeavors, and wonderful friendship.

My thanks to Charles Spicer, my editor at St. Martin's Press, for enthusiastically "getting it" and believing in the possibilities. An additional heartfelt thanks Charlie, for your patience, flexibility, and good cheer. My thanks and appreciation to associate editor Dorsey Mills for her spirited interest in the material and her remarkable tolerance for obsessiveness. And to assistant editor extraordinaire Anderson Bailey, who rode in with the calvary (oh wait . . . he *was* the calvary), my deepest thanks for engineering such a smooth and gratifying completion. It was a joy to work with you. And thankful kudos to publicist Jennifer Reeve for her assiduous "who, what, when, where" savvy and buoyant optimism.

I'm grateful to the following health professionals for their time, knowledge, and wisdom in compiling various sections: Dr. Lonnie Barbach, Dr. Helen Fisher, Dr. Gary Rheinschild, Dr. Roger Seibert, Dr. Lauren Streicher, Dr. Baolin Wu, and Dr. Bernie Zilbergeld.

I'm grateful also to the thousands of human sexuality students who contributed to both the spirit and substance of this book. Teaching was one of the great joys of my life, and I thank you all for allowing me to be a part of your educational journey.

A special thank-you to my parents, Ernie and Mary DiMatteo, my loving rocks in a sea of hard places. I'm blessed and somewhat humbled by their enthusiastic support for my various life adventures, this book being the latest on a long and eclectic list (any day now I'm going to tell them what I wrote about). Thanks also to my sister Sue Snell for her endless encouragement . . . and for keeping the name Snell.

And finally, my thanks, my gratitude, and my forever love to the man who gives meaning, joy and passion to my life, my husband Bill. In an uncertain world where absolutes are scarce, I know this for sure: I am loved and treasured as I love and treasure. I'm one of the lucky ones who chanced upon my soul's companion and heart's desire in this lifetime, and for this I am grateful every day. I was supported in this undertaking as I am in everything I do . . . with love, with encouragement, with enthusiasm, with understanding, with thoughtful input, with comic relief, and always, with much needed neck rubs and tasty breakfasts. I am a woman to be envied.

INTRODUCTION

Throughout history, male and female genitalia have been shrouded in mysticism, celebrated in ritual, enjoyed in intimacy, contemplated in poetry, worshipped, mutilated, scorned, feared, and adored. Indeed, even as we stand at the dawn of a new millennium, our fascination with private parts has not abated. We *name* them. We *talk* to them. We *write* about them. We are *ruined* by them. Sometimes, *we even die for them.* The level of attention bestowed upon—and obsession with—the penis and vagina challenges even the most progressive thinker. It also makes for really good book fodder. And that, honestly, is all this book intends to be. Good fodder. Not a deep, probing gender treatise. Not an analytical dissection of pudendal parts. Not a foray into sociological underpinnings. Just . . . an entertaining read. One that I hope will alternately amuse, educate, soothe, challenge, inspire, and, occasionally, wow.

I chose to write about genitalia because I could. I didn't wake up one morning filled with an urgency to pen prophetic words about the penis. I didn't hear hallowed voices compelling me to extol the virtues of the vagina. Truthfully, I didn't even know the subject would be all that interesting until well after I had committed myself to the task—a feat which took more than a few contemplative moments, I might add. But in the end, penises and vaginas were a natural choice for my initial foray into the author abyss.

The seed for this work was actually planted many years ago, in a university classroom filled with nervously tittering students embarking upon an academic journey into the nebulous world of human sexuality with me as their guide. Before they could arrive at the imagined nirvana, however, they first had to overcome daunting obstacles, such as speaking aloud taboo words like "penis" and "vagina." To further this endeavor, the budding scholars participated in an exercise designed to lessen their anxiety, expand their social comfort zone, and desensitize them to the sexual vernacular. This activity involved clustering students together in groups of six to eight, and telling them they had five minutes to come up with as many synonyms for "penis" as they possibly could.

After a few timid utterances, the room was soon awash in the camaraderie of chuckles and chortles as a wondrous vocabulary began to unfold. At time's end, each group's anointed scribe would stand and read their selections aloud. Round two followed the same procedure with "vagina." By the time the groups dispersed, the word barrier was broken, unspeakables had been spoken . . . and a curious collection was spawned.

Many years, and well over seven thousand sexuality students later, the collection was . . . big (much of which can be viewed in chapter two). And while I never thought of it as anything more than just an interesting lecture moment, my savvy sister, Neva— an idea guru of unparalleled proportions—thought otherwise. One day, when our conversation drifted (as it often did) to the as yet unnamed, unexplored, unselected book I was perpetually going to write, she (as she often did) said, "Here's an idea: why don't you write something about your giant collection of penis and vagina words?" Well, we laughed and laughed . . . and then she said, "No, really. I'm serious." And so, instead of dismissing the notion as insufficient, inconsequential, even a tad insipid, I mulled it over. And in doing so, I realized that as a sexuality educator for twenty-something years with a penchant for overdoing the anatomy front (doggedly trying to undo the "nasty, shameful, and disgusting" mindset so many kids grow up with) I had collected more than just penis and vagina words. I had a lot of stuff about genitalia. Facts. Fallacies. Folklore. Useful tidbits. Odd things. And darned if it wasn't all pretty interesting, too.

Thus the book began to unfold. From glib genital words (and why we feel compelled to have glib words for the genitals) to ghoulish genital activities, to more than anyone could possibly want to know about pubic hair. What began as a whimsical portrait of private part trivia evolved into an eclectic excursion into the genital cosmos—a world filled with sacred rituals and traditions, mythological gods and goddesses, countless symbols, confused anatomists, obsessed worshippers, fascinating folklore, bizarre behaviors, "gifted" celebrities, and a goodly sum of genital gobbledy gook.

One last thing. When I first conceived *Skin Flutes and Velvet Gloves,* penises and vaginas had yet to achieve their reluctant status as media darlings. It was only a few short years ago that all things genital were relegated to the dark corners of the forbidden zone, banned from the likes of social gatherings, mainstream magazines, and daytime television. We heard of them only vaguely, through abstract euphemisms usually delivered with a bashful blush and a knowing wink. But that was then. A flurry of "activities" in the late 90s, most notably the appearance of Viagra, the presidential "Zippergate" fiasco, and the poignant theatrical play *The Vagina Monologues* have since catapulted the genitals from "down there" obscurity into the national conversation.

Now, even polite folks talk about genitalia. A lot. But I'm thinking they still don't really know very much (despite all my years in the sex ed trenches, even I didn't know half this stuff). So while I have no illusions that this book will profoundly change anyone's life, by golly, I'm confident that people who read it will definitely *know* more. And, given *what* they'll know, I'm also thinking—and hoping—they just might be smiling more, too.

Skin Flutes & Velvet Gloves

IN THE
BEGINNING . . .

*"Let's face it, the sex organs
ain't got no personality."*

—MAE WEST

In the beginning . . . there were no penises. There were no vaginas. There were only (brace yourself) *cloacae*—sort of multipurpose cavities that handled both the animal's bathroom and sexual responsibilities. Private parts as we now know them took another hundred million years to evolve. (Imagine this conversation between Eve and Adam—Eve: *"Adam, is that a cloaca in your pocket, or are you just happy to see me?"* Adam: *"What's for dinner?"*) Nature saw fit to attach the first actual genitals to a group of primitive reptiles known as saurians. Members of this honored group include lizards, tortoises, and crocodiles.

SPEAKING OF PRIMITIVE

In the beginning . . . Man knew nothing of the Saurians, nor did he care to. However, according to primitive folklore, he was curious about the penis and vagina, and thus devised a variety of colorful explanations regarding their origins. One of the more charming of these—which appears in the book *Femina Libido Sexualis*—is the legend of the Bakongo tribe located on the Loango Coast (in southwestern Zaire). It seems the Creator, Nzambias, purposefully left a kola nut laying about, apparently as a test for the first man and woman. However, when the first woman found the nut, she resisted the temptation, and wisely warned her partner not to eat it, as well. As the story goes:

DID YOU KNOW?

It's impossible to tell the sex of a fetus simply by looking at its external genitals during the first two months of development. At that stage, all fetuses look alike, possessing nothing more than a single mass of protruding tissue nondescriptly called a "genital tubercle" (destined to become either a clitoris or a penis head), along with a pair of folds (which will become either labia or penile shaft and scrotum). It isn't until the third and fourth month of fetal development that this mass of tissue will become genitalia visually identifiable as hers or his.

Nzambias praised the woman's steadfastness but he did not wish her to be stronger than the man, that did not please him. So he cut her open and took out some of her bones, making her smaller and softer to touch. Then he sewed her together again, but with too short a thread, so a piece remains open to this day.

The Boys' Club

"Anatomy is destiny."
—SIGMUND FREUD

Aristotle Discovers *What* Women Are

In the fourth century B.C., the influential Greek philosopher and bastion of original thought Aristotle (384–322 B.C.) had an epiphany: the female . . . was an imperfect male! This conclusion was based on his theory that women's sexual organs were similar to men's well-developed appendages, but *hers* were stuck *inside* the body, having failed to develop sufficiently to emerge into the daylight. And so was born a deformed child, as it were. Or so said Aristotle:

> *Just as it sometimes happens that deformed offspring are produced by deformed parents, and sometimes not, so the offspring produced by a female are sometimes female, sometimes not, but male. The reason is that the female is as it were a deformed male . . . we should look upon the female state as being . . . a deformity.*

With those words, Aristotle spawned a male-oriented way of thinking that flourished for well over two thousand years.

Following in his wake came Soranus, the second century physician whose book, *Gynecology*, was one of the most widely cited texts until the late seventeenth century. Soranus agreed that women had "interior male organs," and reasoned that since the woman's penis was hidden inside of her body, the vagina was therefore its foreskin, which grew around the neck of the womb "like the prepuce in males around the glans." In other words, Soranus imagined the vagina as a giant foreskin draped over the head of her penis (now known, of course, as her cervix).

Galen Discovers *Why* Women Are the Way They Are

By far the most powerful and enduring model of male and female reproductive organs was developed by the Greek physician Galen (130–200 A.D.), considered the most influential anatomist of early antiquity. Elaborating on previous notions, the estimable Galen agreed with his predecessors that the female genitals were a less perfect, inverted and mutilated version of the male's, with a slight twist. Galen also described the female genitals as a penis turned inside out, but viewed the labia as foreskin, the uterus as scrotum, and the ovaries as testicles. "Turn outward the woman's, turn inward, so to speak, and fold double the man's genital organs and you will find the same in both in every respect," he insisted. The good doctor argued relentlessly that women have exactly the same organs in exactly the wrong place. (Of course, it never occurred to any of these folks that *men* might be the one's misplacing their parts, much in the same way they're forever losing their keys.)

The mindful Galen also developed a theory as to the *reason* for male genital superiority: heat. "Now just as mankind is the most perfect of all animals, so within mankind the man is more perfect than the woman, and the reason for his perfection is his excess of heat," he said to polite applause. Galen attributed great importance to the role of heat, considering it to be "Nature's primary instrument." Women, he concluded, were much colder, "and so it is no wonder that the female is less perfect than the male." When those in power speak, people listen, and these spoken words stuck around for a good fifteen hundred years before folks finally said, "Say what?"

SON OF SEMEN

• The role of reproductive fluids was also potent gender fodder for the ancient thinkers. Aristotle believed that man contributed the "active substance," semen, while women offered menstrual blood as "passive material" for the semen to work on (although he was clear that man *alone* controlled the magical force of conception, and was the true parent of the child). Galen, on the other hand, thought *both* sexes produced semen, but believed man's seed was "hotter and thicker," and women's, naturally, was inferior. Not surprisingly, Galen also believed that male semen was the sole force responsible for producing life . . . and so did everyone else for almost two thousand years.

• Some physicians later theorized that the milky fluid contained *homunculi,* fully formed offspring that were simply deposited, through intercourse, inside the female "incubator," where they were nourished. Daughters, it was decided, were the result of a mother's errant behavior during pregnancy, i.e., eating the wrong foods, thinking the wrong thoughts, or as Galen posited, having a "chilled" body. One thing was obvious: girls were unequivocally "a mistake of Nature's intentions."

• Tertullian (155–225 A.D.), considered one of the greatest Western theologians and writers of Christian antiquity, believed that the formation of a person happened at the moment of ejaculation. Consequently, the practice of fellatio—which culminated in swallowing the semen—was an act of *cannibalism.*

THE BIG "OH"

It was not until 1877, when a Swiss biologist by the name of Herman Fol observed the entry of sperm into an ovum (of a starfish), did the scientific world utter a collective "Oh . . ." regarding the process of reproduction.

BOY OR GIRL? GENETIC SEX 101

Once science determined that both eggs and sperm were necessary for reproduction, their curious minds turned to the question of sex: how and when do we get a boy or girl? The question is a complex one with few solid answers. However, we can safely say this: the *genetic* sex of a child is determined at the moment of fertilization and depends upon chromosomes carried inside the egg by the one winning sperm in the biological game of life. (A contest, by the way, that begins with about five hundred million sperm desperately vying for the honor.) If the lucky tadpole carries a Y chromosome, the child will be a genetic male (XY); if it carries an X chromosome, the result is a genetic female (XX).

Why Men Are Loathe to Admit They're Lost

The Y chromosome has a special gene that carries "penis directions," meaning, a few weeks into fetal life it tells the previously mentioned nondescript genital mass "it's time to make male hormones and turn into a penis." *But,* (and this is a significant "but"), if the directions somehow get lost or damaged, female genital development will take place instead, in spite of the Y chromosome. It seems Nature engineered *all* fetuses to become female in the absence of special instructions indicating otherwise. In other words, contrary to centuries of phallic thinking that ungraciously labeled women as "defective males with inverted mutilated genitalia," the basic blueprint for all embryos . . . is FEMALE. So there.

Yours, Mine, and Ours

Male and female genitals emerge from the same embryonic tissues so it should come as no surprise to learn that they have corresponding parts:

Undifferentiated before 6th week of development

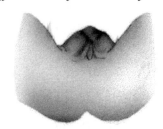

7th to 8th week

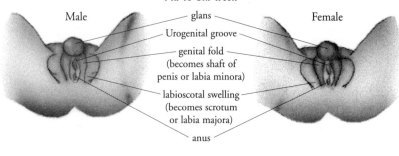

Male · Female

- glans
- Urogenital groove
- genital fold (becomes shaft of penis or labia minora)
- labioscotal swelling (becomes scrotum or labia majora)
- anus

12th week

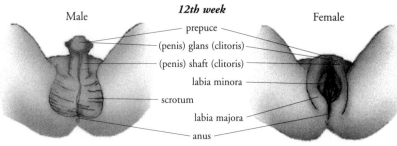

Male · Female

- prepuce
- (penis) glans (clitoris)
- (penis) shaft (clitoris)
- labia minora
- scrotum
- labia majora
- anus

Female	Male
1. Clitoris Glans	1. Glans of Penis
2. Hood of Clitoris	2. Foreskin of Penis
3. Labia Minora	3. Shaft of Penis
4. Labia Majora	4. Scrotum

Does *That* Feel Good?

Ever wonder what your opposite sex partner really feels when you touch certain intimate places of his/her body? The best way to glean some understanding is to simply notice the sensations you experience when he or she touches the corresponding body part on you!

His . . . or Hers?

Private parts may come from the same origins, but does the finished product of one sex have any advantage over the other? This provocative question has long been the subject of heated debate. According to Greek mythology, the great gods Zeus and Hera actually came close to battle while trying to determine who feels the greater pleasure from coitus, man or woman? Zeus argued that the female enjoyed sex more than the male; Hera was convinced the opposite was true. To settle the argument, the two gods consulted the seer Teiresias—who had been both man and woman, and was, therefore, a logical choice. His answer?

"If the sum of love's pleasure adds up to ten,
nine parts go to women, only one to men"

(Hera later had Teiresias blinded for being "disagreeable.")

Battle of the God Sexes, Part 2

Not surprisingly, sexual pleasure was but one of many topics that male and female divinities battled over (golly, just like real life). Indeed, one of the earliest legends of godly conflict apparently occurred over the all important matter of who actually did the "creating." A Hindu myth tells the story of a quarrel between the god Shiva and the goddess Parvati, who each claimed to be the true parent of all human beings. To settle the dispute, each proposed to create a race of people without the aid of the other. As the story goes, according to G. L. Simons in *Sex and Superstition,* the god Shiva, spirit of the lingam (phallus), created the Lingajas, who were weak and stupid, "dull of intellect, their bodies feeble, their limbs distorted." The goddess Parvati, on the other hand, created the Yonijas, spirits of the yoni (vagina/vulva), who turned out to be excellent specimens, "well shaped, with sweet aspects and fine complexions." The two races fought a war, and the Yonijas reigned victorious (needless to say, Shiva was not pleased. Indeed,

Parvati was forced to step in to prevent him from destroying the Yonijas "with the fire of his eyes").

BIG OR SMALL?

During gestation, hormonal influences—specifically testosterone—significantly affect the size and shape of the developing phallus. For the first twelve to fourteen weeks the amount of testosterone produced is determined by Mom's hormones, and if her levels are not high enough, the penis may resemble . . . something else (a sort of cross between male and female genitalia). If something should happen to those levels *after* fourteen weeks (at which time the fetus is creating hor-

---

Approximately 1 in 100,000 baby boys is born with a *diphallus*—alias a double penis.

A diphallus may present itself as a single organ that fissures into two—or as two distinct penises that are located some distance from each other. Those in possession of such an appendage may pass urine from both penises, only one, or through an opening located somewhere in the perineum (the area between the anus and the scrotum). While most diphalluses lay side-by-side, they can also be situated with one atop the other. Alas, men endowed as such tend to be sterile, and are usually unable to perform sexually.

Approximately 1 in 4,000 baby girls is born without a vagina.

mones on its own) the penis ends up looking like a mini-version of the real thing. Fortunately, all is not lost for the boy born with a very small penis due to insufficient amount of male hormones. Believe it or not, it *is* possible to encourage the organ to grow again simply by regularly rubbing it with male hormone cream. This treatment appears to increase the number of cells in the penis thus increasing the size . . . but is only effective when applied *before* puberty. Unfortunately, once the boy's voice has deepened and the pubic hair sprouted, all bets are off for hormonally increasing penile proportions.

Late Bloomers

In the village of Salinas in the Dominican Republic, a large number of children suffer from a rare, inherited enzyme disorder that interferes with the normal development of external genitalia. At birth they appear to be girls, but at puberty their voices deepen and what initially *appeared* to be a *clitoris* enlarges into a sexually functional penis. Thus, the townsfolk call them *guevodoces,* a Spanish term meaning "penis at twelve" children.

IT'S A BOY! IT'S A GIRL!
IT'S A . . . MERM?!

"The sexual organs are easy to locate on the human body. Trace a line with your finger from your navel to your knees. Somewhere along this line you will feel something. If you feel a bump, chances are you're a male. If you feel a dip, then you're probably a female. If you feel both a lump and a dip, then you're a little bit of both but not enough of either."

—DAVE BARRY

DAVE BARRY'S GUIDE TO MARRIAGE AND/OR SEX

What Sex Are You?

Are you . . . *sure?* Typically, a quick glance between the legs of a newborn is all it takes to elicit the jubilant sexual mandate but, surprise, surprise! It's not always the right one. Indeed, millions of Americans are neither male *nor* female at birth. Many of these folks were ushered into the world with ambiguous genitalia—meaning, just looking at the genitals didn't provide the traditional clue regarding the infant's gender.

Today, those who are ambiguously gendered are referred to as "intersexuals," a category that claims an estimated 1.7 percent of modern day babies. In order to understand how and why this happens, first keep in mind that there are at least three ways to define gender:

genetic—determined by chromosomes: males have an X and a Y chromosome (XY); females have two X chromosomes (XX)

biological—determined by genitalia and gonads: male (penis, scrotum, testes) and female (clitoris, vagina, ovaries)

cultural—determined by what we see and do: people who look and act male are males; people who look and act female are females (or so we say)

Now here's the twist: All humans, no matter what their chromosomal makeup might be, can potentially develop either male or female genitalia while in the womb. As bizarre as it may sound, certain developmental mishaps, usually hormonal, may cause an XY (genetic male) baby to greet the world with a clitoris and a vagina, while an XX (genetic female) can arrive sporting a penis. According to a 1993 gender classification system created by developmental geneticist Anne Fausto-Sterling, a child may be 100 percent male, 100 percent female, or *somewhere* in between:

- People born with both testes and ovaries—called "herms"
- People born with testes and some female genitalia, but no ovaries—called "merms"
- People with ovaries and some male genitalia, but no testes—called "ferms"

Thus we have males, herms, merms, ferms, and females. Experts say there may be millions of XX *males* and XY *females* living in the United States. today, with many unaware of their true biological gender. Physicians, exercising the infinite power modern medicine has placed in their hands, generally reassign the gender of intersexual infants at birth, surgically altering them in the fervent belief that the child must leave the hospital as a he or a she. As a result of this medical manipulation, along with nature's own developmental quirks, our population is dotted with cultural males equipped with male genitalia who are genetically female: and cultural females with female genitalia who are genetically male. (It makes my head hurt too.)

His 'n' Hers

(A Greek Tale of Mythtaken Identity)

Before the evolution of specialized gender categories, a person born with both male and female sexual organs was called a "hermaphrodite"—and, in fact, the term is still used interchangeably with the term "intersexual." Hermaphrodite is actually derived from the Greek god Hermes and goddess of love Aphrodite, or more directly, from the *son* the canoodling pair named after themselves, Hermaphroditus. As legend has it, Hermaphroditus—said to be an unusually beautiful young boy—was spotted one day, while quenching his thirst at a spring, by a young nymph who lived in the pool. The nymph—a brazen creature by the name of Salmacis—was immediately lovestruck, and, although she never showed Hermaphroditus her thong underwear, Salmacis nonetheless boldly made a pass at him. Much to her dismay, her propositions merely embarrassed the naive youth, and he rejected her seductive advances. However, the scheming nymph was not so easily dismissed, and she decided to simply bide her time. One

day, while Hermaphroditus was bathing in the pond, the smitten Salmacis flung herself at the startled pretty boy, and clung to him like white on rice. The tightness of that embrace caused the two bodies to fuse into one, and thus Hermaphroditus became both male *and* female, remaining that way for the rest of his/her life.

Among the early Greeks and Romans, babies born with ambiguous organs were usually killed.

The Third Sex

Among the Navajo, those possessing genitalia that falls into neither the male or female category are not only readily accepted, but accorded status and prestige. These folks, referred to as *nadleeh*, are considered sacred and holy, and a family into which they are born is considered fortunate, because a *nadleeh* ensures wealth and success. They are made heads of family, and are given control of family property. Those belonging to the third sex are honored for their ability to do both the work of man and woman.

A HOSE BY ANY OTHER NAME . . .

"Your children have been shown for ten years or more that they are to be ashamed of (their sexual) parts. Some are not even told the proper name for them. They hear everything from 'wee wee' to 'your bottom' to words some of you must strain mightily to invent—all to avoid simply having to say 'penis' or 'vagina.'"

—GOD, AS TOLD TO NEALE DONALD WALSH, *CONVERSATIONS WITH GOD, BOOK 2*

Mr. Happy. Mossy Jaws. Trouser Trout. *Mona.* From pet nicknames fashioned after the appendage's owner (à la "Hank, Jr.")

to euphemisms inspired by the obvious (banana, lollipop, cigar box), naming human genitalia is truly an art form. And a pervasive, not to mention peculiar one at that. (Perhaps you've noticed that our penchant for naming body parts doesn't extend to fingers and toes.) One ongoing research effort boasts a collection in excess of three thousand words . . . and counting. Nor is our propensity for christening the likes of St. Peter a recent fad. Ancient Chinese pillow books dating back some two thousand years provide an enchanting list of erotic and alluring terms for genitalia, although the reasons for the poetic words used by the ancient Chinese was mostly a pragmatic one. Romantic names were chosen because the Chinese found proper names to be too rude, and writers caught using such crude terms for sexual parts were often beheaded. Another exhaustive list of genital nomenclature can be found in the classic sixteenth century work of Indian erotica, *The Perfumed Garden.* And when it comes to attaching *personal* nicknames to a lover's parts, we find that, too, is an old tradition. Martha Cornog, a bibliographer, sex researcher, and pioneer of the genital pet name genre, cites the fictional character Mellors in the 1928 D. H. Lawrence classic, *Lady Chatterley's Lover,* who calls his penis "John Thomas," and refers to the vagina of his love Connie as "Lady Jane":

John Thomas says good-night to Lady Jane, a little droopingly, but with a hopeful heart.

WHY CALL IT A "SKIN FLUTE" OR A "VELVET GLOVE"?

Of course, the question most people tend to ask is not *what* to name a penis or vagina, but rather *why?* Why do we bother anointing our intimate organs? Why do we insist on calling these parts other than their proper names? The reasons, while not as varied as the words themselves, are numerous.

In earlier times and among various cultures, words were often consciously designed to go unrecognized by outsiders, evolving out of a need for secrecy in times when sexual discussion and experimentation were not socially accepted. In other words, people were uncomfortable talking about sex.

Today, there are no secrets; sex is discussed ad nauseum on the nightly news, and people are experimenting sexually on national television. And *still* . . . people are uncomfortable talking about sex. For many, the difficulty lies in expressing themselves with the generic, sterile terms we commonly use for the genitals. Thus, having "special" words makes it easier for people to communicate, and increases their comfort with sexual expression. On top of that, they can talk about sex in public, or in front of clueless friends . . . heck, they can even talk about sex in front of Mom and Dad. An example of this tactic would be the wife who publicly expresses her desire for a burrito supreme to a mate who understands she's not talking about taking a detour to Taco Bell.

On the romantic front, some of the most clever nicknames are created as "terms of endearment" meant only for the ears of one's beloved. These private pet names serve as a secret language

> ⚜
>
> "Pat your man's penis during nonsexual moments. Give it a pet name such as John Thomas; or name it after its owner, calling it 'Junior, e.g., 'David Junior.' A girl I know has long hilarious conversations with someone named Penis Desmond—P.D. for short—who answers her in a high-pitched falsetto voice. This little act is a fun way to humanize a woman's relationship to a man's penis."
>
> —XAVIERA HOLLANDER, *XAVIER'S SUPERSEX: HER PERSONAL TECHNIQUES FOR TOTAL LOVEMAKING*

between lovers, and emphasize the couple's intimate connection to one another.

My Best Friend's Heading

"I really meant it when I dedicated that book of photographs of myself to my dick. It's like my best friend."
—MARK WAHLBERG

Finally, there's what we might call the "little buddy" syndrome, a uniquely male phenomenon, born of man's unrivaled love (and sometimes hate) relationship with his penis. In this scenario, the owner has bestowed upon his organ an identity of sorts, complete with a designated moniker. Thusly spawned, Melvin (or whoever) is accorded responsibility for his own actions (or inactions as the case often is). At times friend and foe, the buddy concept is charmingly illustrated in Jerry Rubin's book, *The War Between the Sheets*. Rubin spent a number of years at war with his penis, which he began thinking of as a "separate person"—with thoughts and feelings of its own—while in the midst of a tumultuous relationship with a woman named Rosalie. As the following dialogue indicates, Rubin's penis/buddy was given to periods of rebellion:

> **My Penis:** *I don't want to get turned on here. This bed is not safe for me.*
> **My Mind:** *Shut up! Perform! Don't let me down! . . . You're humiliating me in front of Rosalie! Shitty, useless thing!*

Which is not to suggest the idea of "penile independence" is a new one. Indeed, in the fifteenth century, no less a luminary than Leonardo da Vinci (a busy man, what with all those talents: engineer, painter, musician, scientist . . .) nonetheless took time from his grueling schedule to jot down in one of his notebooks the observation that the penis:

> *has intelligence of itself, and although the will of the man desires to stimulate it, it remains obstinate and takes its own course, and moving sometimes of itself without license or thought by the man, whether he be sleeping, or waking, it does what it desires; and often the man is asleep and it is awake, and many times the man is awake, and it is asleep.*

Of course, we have yet to discover if Leo had a private sobriquet for his own organ.

A Penis by Any Other Name . . .

THE WORD "PENIS"

Pe•nis (pē'nĭs), n., pl. —nes (nez): the male organ of copulation and, in mammals, of urinary excretion. [1685–95;, L penis tail, penis] –pen*ile (pen'l, pe'nil), adj. (*Merriam-Webster's Collegiate Dictionary,* 1991)

The origin of the word penis is Latin for "tail," and was adopted by the English in the seventeenth century to refer to the male sex organ. Or so most linguists believe. Some, however, say penis came from Latin for "pencil," and that the two words were, in fact, interchangeable. And then again, it's been suggested by still others that penis came from the Latin *penus,* a word referring to

23

a storage chamber sacred to the Roman household gods called the *penates*. Penitus means "something deep inside," and accordingly, the word came to be applied to the "penetrating" male member. (Obviously, the word, like the object it represents, has been the source of scattered fascination and speculation.)

Cock

Certainly the most widespread and well-known of the peniss many nicknames, this popular penile synonym has its own charming and fascinating history. The word "cock" is a centuries old echoic term, derived from the familiar sunrise "cock-a-doodle-doo," of a crowing rooster. According to the Oxford English Dictionary, "cock" hails from both the Old English and Old French "cocc," where it originated as the name for a male chicken. Given the rooster's "responsibility" for bringing up the sun each morning, it's not surprising to learn that among our early ancestors, the cock (a.k.a., the rooster) came to be popularly known as a symbol of the revered orb. The phallus, of course, was *also* known to the ancients as a sacred symbol of the sun (the sun being the ultimate "organ of generation"). Thus, it should similarly come as no surprise to learn that the cock came to be seen as a symbol of the phallus. Think of it this way:

**If COCK = SUN, and PHALLUS = SUN,
then, COCK = PHALLUS**

Accordingly, during the early Roman and medieval periods, the cock (male chicken) was a popular phallic symbol, and sculptures from that era frequently depict cocks somehow transformed into human penises. It was also common to find amulets

DID YOU KNOW?

The cock (rooster) was also a symbol of St. Peter (whose very name came to mean a phallus), which is why the cock's image was often placed atop church towers. And speaking of "Peter," the proper name Peter (Latin *petra*, meaning "rock") was said to be the new name given to the apostle Simon by Christ, who told him "Thou are Peter, and upon this rock I will build my church" (Matthew 16:18). Etymologists speculate that the "rock hard" nature of an erection likely begat the christening of the penis with the name "Peter."

and artwork in the shape of disembodied penises, adorned with cock's wings or bearing cock's legs. But for a glimpse at the ultimate manifestation of the cock/phallus phenomenon, one would have to venture inside the Vatican. In *A Discourse on the Worship of Priapus*, Richard Payne Knight reveals that hidden deep within the hallowed walls of the papal residence is a celebrated bronze image of an oversized penis placed upon the head of a cock, supported by the neck and shoulders of a man's body. On the pedestal of this curious figure is inscribed "The Savior of the World." Knight interprets the composition as representing the powers of generation,

"whose centre is the sun, incarnate with man." Be sure to take your camera.

After Thought
The word "cock" also is said to refer to a "spout" or "tap," such as in a barrel, and some linguists believe this is the sense from which it derived as a nickname for penis.

Dick

In the Oxford English Dictionary, we learn that the ever popular term "dick" came to be used as a penis synonym compliments of seventeenth-century hangman, Godfrey Derrick, who was considered the most ruthless executioner at London's infamous Tyburn Prison. It seems some of the dreaded hangman's victims were sneak thieves who carried short daggers—which for some reason came to be called "dirks," and later "dicks," after Derrick. However, a more colorful explanation for the word's origin is found in Charles Panati's *Sexy Origins and Intimate Things*. While still attributing the word "dick" to hangman Derrick, Panati writes that "since a criminal quickly asphyxiated by hanging can spontaneously get an erection and even ejaculate, Derrick's name was applied to the erect penis that spectators keenly watched for." If the onlookers were lucky, the condemned man died with a "derrick," which in turn became "dick."

Lingam

The Sanskrit (India's ancient sacred language) term for a man's penis is "lingam," a word which implies "sign," and relates to the means by which a male infant is distinguished at birth by his sex organ. Lingam is also a Sanskrit term of reverence for the statues and images of the Hindu god Shiva's genital organ, and the thousands of lingams found throughout India and Nepal on almost every street corner are worshipped even today as sacred symbols of Shiva. People kiss and touch the sculpted stone statues, offering gifts of fruit and flowers.

Penis . . . A.K.A.:

Throughout the ages, the following words have also come to be variously applied to the male member, some for reasons that appear obvious, others for reasons we can only imagine. And while extensive, this list is by no means exhaustive!

Cock, Dick, Peter, Prick, Rod,
Wee Wee, Thing/Thingy, Shaft, Ding-a-Ling,
Wiener/Weenie, Stick, Ding Dong, Hot Dog, Pecker,
Lingam, Phallus,
Pee Pee, Organ, Joint, Schmuck,
Meat, Tool, Dork,
Peanut, Shorty,
Bird, Tree, Worm, Snake,
Wang Dang, Tasset, Knob, Root,
Member, Big Red, One-Eyed Monster,
Sweet Tooth, John, Dipstick,
Goober, Heater Crank, Ram,
Bagpipe, Barge Pole,
Dildo, Punch, Love Pickle, Pisser,
Sausage, Stud, Arrow, Lance,
Expando, Bat, Cactus,

Firehose, Horn, Jack-in-the-Box, Short Arm,
Special Purpose,
Helmet Head, Kickstand,
Pork Sword, Throbbing Python of Love,
Branch of Beauty, Uncle Woody, Schlong,
Bell Beefer, Stun Gun, Injector, High-Hard One,
Ginsu, Bulge, Banger,
George, Magic Wand, Cigar,
Donkey Dick, Dickey (a Junior-Sized Dick),
The Main Vein, Wookie,
Squirmin' Herman, Mr. Happy,
Spare Leg, Third Leg, Tally Wacker,
Unit, Love Muscle, Hot Rod, Joy Stick,
Stinger, Big Bopper, Banana, Squirt Gun,
Monster, Tube Steak, Meat Whistle,
Skin Flute,
Pile Driver, Schwantuken,
Head of the Family, Oscar, Puppy Dog Tail,
Ralph/Ralphie, Pierre, Winny,
Hole Puncher, Pickle, Wally,
Coctus Erectus, Big Mac, Deely Bopper,
Trouser Trout, Crotch Snorkel, Fishing Rod,

"This is my rifle, This is my gun
This is for business, This is for fun."
—MARINE CORPS DRILL
GROUND LITANY (SHOUTED OUT AND
ACCOMPANIED BY APPROPRIATE GESTURE)

Gun, Pistol, Dead Soldier,
Bazooka, Rifle,
Tent Pole, Lifeline,
Manhole Stuffer, Plug, Putter,
Herman, Leroy, Fred, Pete,
Frank(furter), Lollipop, Ying Yang, Fire Cracker,
Plunger, Baseball Bat, Wonder Boy, Sword,
The "Big Ten," Whopper,
Wimp, Limpy, Noodle,
Faucet/Drippy Faucet, Wet Spaghetti,
Hammerhead, Sliver Stick, What-U-Call-It, Rug Bug,
Big Hunk, Cum Gun, Leakin' Lizard, Joe Blow,
Roto Rooter, Heat Seeking Moisture Missile,
Baby Maker,
Charlie, Little John,
John Thomas, Mr. Wizard, Big Thumb, Toy,
Yellow/Brown Submarine, Love Boat,
Melvin, Monkey,
Salami, Peckeroni, Quarter-Pounder,
Bag-Pipes, Iguana, Harry,
Penisaurus, North-Pole, Schlog, Cattle Prod,
Willie, Wilfred (said to be longer than Willie),
Instrument, It, Cucumber,
Cherry Popper, Tree Trunk, Train, Pencil,
Mole, Sex Pistol, Hose,
My Best Friend, Walking Stick,
Wicked Willie, Mr. Microphone,
Jack the Slipper, Hank, Long Dong,
One-Eyed Snake with a Turtleneck Sweater,
Floyd, Ball Park Frank, Purple-Headed Monster,
Mini-Me, Pepito, Binky,

29

Privates,
Satisfier, Flag Pole,
Russell the One-Eyed Muscle,
Herman the One-Eyed German,
Throbbing Crusader, Love Dart,
Doodad, Do-Hickey, Do-Jigger,
Drooping Member, Little Red Waggin',
Candy Cane, Poodle, Probe,
Texas Longhorn, Meatloaf, T-Bone,
Mushroom/Head, Pepe, Skinflick,
Staff of Life, Tree of Life,
Lizzard, Hammer, Harvey, Handle,
Super Dog, Big Fry, Sam, Cobra,
Bufford, Lucky Chuckie, Pirannha,
Rambo, Pokey

Yard: word of choice for the penis between the 1400s and 1800; primarily British. Curiously, yard does not refer to a measure of length, but rather to the arrow, the weapon of choice among men in earlier times.

Bald-Headed Hermit,
Abraham, Almond,
Bean-Tosser, Belly-Ruffian, Blade,
Blow-Torch, Blueskin,
Broom-Handle, Brookstick,
Burrito/Burrito Supreme,
Carnal Stump, Cherry Picker,

The Club, Corps Commando, Cream Stick,
Crack Hunter, Crimson Chitterling,
Flapdoodle, Flip-Flap,
Crotch Cobra, Dangling Participle,
Pink Flute With the Purple Mouthpiece,
Family Organ, Fiddle Bow, Fiddlestick,
Foaming Beef Probe,
Hangin' Johnny, Licorice Stick,
Girl-O-Meter, Godzilla, Goose's Neck,
Dart of Love, Dribbling Dart,
Dingle Dangle, Divining Rod,
Master of Ceremonies, Maypole, Mutton Dagger,
Piccolo, Pilgrim's Staff, Pink Oboe,
Baloney Pony, Battering Piece,
Quim Wedge, Rooster,
Scepter, Stargazer, Swizzle Stick,
Bug-Fucker, Bush Beater,
Butter Knife, Tent Peg, Thingamabob,
Throbbing Thrill Hammer, Rumpleforeskin,
Saint Peter,
Kosher Pickle, Wazoo,
Cecil the One-Eyed Sex Serpent,
Mufasa (King of the Jungle),
Bone Phone, Ginger Bread, Trouser Worm,
Cannon, Solicitor General, Peacemaker,
Thor, Julius Caesar,
Washington's Monument, Little Big-Horn,
Precious One, Faithful Servant,
My Boy, Pride and Joy, Roger and Out,
Bubblehead, Dart of Venus, Spear of Love,
Cupid's Torch, Pants Rabbit, Snake in the Grass,

Funny Doodle,
Ninny, Pud, Diddy Jigger,
Captain Standish, Dam Master,
Hoe Handle, Extension Cord, Rump Splitter,
Thumb of Love, Rocket Thrust, Tent Peg, Hokey-Pokey,
Humpmobile, Big Ben,
Tiny Tim, Little Richard, Little Elvis,
Jade Stalk, Positive Peak, Unicorn,
Sir Knobby, King Dick,
Stanley (as in power tool), Bayonet,
Hammer, Womb Cannon,
Torpedo, Drill, Weapon,
Biggus Diccus

"Frankly, the names of weapons and tools it often goes by are little justified for something that can comfortably be fitted into a sardine can."

—ISABEL ALLENDE,
APHRODITE, A MEMOIR OF THE SENSES

A Vagina by Any Other Name . . .

"It sounds like an infection at best, maybe a medical instrument: 'Hurry, Nurse, bring me the vagina.' 'Vagina. Vagina.' Doesn't matter how many times you say it, it never sounds like a word you want to say. It's a totally ridiculous, completely unsexy word. If you use it during sex, trying to be politically correct—'Darling, could you stroke my vagina?'—you kill the act right there."

—EVE ENSLER, *THE VAGINA MONOLOGUES*

THE WORD "VAGINA"

VA*GI*NA (ve ji`ne), n., pl. –nas, nae (-ne) 1. a. the passage leading from the uterus to the vulva in female mammals. b. a sheathlike part or organ 2. the sheath at the base of a leaf where it surrounds the stalk as in grasses. [1675–85; <NL; L vagina sheath] (*Merriam-Webster's Collegiate Dictionary,* 1991)

The word "vagina" hails from Latin meaning "sheath." In his comedy *Pseudolus,* the Roman playwright Platus (250–184 B.C.) makes joking euphemistic use of the term vagina: "Did the soldier's sword fit your sheath?" Alas, the word folded along with the play, and had to wait a few years before making a "comeback." It didn't reappear again until the mid-sixteenth century, when young Renaissance anatomist Gabriel Fallopio—hoping to clarify just where exactly it was a penis goes when it ventures into the female body—officially conferred the title "vagina" upon the female orifice (perhaps he was a theater buff?). Believe it or not, until that time, *there was no technical term* in Latin, Greek, or in the European vernaculars, for the vagina as the tube or sheath into which its opposite, the penis, fit. Although it took awhile to get an official term, people throughout the ages have not been uninspired when it came to making up their own vagina aliases.

Cunt

"By my life, this is my lady's hand!
These be her C's, her U's, and ['n] her T's;
and thus makes she her great P's."
—WILLIAM SHAKESPEARE, *TWELFTH NIGHT*

The word "cunt" is said to be from the Latin *cunnus,* meaning vulva. Taboo for centuries, the word was banned from print in much of the British Empire until the middle of the 1900s, and is widely considered (particularly among women) to be the single most offensive word in the English language. While early editions of the *Oxford English Dictionary* included records for "cock" and "prick," it did not include "cunt," a term the editor deemed "an injustice to women" (politically incorrect though it may be, the word has nonetheless early on found its way into many great works, most notably those of Shakespeare, who delighted in creating cunt wordplays). Among the many differing views of the word's origins:

- There are those who believe cunnus (cunt) derived from the names of the goddesses known as *Kunthus,* a Greek goddess of fertility, and *Kunti,* an Indian goddess of Nature and Earth.
- Others speculate cunt derived from the Middle Low German *kunte,* meaning female pudenda, and Old High German *kotze,* meaning prostitute. The word has also been said to be a derivative of the Oriental Great Goddess *Cunti,* or *Kunda,* the "Yoni of the Universe."
- Finally, there are suggestions that cunt derives from the Old English *coynte* or *qwaynt,* meaning "a many-layered, in-folded mystery," as well as "wise, ingenious, and cleverly wrought." The use of the word based on this notion was embraced by Chaucer who penned it into several classic works, including *The Miller's Tale* and *The Canterbury Tales.*

Yoni

"The divine yoni is brilliant as tens of millions of suns, and cool as tens of millions of moons."

—SHIVA SAMHITA, SEVENTEENTH-CENTURY INDIA

An honored word from Sanskrit, yoni translates as "origin," "source," "womb," and more specifically, "female genitals" or "vulva." The term is widely considered to be the most respectful word available for the female genitals, in contrast to degrading Western choices such as "pussy" or "cunt," or the clinical detachment offered by words like "vagina." Yoni heralds from a culture and religion in which women have long been regarded and honored as the embodiment of divine female energy, and where the female genitals are seen as a sacred symbol of the great goddess.

Vagina . . . A.K.A.:

Cunt, Pussy, Cherry, Punany,
Ginny, Gina, Love Triangle, Lips,
Canal, Jungle, Tunnel, Pit, Grand Canyon,
Canal, Twat, Bush, Mush,
Keyhole, The Mount, Cunny,
Aunt Maria, Hair Pie, Crotch Cobbler,
Hot 'N Juicy, Honey Pot,
Mossy Jaws, Snatch,
Tuna Taco, Love Machine, Hole, Slit,
Beaver, Bearded Clam, Bearded Oyster,
Poon Tang, Muff,
Fishburger, Fly Trap, Whisker Biscuit,
Black Hole, The "Y" and/or Box Lunch at the "Y",
Red Snapper, Red Sea,
Doll House, Nest, Garage,
Love House, Forest, Hairy Situation,
Sweet Piece, Holster,
Wuss, Giblet,

Love Button, Cocket Book,
Endless Pit, Bottomless Pit, Cock Pit,
Romancer of the Bone,
Cock Alley, Cock Inn, Living Fountain, Lapland,
Home of the Whopper, Happy Home,
Breakfast of Champions,
Honey Hole, Alter of Love, Crack, Fur Hole,
Fountain of Life, Wishing Well,
Gash, Stinky Twinkie, Cookie,
Coo/Coot, Treasure Chest, Drive-In,
Beaver Burger, Juicy Lucy, Meat Taco,
Garden of Eatin', Vegetarian Delight, Cherry Pie,
Tush, Puss,
Oyster Sweat, Slip 'N Slide,
Finger Hole, Pink Eye, Fly Catcher, Quick Sand,
Banana Split, Play Ground, Juice Squeezer, Mona,

Box,
Hot Box, Love Box, Squeeze Box
Sweet Box, Sweat Box, Fish Box
Cigar Box, Bread Box, Tool Box
Toy Box, Box Office, Chatter Box
Jean-In-the-Box, Pandora's Box,

Tube Packer, Pencil Grinder, Vise Pipe,
Egg Releaser 100, Thermometer Holder,
Sweet Meat, Ocean, Home Base,
Cum Catcher, Carnal Trap,
Love Highway, Bull's Eye,
Play Pen, The Deep, Bun Warmer, Slant Eye,
Parking Meter, Furness,

Twitter, Tinki,

Key Hole, Cigar Box, Fishing Hole,

Wine Cellar, Key Hole, Kootchie,

Super Bowl, Wooly Wooly,

Loose Lips,

Salami Rack, Hidden Valley, Gold Mine,

Womb Broom, Hot 'N Juicy,

Cookie Jar, Port of Call, Holy Gate,

Sardine Can, Big Bertha, Harriet,

Peter Pocket, The Gap,

Gopher Hole, Bat Cave, Hair Pie,

Love Canal, Manhole, Spread Eagle, Finger Bowl,

Butterfly, Womanhood,

Penis Eater, Condo,

Catcher's Mitt, The Great Divide,

Escape Hatch,

Crack of Dawn, Garbage Disposal,

Divine Scar, Eve's Custom House, Fig, Fort Bushy,

Open Sesame, Pumpkin Patch, Zipper Snapper,

Sunday Face, Hairyfordshire,

Bumbo, Joy Wagon,

Velvet Glove,

Flesh Blanket, Flower Pot, Fruitery, Beehive,

Black Bess, Janey, Loppy Tuna,

Great Hairy Lasso of Life, Honey Tree,

Bower of Bliss, Cupid's Alley,

Sugar Donut, Cream Jug,

Yeast Biscuit, Yum-Yum Cake, Butter Boat,

Milk Jug, Sugar Scoop,

Jam Pot, Jelly Roll, Bit of Jam,

Golden Donut,

Home Sweet Home,
Lover's Lane, Furnace Mouth,
Temple of Venus, Crown and Feathers,
Cupid's Cave, Cupid's Hotel,
Dark Gate, Ditch, Doorway of Life, Fleshy Idol,
Fufu, Golden Gate, Happy Valley, Hot Lips, Jade Door,
Mystic Rose, Yoni
Pit of Darkness, Pleasure Garden,
Promised Land,
Split Apricot, Sugar Basin, Velvet Sheath,
Fly Catcher, Beauty Spot, Belly Dingle,
Bluebeard's Closet, Apostle's Grove,
Garden of Eden,
Lady Jane, Miss Brown,
Minnie Mouse, Tit-Mouse,
Horse Collar, Bushy Park, Butcher's Shop,
Cabbage Patch, Cape of Good Hope, Center of Bliss,
Cuckoo's Nest, Hairburger, House Under the Hill,
Itching Jenny, Jack Nasty Face, Little Sister,
Molly's Hole, Mouth-That-Cannot-Bite,
Nature's Tufted Treasure,
Old Mossyface,
Palace of Pleasure, Prime Cut,
Rest-and-Be-Thankful, Stench-Trench, Tail-Gate,
Upright Grin, Road-to-Heaven

PENIS 101

·

The Penis Files

"Men are very protective of [their sexual] organs. This is because Mother Nature decided, apparently as a prank, to place them on the outside of the male body, where they are most likely to get hit by baseballs, or punched by small children."

—DAVE BARRY, *DAVE BARRY'S GUIDE TO MARRIAGE AND/OR SEX*

Penis

The male organ of sexual intercourse. A simple definition for an organ that seems, at least to the naked eye, rather simple in its structure. However, appearances *can* be deceptive—and in this case they are—because what you see is only part of what you get. And since the anatomy of the penis includes much that *cannot* be seen, the good news for men (at least those who feel "shortchanged") is that the appendage is also bigger than most people realize. This is because a portion of the organ (known as the "root") actually extends deep inside a man's body . . . back nearly to the anus. Just below the prostate, this root separates into two leglike structures called the *crura* (think: wishbone), which are anchored to the pelvic bones. As they do with towering trees, these roots below the surface give the penis stability.

No Bones About It!

The term "boner" is a misnomer. Contrary to popular belief, there are no bones—nor even an abundance of muscular tissue—inside the penis. Instead, the male organ is made up of three spongy chambers of erectile tissue: two long side-by-side cylinders on the top (called the *corpora cavernosa*), and a smaller chamber on the underside (called the *corpus spongiosum*) along with a rich network of blood vessels. When a man is sexually aroused, the fleshy limp organ undergoes a truly amazing transformation. The nervous system pumps extra blood—eight to ten times the normal volume—into the spongy chambers which in turn, expand, compressing the walls of the veins that normally carry blood away from the penis. And, voilà! A throbbing erection . . . caused by the pressure of all that trapped blood.

THERE WAS A CROOKED
MAN, HE HAD
A CROOKED . . .

Unlike the "rods" and "rulers" often used to describe them, penises are rarely straight and smooth (they're much more similar to fingers and toes in this respect), and when erect, many actually *do* resemble the billowy banana (and we're not talking color). An erect penis may curve to the right, to the left, up, down . . . or some combination thereof, and still be considered perfectly normal. That is, of course, unless there's pain involved. And then we're talking problem—most likely one called Peyronies disease. (Important Note: Penile pain *always* invites a doctor's perusal.)

Peyronies Disease, a.k.a. "twisted penis," is named after Francois de la Peyronie, Italian physician to King Louis XIV of France, who first described it in 1743. It is a strange and relatively uncommon disorder (afflicting 1–2 out of every 100 men) in which fibrous tissue and calcium deposits develop in the space above and between the cavernous (spongy) bodies of the penis. The resulting scar tissue: (1) interferes with the penis's ability to fully engorge during erection, (2) may cause the penis to appear "curved," and (3) often causes some serious pain. If left untreated, plaque can twist the penis a full ninety degrees. The cause of Peyronies remains unknown, but is thought to be triggered by an injury during which the erect penis has been unnaturally stretched or bent (say, a missed thrust or an unlucky rollover in bed).

Claim to Fame

Peyronies (rather, penile curvature caused by Peyronies) had its fifteen minutes of fame when it was widely rumored to be the identifying "descriptive characteristic" of President William Jefferson Clinton's genitalia. The Paula Jones affidavit in her infamous sexual harassment suit alleged that his genitals manifested "a distinctly angled bend visible when the penis is erect." It should be noted that later, doctor's reports gave the presidential penis a clean bill of health, claiming it had "no distinguishing marks, characteristic blemishes, or abnormalities." Only in America . . .

Which Way Does It Point?

• When erect, 20 percent of penises point straight out, 5 percent point downward, the rest point upward. The angle tends to move downward as a man gets older. And one more thing . . .

• A man may be unconsciously influencing the angle of his erection given the angle he places his penis in his underwear. A guy's daily dressing routine (pointing his penis up, down, or off to the side) will eventually affect the aroused organ's tendency to go that way on its own. Kind of gives a whole new meaning to the word "jockey."

• According to Japanese folk wisdom, the fingers of an open hand (with the thumb facing up) give tell-tale clues about erection direction throughout the masculine life-span. Each finger is said to represent the angle of the erect penis during a decade of man's life, from his twenties (the thumb) to his sixties (his pinkie).

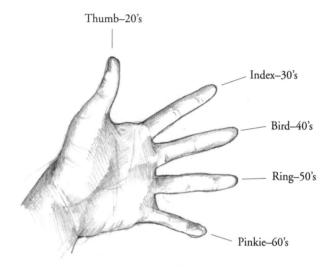

Thumb–20's

Index–30's

Bird–40's

Ring–50's

Pinkie–60's

Decades of a Man's Erection Angle

If Roxanne Had Only Known

In *The Tao of Sexology,* Dr. Steven Chang claims that numerous physical characteristics provide tantalizing clues as to the length and shape of a man's penis. He insists these are accurate about 90 percent of the time. According to Chang:

- Long nose *and* long fingers = LONG PENIS
- Short nose *and* short fingers = SHORT PENIS

- Fat tip of the nose = FAT PENIS (likewise, thin tip = THIN PENIS)
- Thick, wide lips = LARGE PENIS
- The shape of the thumb reflects the shape of the penis (e.g., a mushroom-shaped thumb signals a penis with a large head and narrow shaft)

☙

THUMB QUEEN:

Term used in the Gay community—refers to a homosexual claiming the ability to correctly guess the length of another's penis based on the size and shape of the owner's thumb.

Big Nose=Big Hose?

Despite numerous attempts, Western medicine has yet to uncover any correlation between facial structures—nasal or otherwise—and penile characteristics. Scientists who study such things are equally adamant about finding no relationship between penis size and shoe size, height, hairiness, ear lobe length, or thumb size. However, there *are* some titillating clues to be found in another hand digit—the index finger—specifically, the *length* of the index finger when a guy makes a "gun" with his hand. Actual research from Boston University (seemingly conducted by some guys with too much time on their hands) suggests that the distance between a man's thumb-finger crease and his index fingertip roughly correlates to the length of his sexual appendage.

Sticks . . .

Glans Penis

The glans, from Latin for "acorn" (because of its keen resemblance) is also known as the head. This is the knob-shaped—some might say helmet-shaped—tip of the penis. This area contains an extensive nerve supply and therefore is extremely sensitive to physical stimulation. However, direct, prolonged stimulation can become irritating, as evidenced by the preference of most men to masturbate by stroking the shaft rather than the glans.

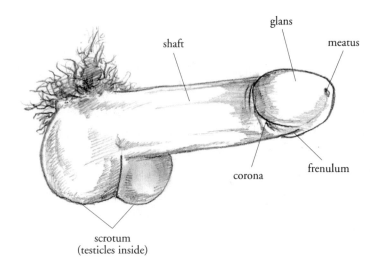

The Penis (circumcised penis)

Corona

From Latin for "crown" (sometimes referred to as the "coronal ridge") the corona marks the area where the glans rises abruptly from the shaft—basically separating the glans from the body of the penis. It is *extremely* sensitive to sexual stimulation in most men.

Frenulum

From the Latin *frenum,* meaning "bridle," the frenulum is the thin, highly sensitive strip of tissue that connects the underside of the glans to the shaft (where the seam meets the crown). The frenulum is generally considered to be the winner of the coveted "most sensitive spot on the penis" award, and is particularly responsive to oral caressing.

Prepuce

From Latin meaning "before a swelling," the prepuce, commonly called the "foreskin," is a loose-fitting, retractable, double-layered fold of skin that forms a hood, or cuff over the glans (think: oversized turtleneck). Measuring in at about 15 square inches, or the size of a 3 × 5 inch index card, the surface of this unique organ represents at least 50 percent of all (adult) penile skin. In some males, it covers the entire head, while in others only a portion is covered. Like the undersurface of the eyelids, the undersurface of the foreskin consists of mucous membranes, and contains glands which secrete antibacterial and antiviral lubricants called "smegma" (a.k.a. "dick cheese"), a Greek word meaning "that which is wiped off." This much maligned substance is designed to protect the sensitive glans from friction and infection (believe it or not, the glans has no skin; it's actually covered by a very thin, moist mucous membrane, much like the inside of the lip. If the foreskin is removed, the mucous membrane of the glans thickens in response, forming scar tissue.

foreskin

Uncircumcised penis

BET YOU DIDN'T KNOW THIS:

The foreskin contains a richer variety and greater concentration of specialized sensory nerve receptors, called Meissner's corpuscles, than any other part of the penis, making it *the most erogenous area of the organ*. Unfortunately, given the frequency of circumcision in this country, most men are clueless about their long-lost foreskins. (For more on circumcision, see Circumcision chapter.)

Shaft

The pendulous portion of the penis between the glans and the body that also makes up the bulk of its size.

. . . And Stones

Testes

Colloquially referred to as "balls," the testes serve two functions: they (1) manufacture sperm, and (2) produce the male hormone testosterone (responsible for producing some 95 percent of the total amount). About the size of a large grape, the average testicle length is around 1½ to 2 inches and just about 1 inch wide. One ball weighs in at around 22 grams (about as much as a palmful of paperclips). Extremely sensitive and vulnerable, testicular injuries (i.e., a kick in the balls) are considered by many experts to be a major factor in infertility, accounting for 17 percent of all cases in one major study. Anabolic steroids, often taken by bodybuilders to *bulk up* the body, frequently cause the testicles to *shrink down.*

In China, the average weight of the right testicle is 10 grams, compared to the European average of 22 grams.

Scrotum: From the Latin *scorteus,* "of leather" (most likely relating to the pouch's leathery texture). The scrotum is the fleshy pouch of thin, fibrous, almost fat-free skin whose primary function is to act as a climate control center for its occupants, the testicles. The word is also related to the Latin *scrautum,* meaning "quiver" (referring to a sack in which arrows are kept, which of course begs the image of sperm as little arrows of love). Typically, scrotal temperature is about 93 degrees Fahrenheit (about 5.6 degrees lower than average body temperature) which is the thermostat setting required for sperm production. The loose hanging scrotum is a flexible organ that contracts and relaxes reflexively in response to temperature changes (a characteristic readily illustrated when a man emerges from, say, a swim in chilly waters, and a source of the expression "I'm so cold I don't know if I'm Agnes or Angus"). During sexual arousal, a great deal of blood is pumped into the testes, causing them to increase in size (almost double) and rise up in the scrotum. If a man's arousal does not end in the body's hoped for ejaculation, the swelling may remain and the skin of the scrotum takes on a purplish-blue tint, an uncomfortable condition popularly known as "blue balls."*

Testicular Terms of Endearment

Balls, Nuts, Family Jewels, Ballocks, Bird-Eggs, Boo Boos, Cojones, Danglers, Gooseberries, Gonads, Love-Apples, Marbles, Marshmallows, Oysters, Rocks, Tally Wags, Thingumbobs

*Singin' the Blues—Blue balls—slang for "epididymo-orchitis"—technically refers to an inflammation of the testicles and the epididymis (an oblong organ attached to the testicles). As mentioned above, extended arousal that does not result in orgasm may cause a lingering sensation of heaviness, aching, or discomfort in the testicles . . . but that's about all. The "condition" usually does not last long, and is easily cured by ejaculation . . . through any means (in other words, most men can "handle" it themselves).

The "Right" Stuff

Some early philosophers and anatomists believed that the *right* testicle produced "masculine seed," with the *left* favoring female development. It is not surprising, therefore, to learn that they also believed the perfect man displayed the right testicle hanging on a higher level than the left, as evidenced in correctly designed statues of Apollo, the Greek and Roman hallmark of male physical beauty.

Percentage of men in which the left testicle hangs lower than the right: 85

Some maladies can cause the testicles to swell to unbelievable size. For example, those unfortunates who happen to fall victim to Elephantiasis (a disease caused by parasitic filarial worms) may find their gonads swelling to the size of watermelons. Medical records describe the case of an African man whose scrotum alone weighed in at 154 pounds and measured almost 2 feet in diameter, forcing him to tote his jumbo balls around in a wheelbarrow.

At one time, the Hottentots of southern Africa routinely cut out one testicle to prevent—or so they believed—the birth of twins (thought to be bad luck)

Say It with Flowers

The Greek word for testes is *orcheis,* not uncoincidentally, also the origin of the word "orchid," as in flower. This floral favorite of prom dates and wedding bouquets was duly named after the testicles because the bulb at the base of the plant looks like a little wrinkled scrotum. Roman historian Pliny (23–79 A.D.) claimed that holding orchid roots in one's hands would arouse sexual desire, and parts of the plant were frequently used in love potions. According to *The Woman's Dictionary of Sacred Symbols and Objects,* when a man of early Roman or Greek society gave a woman an orchid as a gift, he was expressing his intention to seduce her (in the language of flowers).

I Cannot Tell a Lie

In early times, it was common practice for men to hold their genitals when swearing or taking an oath. The Latin word for testicles and for witness is one and the same: *testes.* The words "testify," "testimonial," and "testament" all originate from *testes,* as well. This practice was born of the belief that unborn generations (those yet to erupt from the genitals) would seek revenge if a promise was broken or a lie was told. To that end, during Greek and Roman times, eunuchs (men "relieved" of their testicles) were not allowed to testify in court.

The Bible is filled with accounts of balls-in-hand oaths, with assorted biblical editions referring to the testes variously as "stones," "loins," or "thighs":

And Abraham said unto his eldest servant of his house, that ruled over all that he had "Put I pray thee, thy hand under my thigh: And I will make thee swear by the Lord, the God of Heaven, and the God of the earth, that thou shall not take a wife unto my son of the daughters of the Kanaanites, among whom I dwell. (Genesis 24:1–3)

Hands Off, Wench!

As prized male possessions, the testicles were so revered they were protected by the courts in many lands, and, in fact, prompted a biblical injunction against possible female groping during the heat of an argument (something many women were apparently inclined to do). The Old Testament confirms the fact that the punishment for mishandling testicles was, to put it mildly, harsh:

When men fight one another, and the wife of the one draws near to rescue her husband from the hand of him who is beating him and puts her hand and seizes him by the private parts, then you shall cut off her hand. (Deuteronomy 25: 11–12)

That's right, according to the Bible, any woman bold enough to latch onto an aggressor's gonads in an effort to defend her spouse could potentially have her hand chopped off. (Husband: *Honey! Hurry! Mine enemy beateth me senseless with large stones. My blood pours forth in abundance. Help me . . . aiiieeeee!* Wife: *Sorry dear, but this I cannot do. For verily I tell them, if by accident I handle thine enemy's stones my hand will be his—and I don't mean that in a good way. Thy fate is thy own, babe.)* Kind of makes one wonder why Moses didn't ask God to provide an eleventh commandment stipulating "Thou Shalt Not Touch Balls."

MAY THE LIFE FORCE BE WITH YOU

In early Greek and Roman times, semen was called *cerebri stillicidium,* which roughly translates to "distillate of brains," and those in the know believed that every time a man ejaculated he lost a small amount of his brains. This concept was likely born of Hippocrates' belief that semen was first refined out of the blood; it then passed to the brain; from the brain it made its way back through the spinal marrow, the kidneys, the testicles, and finally into the penis.

Two Parts Fructose, One Part Sperm

Seminal fluid may not look like anything special, but, in truth, it is composed of a precise combination of proteins, citric acid, fructose, and sodium chloride and lesser amounts of ammonia, ascorbic acid, acid phosphatase, calcium, carbon dioxide, cholesterol, prostaglandins, creatine, other minerals, and, of course . . . sperm. Although sperm constitute only about 3 percent of the total volume, the term is often wrongly used as a synonym for semen.

Vitametavegamin?
According to scientific research, the nutritional value of a tablespoon of semen is equal to that of two pieces of New York steak,

ten eggs, six oranges, and two lemons—combined. All that, and it's so tasty, too!

The flavor of human male ejaculate varies from person to person, and is highly influenced by the following factors:

- BITTER: cigarette or marijuana intake; coffee, alcohol (Bitter tasting ejaculate may also be due to urinary or prostate infections.)
- SHARP: red meats, asparagus, broccoli, spinach, dairy products, chocolate, garlic, greasy foods
- MODERATE: having only one or two of the sharp ingredients and none of the bitter ones
- MILD: vegetarian, celery, fruit (especially pineapple and apples), no sperm, parsley, spearmint, peppermint
- SWEET: diabetic or borderline diabetic; naturally fermented beverages

Smells Like Conception

Belgian researchers discovered that sperm cells possess the same kind of receptors that the nose uses to sense odors, suggesting that sperm may find their way to an egg by detecting its scent.

Another group of folks in white coats discovered that an essential protein of sperm which enables it to bind to the egg is molecularly similar to . . . snake venom.

Seeds of Life

- Average age a male starts producing sperm: **12.5**
- Average number of sperm produced each minute of life: **60,000**
- Average number of sperm produced each day: **86,000,000** (The testes churn out 1,000 sperm per second, or 30,000,000,000 per year.)
- Average number of sperm per ejaculation: **300–500,000,000** (Mathematically speaking, 10 to 20 ejaculations hold enough sperm to populate the Earth.)

Population Control?

In the early 1990s, a group of Danish scientists reported that sperm counts had declined by almost 50 percent worldwide between 1938 and 1990. The reason? Increased exposure to chemicals with estrogenic effects, think the Danes. While the study remains controversial, one recent analysis of the original data actually found an even *steeper* decline in man's tiny tadpoles.

- Average sperm count in 1949: 113,000,000 per milliliter
- Average sperm count in 1990: 66,000,000 per milliliter

The number of sperm produced *is* related to the size of a man's testicles. Oh, and one more thing: the size of a man's testicles also determines the strength of his sex drive.

The Fertile Finger

Curiously, the number of sperm produced may also be related to the size of a man's ring finger. Researchers have discovered that the same genes that tell the testes to grow in utero also stimulate the growth of the hand's third finger. Recent studies indicate that men sporting a ring finger that is longer than the index finger tend to have higher levels of testosterone and produce more sperm, and thus have bigger balls than men with shorter ring fingers.

- Average life span of sperm: **1 month** in the male; **1 to 3 days** (once deposited) in the female
- Average size (length) of sperm cell: ⅟₅₀₀ of an inch
- Average percentage of ejaculate made up of sperm: **3**
- Average amount of semen per ejaculate: approximately **3–5** cubic centimeters (about 1 teaspoon)

The 80s rock group 10cc named themselves after the amount of semen ejaculated per orgasm, suggesting they were either very optimistic or very naïve!

Sperm Terms

Cum/Come, Scum, Cream, Jisim, Jizz, Mettle, Spunk, Baby-Juice, Bull Gravy, Dick Wad, Duck Butter, Home Brew, Hot Milk, Load, Love Juice, Nature's Oil, Pudding, Snowball, Oyster Paste, Sperm Juice, Seed, Spend, Spoo, Whipped Cream, White Honey, Yogurt, Phallus Phlegm

THE MALE G-SPOT

The *perineum*, nicknamed the "tain't" ("'tain't the balls, 'tain't the anus") is the hairless quarter-sized area below the scrotum and above the anus bordered on the sides by the thighs. Although not technically a penis part it's certainly close enough to bear mentioning. Widely regarded to be a sensitive erogenous zone, the perineum is sometimes called the male G-spot. Pleasure enthusiasts have long known that massaging the area (commonly referred to as an "external prostate massage") during sex play can intensify and heighten male orgasmic response.

For the Advanced Perineal Pupil

According to Taoist sexology, pressing an acupuncture point located halfway between the scrotum and the anus (right in the heart of the perineum) will cause a man's ejaculation to be *reversed,* resulting in an improved orgasm. In *The Tao of Sexology,* Dr. Stephan Chang says that when this point, known as the *Jen-Mo* (conception meridian) acupuncture point is pressed just prior to an anticipated ejaculation, the man will "injaculate," instead. Why is this good? Well, according to Chang, this maneuver causes the semen to be reabsorbed into the blood, which in turn causes the energy (contained by the semen) to go *up into* the body instead out of the body, as it does during ordinary ejaculation. While ordinary ejaculations are certainly not a bad thing, there is an "exhausting" downside. In Chang's words:

> *Ejaculation is often called "coming." The precise word for it should be "going," because everything—the erection, vital energy, millions of live sperm, hormones, nutrients, even a little of the man's personality—goes away. It is a great sacrifice for the man, spiritually, mentally, and physically.*

As a bonus to reserving energy for the body, men who employ the Taoist technique are said to enjoy longer (up to five minutes) and more intense orgasms. So pleasurable is the resulting sensation, the *Jen-Mo* point has been nicknamed the "million dollar point." (To avoid a "bargain basement result," be advised this technique requires a practiced touch. Pressing too close to the scrotum will cause semen to enter the bladder, whereas pressing too close to the anus will not stop the ejaculation at all. Either way, the benefit of the technique will be lost.)

Ancient Chinese Emperor Chou-hsin was reputed to have lived his profoundly sexual life adhering to the Taoist views of "injaculation." The Emperor, said to possess a humongous penis (legend had it he could walk around a room with a naked woman sitting on his erection), reportedly copulated with ten women every night—religiously adhering to the "essence saving" practice. Alas, Chou-hsin nonetheless became impotent—casting blame for his misfortune on the medical adviser who counseled him. The disgruntled Emperor relieved the incompetent medic of his duties . . . along with his head.

My Penis, Myself (The Tao of Penis)

According to Taoist philosophy, there are specific reflexology points (meridians) on the penis that correspond to different organs of the body. When these specific points are massaged (okay, *masturbated*), energy is delivered to the desired organs. In *Sexual Energy Ecstasy,* authors David and Ellen Ramsdale write about the Taoist sexology of the Su Nui Ching, which teaches that sexual intercourse is actually a form of "mutual ecstatic acupressure . . . when male and female sex organs unite, a wonderful pressing together of acupuncture takes place." The various points are illustrated in the diagram on the next page, where Lung (L) includes the large intestine and skin; Heart (H) includes the small intestine and blood vessels; Spleen-Pancreas (SP) includes the stomach and muscles; Liver (L) includes the nerves and gall bladder; and Kidney (K) includes urinary bladder and bones.

Taoists believe that when a physically and emotionally compatible man and woman unite (via their sexual organs), his kidney communes with her kidney, his liver communes with her liver, etc., resulting in an "all-points alignment." Feeling less than spunky? Not to worry. Even if a couple just lies still, Taoists say "abundant bio-energy is exchanged" and both partners are obtaining the equivalent of a free acupressure treatment.

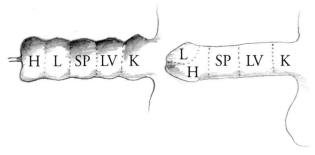

Taoist "sex organ" Acupressure

FROM THE PENIS FILES

*"Women do not have nearly as much penis envy
as men do. Men are all deep down very preoccupied
with their penis—how big it is, how long,
how thick, and how deep it goes."*

—EMANUEL H. ROSEN

PSYCHIATRIST

- Smallest natural (functional) penis recorded on a man: ⅝ inch
- Largest natural (functional) penis recorded on a man: **13.5** inches
- Cost of replacement surgery: About **$50,000**

The word "flaccid" is from the Latin *flaccus*, meaning "flabby."

- Pecentage of U.S. men who are circumcised: **64**
- Amount of blood in the flaccid penis: ⅓ ounce
- Amount of blood in the penis when erect: **3** ounces (The erect penis holds eight times as much blood as a flaccid one.)
- Other organs that can increase their capacity by as much: **none**
- Number of penile implants currently in use in the United States: about **250,000**
- Percentage of men who say they masturbate at least once a day: **54**
- Average number of times a man will ejaculate in his lifetime: **7,200**
- Average total amount of lifetime ejaculate: **14** gallons (The average male will ejaculate 30 to 50 quarts between the ages of 15 and 60.)
- Average speed of ejaculation: **28** mph
- Average speed distance traveled by sperm once in the vagina: **1** to **4** millimeters/minute

---

The word "ejaculate" is from the Latin *ejaculari*, meaning to "throw or shoot out."

- Farthest medically recorded ejaculation: **11.7** inches (The uncontained penis is said to be capable of ejaculating semen a distance of 12–24 inches.)
- Average number of ejaculatory spurts during orgasm: **3** to **10**

- Average number of calories in a teaspoon of semen: **36**
- Amount of time needed for a man to regain his erection after orgasm: from **2 minutes** to **2 weeks** (depending on his age and physical health)
- Average number of erections per day for a man: **11**
- Average number of erections that occur while a man is sleeping: **5** (Erections occur at 90-minute intervals during REM sleep and last between 20–30 minutes.)

Snap, Crackle, Pop!

If the erect penis should find itself bending in a way it was not intended to bend (insert your own visual imagery here), it may be accompanied by a curious "cracking" or "popping" noise followed by swelling and bruising (likely to occur just after the owner's shrieks of pain). The disturbing sound—as well as the pain—is most likely due to a snapping ligament in the penis, which unfortunately, *is* cause for alarm. A fractured penis can result in internal bleeding, which in turn may cause permanent damage to the organ. The owner is advised to place towel-wrapped ice around the throbbing part and *get thee quickly to a doctor.* Timely intervention is a must.

Intercourse position that poses the most serious threat to the penis (i.e., causing it to fracture): woman-on-top

A Few More Phallic Phacts:

• Male genitalia reach adult proportions at approximately 14.9 years of age. A male reaches full adult proportion by age 17, with *no* subsequent growth.

• Zip-a-dee-doo-dah! Contrary to conventional wisdom—along with the infamous scene in the movie *There's Something About Mary*—most zipper injuries to the penis occur on the downstroke. Men who get stuck should attempt to free themselves by pulling the zipper in the direction it came from in one swift motion.

• When sexually stimulated, males under the age of forty are capable of achieving an erection in less than 10 seconds. Kinsey and associates also recorded a few individuals who could achieve an erection in as little as 3 seconds!

Odors that can increase the flow of blood to the penis:

Odor	Penile Blood Flow Increase
Pumpkin pie and lavender	40%
Black licorice and doughnut	32%
Orange	20%
Black licorice (alone)	13%
Buttered popcorn	9%
Cheese pizza	5%
Cinnamon buns	4%

Conditions/activities that can shrink the (flaccid) penis by as much as two inches:

cold weather
chilly bath or shower
sexual activity
non-sexual excitement (i.e., sporting events)
illness
excess body fat
stressful situations
exhaustion

With all of the attention, concern and overall general importance given to the topic of penis size, one would think volumes of research exist on the subject. But according to the folks at the Kinsey Institute, surprisingly, this is *not* the case. In addition, of the few studies that have been done, most were not done well (i.e., they used small numbers of men or had volunteers measure their own penises without any monitoring by the researcher). All of this, of course, makes the numbers somewhat suspect, and accounts for the variety of figures one is likely to see from one source to another. This means that most of the available data relating to penis size are pretty much "give or take a centimeter" ballpark figures. When discussing averages, one can correctly assume there will be many people who are somewhat shorter, and likewise, many people who will be somewhat longer. With that thought in mind, the following reflects the most recent, and reliable stats:

- At birth, the male infant penis (stretched) average: **1.5** inches
- Average length of adult penis (from base of pelvis to top of penis) when flaccid: **3.5** inches
- Average diameter of flaccid penis: **1.25** inches

- Average circumference of flaccid penis: **3.9** inches
- Average length when erect: **5.4** inches
- Average diameter of erect penis: **1.5** inches
- Average circumference of erect penis: **4.4** inches
- From the flaccid state, the fully erect penis increases in length by an average of about **2** inches
- Increase in the average penis length upon erection: **63%**
- Increase in the average penis circumference upon erection: **32%**

Approximately 1 in 100 males is capable of self-penetration (inserting his penis in his own rectum)

For the Record

There is a greater range of size variability among flaccid penises than erect ones. Penises that are small when flaccid tend to gain more in size when they become erect. Larger flaccid penises gain relatively less. In other words . . . erect, most men *are* created equal.

Penis size is largely a matter of heredity . . . if Dad is well hung, there's a good probability his sons will be too . . . or, to put it another way: What's in the Jeans is Due to What's in the Genes.

And Finally . . . How Long Is It?

"Men have always detested women's gossip because they fear the truth: their measurements are being taken and compared."

—ERICA JONG, *FEAR OF FLYING*

Approximately 5% of the adult male population has a penis that measures less than 4 Inches in the erect state

---

An "average sized" penis measures 4.5–6.5 inches when erect . . . well over 75% of all men fall into this range.

NOTE: Reliable studies of penile measurements beyond average simply do not exist, although penis researcher extraordinaire Gary Griffin has tracked down some interesting guestimates. According to his work *Penis Size and Enlargement*:

- Only 15% of men have a penis over **7** inches when erect
- Only 3% of the male population can claim **8** inches
- A **9** inch penis is found in 2 in 1,000 men
- A **10** inch erection is a rarity, possessed by less than 1 in 10,000 men

• Less than 5,000 penises worldwide measure **12** inches when erect

"Whether a long one or a thick one it matters not, as long as it satisfies in abundance!"

—ISLAMIC PROVERB

Bigger Than a Breadbox

"Size Does Matter"

—MOVIE POSTER SLOGAN FOR
GODZILLA, 1998

In the popular game of word association, utter "size" and the response you're likely to get is "big." Like it or not, ours is a culture that reveres all things big. Big cars. Big-screen TVs. Big muscles. We punctuate these preferences with mandates to "Think Big" and "Dream Big," and of course, we've all heard—and *most* men believe—that "bigger is better." Thus, it really can't be all that surprising to know that as man's most prized possession, the penis sits comfortably atop man's "wanna big one" wish list. And lest you think this is a recent yearning, born under the influence of the strutting studs who inhabit the porn industry, think again. Man began coveting the Big One well before John Holmes, Long Dong Silver, and the fourteen-inch *Boogie Nights* schlong became phallic phenomena.

In the *Big* Inning . . .

Man's obsession with and concern over the proportions of his penis has an extensive and rich history, dating back to the earliest mythological tales. Some suggest the probable origin of his phallic fixation can be linked to the god Osiris, considered to have been the favorite of all Egyptian deities. According to legend, Osiris was murdered by his brother Typhon, who dismembered the fallen god and scattered his body parts throughout the four corners of the Earth. Picking up "the pieces formerly known as Osiris" was his sister/lover/wife, the goddess Isis, who managed to recover everything but . . . his penis, which had apparently been eaten by a fish. Seeking to make him whole once again, the inventive Isis had a replica constructed to replace the missing organ, and ordered all Egyptians to revere it like the original. (Isis subsequently used the large golden understudy to conceive her divine child, Horus). When Isis later reassembled Osiris and brought him back to eternal life, her first concern was to restore his ample phallic spirit. Thereafter, Osiris, in all his godlike glory, was hailed as a bull of lust, "The mummy with the long member."

The myth of Isis and Osiris was vastly important to the Egyptians. Each year the death of Osiris was enacted in a public ceremonial during which a mammoth representation of the phallus (gilded and 150 cubits high) was carried through the streets in solemn procession.

Mountain Man

In the first century B.C. the people of England undertook an outdoor art project of monumental proportions. Carved into the chalk hillside above Cerne Abbas, Dorset, is an earthen sculpture representing a fertility god named Hercules. Known today as the "Giant of Cerne Abbas," this enormous figure is 180 feet high with a penis measuring 36 feet . . . about 20 percent of the total mass (in human proportions, Mr. Giant would be sporting a 14½-incher). The fact that the carving has survived through

the centuries—despite the church's ardent repulsion—is a tribute to its powerful legend as a fertility symbol (indeed, at one point in history the "pagan horror" was obliterated by the Christians, but was later restored in all its magnificence). Local women wanting to become pregnant were known to sleep on the giant's penis overnight, and even today, young couples about to be married often have sexual intercourse within the hollows of the vast phallus, hoping to ensure fertility.

A Sign of the Times

The ancient Romans were notoriously preoccupied with oversized phalluses. A stroll down almost any city street revealed a plethora of giant penises: on statues, on the walls of buildings, adorning clay pots, nestled in parks, perched along roadsides. They were hung—with bells dangling underneath—in business shops to bring good fortune. They were painted on the walls of private homes, suspended over doorways, and stylishly worn about the neck as jewelry. All of this was for good luck, protection from thieves, and, most important, for protection from the dreaded evil eye. Many Roman shops and homes had large phallic replicas above their doors that contained the inscription *Hic habitat felicitis,* or "Happiness dwells here."

Priapus, the Original Big Guy

The early Greeks and Romans ardently worshipped the god Priapus, who was endowed with an exaggerated phallus and widely regarded as the personification of the male sexual impulse. The most celebrated of the phallic deities, (yes, there was more than one), Priapus was thought to be the result of an "adventure" between Aphrodite and Dionysus. His mother, Aphrodite, was said to be horrified by the hugeness of his appendage, and disowned and abandoned Priapus. The deserted youth was raised by shepherds—later presiding over the fertility of both fields and livestock. Numerous statues of Priapus in all his penile splendor dotted the countryside and small public chapels, and were incessantly gifted with flower garlands by his many female devotees. Folks suffering from genital afflictions (impotence, venereal disease, infertility) would offer reproductions of their own private parts along with prayers for his help.

Speaking of Genital Afflictions

As if sporting a monstrous penis wasn't burden enough, Priapus also suffered the nuisance of an incessant erection. As told by the

Roman poet Ovid, Priapus was doggedly courting a young nymph, and just when she was on the verge of giving in to him, she was frightened by the sudden braying of a donkey nearby and ran away, leaving the young god with a perpetual hard-on.

Today, the one in forty thousand men who suffer from persistent, abnormal erections are said to be suffering from "Priapism," so named in honor of Priapus (although most of the disorder's causes have nothing to do with sexual arousal, and thus the name is truly a misnomer, given Priapus had a voracious sexual appetite). Modern priapism is most often caused by drugs, ironically, those used for certain types of impotence therapy, usually the penile injection type. Additional causes include sickle cell disease, leukemia and other cancers, and occasionally, a stonelike penis may be the result of trauma to the organ.

Make no mistake about it, this is not a desirable phenomenon. Priapism is a painful condition that may become a medical emergency given that a prolonged erection (beyond six hours) can rob the penis of oxygen which may result in permanent tissue damage. This means a guy can kiss any future erections goodbye unless medical treatment is prompt and effective. FYI: The favored remedy generally involves injecting the penis with drugs to decrease the inflow of penile blood, and failing that, "bleeding" the penis by making tiny incisions along the base of the engorged member.

The fig was consecrated by the Romans to Priapus. They believed the small sweet fruit to be the cause of his abundant production.

The Phallus God as "Phallus Guard"

In addition to adorning religious chapels, statues of the god Priapus—boasting the requisite titanic phallus—were also frequently erected in ancient Roman gardens. In this setting, however, the purpose was a more ominous one, with Priapus presiding as a mock scarecrow intended to ward off fruit scavengers and thieves. The statues were often inscribed with crude poems written in the admonishing voice of the intimidating guard. Approximately eighty of these epigrams survived from the reign of the Emperor Augustus, found in a collection called *The Priapeia.* An example:

> *When you get the urge for a fig,*
> *And are about to reach out to steal one,*
> *Stare long and hard at me*
> *And try to guess what shitting*
> *A twenty-pound, two foot long turd would feel like.*

REAL PENISES VS.
FANTASY PENISES

"Penises in Fantasyland come in only three sizes: large, gigantic and so big you can barely get them through the door."

—BERNIE ZILBERGELD,

MALE SEXUALITY

The Pen Is Mightier Than the Penis

Writers have been penning erotic prose for centuries, hoping to titillate and stimulate with their lasciviously graphic imagery. As one might expect, the penis is routinely featured in the genre, although it's fair to say the organs starring in these ithyphallic tomes are a far cry from those commonly found in real life. This point is vividly illustrated in the following excerpts:

> *That penis was like a dark python sliding out of a nest of brown-red leaves. It gave me a slight shock to see it, it was so enormous. It was soft, yet it must have been at least three inches wide and eight inches long. The testicles were correspondingly huge . . . [his penis] rose so swiftly it looked as if it were being hauled up on a string. It swelled like a cobra, the blue veins pulsed, and the great red glans glistened. (Philip Jose Farmer, A Feast Unknown)*

> *Gently, her fingers opened his union suit and he sprang out at her like an angry lion from its cage. Carefully she peeled back his foreskin, exposing his red and angry glans, and took him in both hands, one behind the other as if she was grasping a baseball bat. She stared at it in wonder. "C'est formidable. Un vrai canon . . ." (Harold Robbins, The Betsy)*

(. . . and we wonder why men worry about penis size?)

Psychologist Bernie Zilbergeld has written extensively on male sexuality, and in his groundbreaking book of the same name, he suggests that the unrealistic portrayal of penises in literature, par-

ticularly erotic literature, may be at the heart of the male's seemingly endless dissatisfaction with the form and function of his
own endowment. In Zilbergeld's words:

> *Real men with real penises compare themselves to the [fantasy]*
> *model and find themselves woefully lacking. Most men believe*
> *that their penises are not what they ought to be. They are not*
> *long enough or wide enough or hard enough, they do not spring*
> *forth with the requisite surging and throbbing, and they do not*
> *last long enough or recover fast enough.*

AND NOW, THE REAL REASON REAL MEN WANT A REAL BIG PENIS

While the bedroom abilities of the penis figure prominently in
man's assessment of his organ, the *true* test of his overall penile
satisfaction generally lies in another room—that hallowed bastion of maschismo, the locker room. Numerous studies reveal
that the size of a man's endowment is significantly less important
during sex with a female than in the hormone-charged competitive atmosphere of the changing room. It is here, amid jockstraps
and Jockey shorts, in soapy showers and open-towel saunas that
legends are made and egos are swallowed. To these men, the big
penis oozes masculine power and sexual prowess, and the small
penis just . . . oozes. This helps to explain why the majority of
men who seek penile augmentation surgery (discussed below) do
not in fact have small penises. Nay, phalloplastic surgeons' waiting rooms are full of average- to above-average-sized penises

attached to men who believe the oversized organ is a badge of honor and a coveted trophy—and they want one to put on full display. It's a guy thing.

Penis IQ

In *The Kinsey Institute's New Report on Sex*, researchers asked both men and women to estimate the length of the average adult penis in its erect state. While 60 percent answered correctly (5–7 inches), those guessing wrong were twice as likely to overestimate than underestimate, with 12 percent hazarding the erect organ was 8–12 inches. On the other hand, women were almost twice as likely as men to think the average erect penis is 4 inches or less. . . .

Questions about the size and shape of the penis are the second most frequently asked of the staff at the Kinsey institute. The only area of greater concern to men is problems getting and/or keeping an erection.

Genital Incompatibility

During the reign of Pope Innocent III (1198–1216), the law held that a marriage could be dissolved when the genitals of a husband and wife did not manage to "fit" properly. If the difference in the size of the genitals made it dangerous or impossible to have intercourse, the marriage was annulled. While not frequently utilized, the law remained in effect for quite some time. "Genital incompatibility" generally involved an oversized penis and an understandably fearful wife, as occurred on December 24, 1613, when the Ecclesiastical Court granted Magdeleine de Charbonnier a separation from her husband, Jean Fauré "because her said husband's virile organ was too huge and beyond the capacity of any virgin to accommodate it."

Crotch Dressing

In post-Renissance Europe, it became fashionable for men to wear codpieces, which were essentially primitive jockstraps stitched to the outside of the male costume, designed to emphasize the bulge of the male anatomy and serve as a visual aphrodisiac. Not surprisingly, men of modest endowment often compensated by padding their codpieces with handkerchiefs, coins, and keys in such a way as to simulate a perpetual erection. Attention grabbing gents would also have their codpieces made up in attractive colors and sometimes decorated them with ribbons, gold or jewels. The largest codpiece on display at the Tower of London allegedly belonged to Henry the VIII.

SIZE AND SIGHS

"Women, we are given to believe, crave nothing so much as a penis that might be mistaken for a telephone pole."
—BERNIE ZILBERGELD, *MALE SEXUALITY*

For thousands of years, curious minds have pondered the nature and evolution of the human penis, the zealous preoccupation with its large (by evolutionary standards) size, and how it got to be that way. After all, a big penis wasn't necessary for survival. It didn't deliver crushing blows on the battlefield. It can't cook or clean. In her book, *The Sex Contract*, noted anthropologist Helen Fisher provides perhaps the most succinct, if not one of the most reasonable and obvious explanations for this unusual evolutionary development:

> *Of all the primates the human male has by far the largest penis—much larger even than that of a gorilla, a primate three times a man's body bulk. The width of the normal penis provides extreme sexual pleasure to the female. . . . It seems that the largeness of this male anatomical part has no practical function, other than for sex, and undoubtedly it evolved in size long ago because women like men with large penises.*

A statement like this is likely to rile men with penile insecurities, causing them to puff up and bellow "Aha! I *knew* it!" This is because men continue to grapple with a reasonable definition of "large." So here's the deal. In terms of evolutionary penises, 5–7 inches is considered large. Therefore, we can unequivocally say, most men have "large penises." In fact, Fisher herself has elaborated further on this point by emphasizing that when it comes to penises, the size most women are *actually* concerned with is the "right" one. Not too big. Not too little. For women, the right one is the one that *fits* right.

Size Queens

*"I'm a size queen. Honestly. If I'm on a
date and I see the guy is not packing,
that's when I fake a backache."*
—JANET JACKSON

Although the majority of women tend to report that they are, in
fact, *more* turned on by other manly features (intriguing face, small
bottom, toned arms, broad shoulders) and that the sight of the
penis is, if anything, silly and unattractive, suffice it to say, there are
indeed *some women* whose phallic fancies do favor the Big One. As
men are prone to do, many of these women also equate the size of
the penis to a man's masculinity and sexual prowess. Throughout
history, biographers have taken special note of females enamored of
the large penis, a passion especially prevalent among the aristocratic crowd. This type of penile predilection is charmingly illustrated
in an anecdote found in Richard Zack's *History Laid Bare*:

> *(Roman Historian) Lampridius describes big nosed men as
> being more virile and well hung than others, and it was with
> these sorts of men that Queen Johanna of Naples (1326–1382),
> a woman of unbridled lust, most enjoyed having sexual inter-
> course . . . the poor woman believed the old saying "Nasatorum
> Peculio" [crudely put: "Big Nose, Big Hose"] and [upon her
> marriage to Prince Andrew of Hungary] she expected the mag-
> nitude of her new husband's member to match the size of his
> nose, but alas, she wound up very frustrated. "Oh nose," she
> cried, "how horribly you have deceived me!" [Johanna subse-
> quently had Prince Andrew strangled.]*

It's Good to Be the Queen

The Queen of Naples was in good company among history's female ruling factions preferring generously endowed lovers. Catherine II of Russia, better known as Catherine the Great (1729–1796) also had a voracious sexual appetite with a propensity for very young, very virile partners. It was rumored that a former protégé and onetime adjutant general (i.e., "official favorite" lover) of Catherine's handpicked "boy toys" for the Great One, selecting the most well-endowed and sexually capable men from within the Imperial Horse Guard. A practice, by the way, that continued unabated until her death at age sixty-seven. (Note: Contrary to popular rumor, Catherine did not die while attempting intercourse with a horse. The lusty Russian ruler in fact had a stroke.)

Pauline Bonaparte (1780–1825), beloved sister of the French Emperor Napoleon, was well known as an unremitting nymphomaniac with a passion for very large penises. Following the death of her first husband, Charles Victor Leclerc, her second (arranged) marriage to a wealthy Italian Prince went rapidly downhill following a honeymoon that yielded a disappointingly small penis. A disgusted Pauline wrote to an uncle, "I'd far rather have remained Leclerc's widow with an income of only twenty thousand francs than be married to a eunuch." Pauline later found what she wanted in a mightily endowed thirty-year-old painter, Louis Philippe Auguste de Forbin, with whom she copulated endlessly at the expense of her health. According to one of her biographers, Forbin's huge organ was inside Pauline so often she suffered acute vaginal distress "based on nothing but undue friction, mostly brought on by M. de Forbin, who was endowed with a usable gigantism."

> MALE: It's not the size of the ship that's important, it's the motion of the ocean.
> FEMALE: But, only a fool would take a Dinghy out on a stormy sea.

The Club

Those men and women enamored of the large penis may be interested in a heterosexual dating club called "The Hung Jury." To become a member, men must measure at least 8"/20 cm in length (measured from bottom of shaft). Benefits include a monthly newsletter aptly entitled "Measuring Up."

A Sign of Masculinity?

One of the most curious findings of noted sex researchers Masters and Johnson, was the discovery that homosexuals had larger flaccid penises than their heterosexual counterparts. On this subject the famed duo wrote:

> *The organ of these [homosexual] men was both in length and width, distinctly larger than that of the control group of heterosexual men: 3.3 inches (8.5 cm) as against 3.0 inches (7.5 cm). . . . It is difficult to offer an adequate explanation for this finding.*

Some thirty years later, a 1999 study that took a second look at archived Kinsey data came to a similar conclusion regarding homosexual vs. heterosexual penis size. According to the findings, *erect* organs of gay men are *also* bigger than straight men. One-third of an inch bigger. More important, these authors did offer up an explanation for the size discrepancy, proffering the notion that variations in prenatal hormones (or other biological mechanisms) that affect reproductive structures also affect the development of sexual orientation. And vice versa.

Synonyms for well hung (more than seven inches) in the gay community:

Choker, Honker, Gallons, Donkey, Tallywacker, Lumber, Swanska, Texas Longhorn, Whalebone, Longfellow, Goliath

Speaking of synonyms . . .

Among the most popular pet names for penises are those preceded by the word "big":

Big Daddy, Big Red, Big Bopper, Big Mac, Big Ben, Big Hunk, Big Burrito, Big Thumb, Big Fry, Big Ten

Also favored are those with those which clearly refer to extra large size:

Godzilla, Thor, Whopper, Megalopenis, AstroDome, Washington's Monument, Jumbo-Dick, Zeppelin

Nasatorum Peculio, Part 2

The queen of Naples (mentioned earlier) wasn't the only one who believed the "big nose/big hose" precept. The young Roman Emperor Heliogabalus also believed that men with large noses had large penises, and thus he considered them to be superior fighters. According to the eighteenth-century physician and scholar Dr. Nicholas Venette, Heliogabalus chose "big-nosed soldiers, that he might be able to undertake great expeditions with small numbers, and oppose his enemy with greater vigor." Venette then went on to point out the folly and flaw in Heliogabalus' thinking: "At the same time he did not take notice, that well hung men are the greatest blockheads, and the most stupid of mankind."

LONG DONG SILVER

"A scene between Cleavon Little, the black sheriff, and Madeline Kahn. The scene takes place in the dark. 'Is it twue vot dey say' Madeline asks him seductively, 'about how you people are built?' Then you hear a zipper. 'Oh! It's twue! It's twue!' That much is in the picture. But then comes the line we cut. Cleavon says, 'Excuse me ma'am. I hate to disillusion you, but you're sucking on my arm.'"
—MEL BROOKS, ON *BLAZING SADDLES*

During my long tenure as a university professor teaching human sexuality, I frequently utilized a slide presentation of variously sized, shaped, and colored penises aptly titled "Plain and Fancy

Penises." One memorable photo in the collection depicted a black male of average-on-the-small size penile endowment, who had offered the following comment to the photographer after previewing the collection: "If I am killed in an accident on my way home tonight, I feel I will have done my service to humanity by dispelling the myth of the big black cock." And a widespread myth it is. One consistently expressed by students in my classroom along with most of the other folks in the world. A myth that gained international momentum at no less than the 1991 confirmation hearings of Supreme Court Justice Clarence Thomas. The judge-to-be was alleged to have a keen interest in the legendary penis of porn star Long Dong Silver, a black Jamaican man who amused fans by tying his reputed eighteen-inch (although some say it was "only" fifteen inches) appendage in a knot. Forgotten Long Dong porno loops were rereleased and the big black cock mystique revived anew.

So. What do the men-in-white-coats (since they're usually the ones wielding those cumbersome tape measures) have to say on the subject? The fact of the matter is, there are *no* substantive studies (although many have certainly tried) corroborating the public's widely held views on the racial penis matter. What we *do* know is this: in the *flaccid* state, black men do appear to have slightly larger penises. Kinsey researchers found the average length for flaccid black penises was four and a half inches; for whites, the average flaccid length was four inches. The average girth for blacks was one and three quarters inches; the average girth for whites was one and a quarter inch (give or take a quarter inch, these findings are confirmed in several other studies). However, the racial size discrepancy is eclipsed when researchers put *erect* penises to the tape test. In other words, the data show very little difference between the erect penises of whites and blacks (also, remember that there is a great deal of variation within the races, and that averages tend to obscure individuality). Most men, whether white, black, or other tend to observe each other nude while in the nonerect state (usually via furtive glances made in the locker room), and base assumptions regarding each other's probable erect size on this observation. In this regard, their conclusions would be very wrong. End of story. End of myth.

Two Guys and a Tape Measure

Suspicions and speculations about penis size and race no doubt derived in part from the astute findings of two nineteenth-century adventurers, each scouring the world in search of answers to life's varied mysteries.

The bulk of what we know comes from Dr. Louis Jacolliot, a French army surgeon sent by the French government to serve in various colonial outposts. Dr. Jacolliot, who wrote under the pseudonym of "Dr. Jacobus X." dedicated almost three decades of his life to examining and measuring the genitalia of semi-civilized people around the globe (one wonders how he settled on this task in the outposts). After gathering an amazing amount of information, he eventually determined that the African male was the race in possession of the coveted largest penis award. First putting his findings to ink in 1893, the diligent doctor concluded:

In no branch of the human race are the male organs more developed than in the African Negro. I am speaking of the penis and not of the testicles, which are often smaller than those of the majority of Europeans. The genital organ of the male is in proper proportion as regards size, to the dimensions of the female organ. In fact with the exception of the Arab, who runs him very close in this respect, the Negro of Senegal possesses the largest genital organ of all the races of mankind . . . The Negro is a real "man-stallion," and nothing can give a better idea (both as to colour and size) of the organ of the Negro, when erect, than the tool of a little African donkey.

SIR RICHARD'S SIGHTINGS

At the other end of the proverbial tape measure was legendary British explorer Sir Richard Burton (1821–1890), noted among other things for his translations of the classics of erotic literature, including *The Kama Sutra,* and the sixteen volumes of the tales of *The Arabian Nights.* He also spent a considerable amount of time observing and collecting notes on the measurements of African, Arabian, Indian, and South American penises. On this subject Sir Richard wrote:

Debauched women prefer Negroes on the account of the size of their parts. I measured one man in Somali-land who, when quiescent, numbered nearly six inches. This is a characteristic of the Negro race and of African animals; e.g., the horse.

Up-Sizing

"I want to be big"

—TOM HANKS'S ADOLESCENT COUNTERPART, *BIG*

Is There a Hallmark Card for That?

In a world where medical miracles abound and wishes really can come true, it's not surprising to find numerous men zealously pursuing their big dream. Over the past several years, literally thousands of phallically dissatisfied lads have opted to place their most coveted possession in the hands of a white-coated knife-wielding stranger, in order to undergo what are still considered experimental and risky procedures—all in the fervent hope of adding the words "well hung" to their descriptive portfolio.

Lengthening the Penis

Today's most common penile lengthening procedure, called a "ligament transection," involves severing the main suspensory ligament anchoring the penis to the pelvic bone—allowing a portion of the penis that normally hangs *inside* the body to hang *outside.* This sixty- to ninety-minute procedure generally creates the illusion of being endowed with an extra half inch up to a possible two inches (but usually about an inch). Following the procedure patients generally wear specially designed two-pound weights (gradually working their way up to eight to ten pounds) around the penis several times a day for up to one year. It should be emphasized that most gains in size are apparent only in the *flaccid* state, with very little noticeable gain in the *erect* state. A 1960s' version of this procedure was referred to as a "Bihari modification," named after a surgeon in Cairo who reportedly performed it on legendary porn star John Holmes.

The Bad News

Severing the ligaments causes the penis to lose its ability to stand suspended during erection, as well as causing the penis to hang directly down, even when erect. In other words, an unsupported penis is a floppy penis. Complications can include infection, scarring, loss of sensation, impotence, and heaven forbid, a *smaller* penis. Yep, postsurgical scarring sometimes pulls the penis back into the body, causing it to appear even smaller than it was before the expense and trauma of surgery. Oh, and one more thing: the newly exposed penis will have pubic hair at the base (which will need to be shaved routinely to preserve the illusion).

> "... to men, length is what matters. It is the numbers game by which men compare themselves to others. On the other hand, if women were doing the measuring, the important statistic would be girth."
> —GARY GRIFFIN, *PENIS SIZE AND ENLARGEMENT*

Note: Penile enhancement surgery is *not* endorsed by the American Urological Association or the American Society of Plastic and Reconstructive Surgeons (or even the American Board of Psychiatry). These organizations emphasize that the procedures have not been shown to be safe or efficacious.

A recent study in the *Journal of Urology* concluded that penile lengthening procedures should be advised only for men whose penises are 1.56 inches, flaccid; 2.9 inches, erect.

FROM THE UP-SIZING FILES

"This is going to change your self-image, change the way you walk, sit, do business, pursue women. You will now act like a man with a big penis."

—DR. JAMIE CORVALAN,

UROLOGIST/PHALLIC SURGEON

ON THE BENEFITS OF PENILE AUGMENTATION

Most common reason cited for undergoing penis augmentation: self-image

- Percentage of men seeking augmentation surgery who feel *length* is most important: **72**
- Percentage of men seeking augmentation who feel *girth* is most important: **27**
- With penile enlargement surgery, average gain in size when flaccid: about **1 inch**
- Average gain when erect: **.5** inches

- Cost of enlargement surgery: between **$5,000** and **$20,000**
- Estimated number of U.S. men's penises going under the knife since the early 1990s: **25,000**
- Average length of flaccid penis prior to augmentation surgery: **2.6** inches
- Average length of flaccid penis after surgery: **3.8** inches
- Average circumference of flaccid penis before surgery: **3.1** inches
- Average circumference of flaccid penis after surgery: **4.1** inches
- Average length of erect penis before surgery: **5.4** inches
- Average length of erect penis after surgery: **5.7** inches
- Average length of ideal penis as cited by men seeking augmentation: **7.9**
- Percentage of men dissatisfied with results of penile augmentation: **68**

"As long as men think, wish, and hope that the size of the penis really counts, then it does. That is the be-all and end-all of the argument. Their minds are made up. It is useless confusing them with facts."

—BRIAN RICHARDS, *THE PENIS*

Do It Yourself

For those big penis wannabes who hyperventilate at the thought of doctors cutting into intimate tissues, breathe easy, there *are* nonsurgical options, although candidates in search of a bigger banana must possess equally large amounts of patience and perseverance in order to notice (questionable) results that take generally anywhere from six months to two years.

Fans of the Internet can now log on to more than a hundred Web sites featuring information, instructions, and a cadre of penis enlargement chat rooms. True to the saying "there's nothing new under the sun," most of these programs are simply an amalgamation of previously tried and tested practices, all rolled into one (i.e., imagery, milking, compresses, thigh-slapping, and stretching exercises). The regimens can be time consuming (up to three hours a day, every day) but the promise is enticing (up to one to four inches in length, and up to one inch in girth—with heavy emphasis on the words "up to"). Two words: *caveat emptor.*

Pardon Me, Is That an Austin Powers Swedish Penis Enlarger?

A popular element of many self-grow regimes is the vacuum pump. The theory around penile pumping is a fairly simple one: by creating negative pressure around the penis, blood is forced into the organ, thereby engorging the tissues. The goal of pumping is to maintain this engorged state for long periods of time, preferably thirty minutes to an hour.

Consumers can choose from an array of macho-named devices, from the "Fireman's Pump" (for the man who wants a real fire hose hanging between his legs), to the "Bull Fighter" (be a master in the arena!). **Warning, Will Robinson:** This activity is not without risk and often without permanent results. Pumpers may experience temporary impotence, bruising, broken capillaries, and painful blisters.

"Lose" to Gain

Here's another nonsurgical idea: lose thirty-five pounds. According to urologists (and they ought to know), doctors "never see fat men with big penises or emaciated men with small penises." As a man gains weight, the pad of fat surrounding the base of the penis gains as well, which diminishes the appearance of the penile shaft. For every thirty-five pounds *gained,* it's said an inch of penis length is *lost.*

If all else fails, create the illusion of a longer penis by removing some of the shaft-obscuring pubic hair surrounding the base of the penis. Shave directly straight up the penile shaft about an inch onto the pubis (not too high, for a natural look) . . . and bingo! An instantly longer penis (only your hairdresser knows for sure).

"If you've run out of luck, it doesn't matter how long your penis is."
—JUVENAL, ROMAN SATIRIST

WHAT BECOMES A LEGEND MOST?

No chapter on big penises would be complete without at least acknowledging a few famous flutes notable for more than their talent and prestige. Of course, it should be noted that this type of private part information is *purely* speculative, garnered through dubious methodology that wouldn't stand up to rigorous critique.

And while curious minds may wonder about the attributes of contemporary celebrities, polite courtesy shall leave them respectfully zipped. Thus, the list below—with one legendary exception—includes only those "gone but not forgotten" gents who were truly . . . larger than life.

Most of the following names can be found in Leigh Rutledge's, *The New Gay Book of Lists*.

May They Rest with Their Piece

Charlie Chaplin (1889–1977), *comedian/actor/director.*
This celebrated 1920s artist may be best remembered for his silent screen antics as a mustachioed clown, but when it came to his genitalia, the "Little Tramp" was anything *but* little. Chaplin was known to cheerfully boast of his purported twelve-incher, referring to it as "The eighth wonder of the world" (which probably accounts for his success as one of Hollywood's most prolific womanizers).

Frank Sinatra (1915–1998), *singer.*
When the famed crooner's second wife, voluptuous actress Ava Gardner, was asked by the press what she saw in the "one hun-

dred and twenty pound runt," the brazen beauty replied, "Well, there's only ten pounds of Frank, but there's one hundred and ten pounds of cock!" The multiwed Gardner was equally effusive about Sinatra's skill with said organ, referring to him in her auto-biography as her "greatest lover."

Aristotle Onassis (1906–1975), *Greek Shipping Tycoon.*
A man said to be obsessively proud of his endowment, Onassis often referred to his huge penis as "the secret of my success," and once dragged an obnoxious reporter into a men's room to prove just how well-hung he was. In the Terrence McNalley Broadway play *Master Class* (1995), the Maria Callas character (Callas, of course, was Onassis's soul mate and lover of many years) sighs that Onassis was hung "like a fucking bull—and he let everybody know it."

Lyndon Baines Johnson (LBJ) (1908–1973), *former president of the United States.*
Quite possibly the original Texas Longhorn (although he referred to his own organ as "Jumbo"), the Democratic president enjoyed nude group swim sessions with his often reluctant Cabinet, and enjoyed intimidating his subordinates with his presidential penis. Johnson obviously reigned at a time that knew not of political correctness or special prosecutors, as evidenced by his reported fondness for spewing phallic comments such as "Gentlemen, I have a hard-on for the Presidency" and "I don't trust a man until I have his pecker in my pocket."

Jimi Hendrix (1942–1970), *acid rock singer/guitarist.*
The rock 'n' roll guitar virtuoso was known as one of the most sexual performers in history. During his outlandish perfor-

mances, the musician frequently played his guitar with his crotch—thrusting the instrument against his groin, rubbing it between his legs, and ending the orgasmic episode by smashing the guitar to bits. According to legend, Hendrix was the consummate superstud, with a massive corresponding member described by groupies as "damn near as big as his guitar."

Groucho Marx (1890–1977), *comedian/actor.*
A brilliant quipster, this sardonic funnyman was well known in Hollywood circles to be gifted with *more* than considerable comedic talent. Indeed, as a master of sexual innuendo, the irreverent Marx was surely alluding to his "sizable cigar" in the classic film *A Night at the Opera,* where, while shredding some paper to a certain size, he cracks, "mine's a twelve and a half." (One can't help but wonder if "I just shot an elephant in my pajamas . . . how it got in there I'll never know" was yet another veiled reference to his own splendid "trunk.")

John Dillinger (1902–1934), *bank robber.*
The notorious 1930s gangster was said to relish rumors that circulated regarding the "big gun" he packed in his pants—rumors which persisted long after the law caught up with public enemy number one. For years it's been thought Dillinger's legendary penis—which "grew" with each new round of gossip until it reached a whopping fourteen inches—was preserved in a glass container filled with formaldehyde, and hidden in a back room of the Smithsonian Institute. Although the Smithsonian folks say they have no such exhibit in their possession, they nonetheless receive over a hundred inquiries a year to see the fabled organ.

Gary Cooper 1901–1961), *actor*.

He became a star by portraying strong and silent heroes in such classic films as *High Noon* and *Sergeant York,* but it was his heroic endowment that made Coop a star among Hollywood's leading ladies. His penile proportions could often be seen under his slacks, while many an actress reported feeling it during love scenes—even through heavy skirts. Clara Bow, his first lover of note, once boasted to Hedda Hopper that Cooper was "hung like a horse and could go all night"; and sultry Tallulah Bankhead, when asked why she was leaving New York for Hollywood in the 1940s, retorted, "for money . . . and to fuck that divine Gary Cooper."

HALL OF FAMER

Milton Berle's generous endowment is a well-established fact in the entertainment industry, having garnered the unofficial title "King Cock of Hollywood." Along with late actor Forrest Tucker, Berle co-founded The Long Schlong Club of Bel Air, which had a standing rule that one must be hung at least ten inches to join. (Glamorous 1940s star and pinup gal Betty Gable reportedly once remarked "They say the two best-hung men in Hollywood are Forrest Tucker and Milton Berle. What a shame—it's never the handsome ones. The bigger they are, the homelier.")

Show 'N' Tell . . .

One of the most popular stories related to Berle's impressive attribute involves a men's room encounter with a penile challenger demanding a "show and measure." According to Berle (who tells his own version in his autobiography) the confrontation actually took place in a steam bath locker room. A "friend of a friend" wanted to bet his penis was larger than Berle's, and kept pestering the comedian until their mutual friend interceded. "Go ahead Milton," he said. "Just take out enough to win." Ba-rump-bump.

Les Petites

"I am six feet tall and weigh 185 pounds. My penis is four and a half inches erect. Exposing it to another person is like showing up at the Indianapolis 500 in a VW Bug."

—PAUL LYONS, WRITER,
DETAILS MAGAZINE

While most of the male population throughout the ages was (and of course, still is) deeply enamored of the prodigious penis, it's important to note that the overly large appendage was not, historically speaking, a universal preoccupation. Curiously, the ancient Greeks, whose culture was epitomized by the erect phallus, preferred the small dainty type. A peek at the Greeks' effusive painted history reveals that although these ancients frequently adorned their gods with massively endowed penises, *humans* were admired for their small, firm penises. Large members were considered to be abnormal, aesthetically unappealing, even comical, and were banished to the likes of caricature or barbarians. Part of the predilection for small genitals came from Aristotle's speculation that a small penis was capable of greater fertility than a large one, because sperm had less distance to travel and therefore was more "hot and potent." Likewise, the early Hindus also esteemed the small human penis as the epitome of manhood, reserving their worshipful admiration of large phalluses to icons. Indeed, men who feel under-endowed may find penile solace in these prophetic words found in the *Ananga Ranga* (the classic medieval Indian sex manual):

> *"The man whose lingam is very long, will be wretchedly poor.*
> *The man whose lingam is thin, will ever be very lucky.*
> *And the man whose lingam is short, will be a Rajah."*

THE SMALL PENIS SYNDROME

[The Penis] is the objective correlative of self-esteem,
both the source and the embodiment of virility.
The man who feels inadequate is convinced his penis
is small, just as the man with the small
penis feels inadequate.

—JACQUES LACAN,
THE MEANING OF THE PHALLUS

Power. Virility. Fertility. Sexual magnetism. Sexual prowess. Success. To countless men, these concepts are associated with, and rooted in, the big penis. Ergo, the origins of the dreaded "small penis syndrome." Simply put, the more importance men attach to the penis, the smaller it becomes (or so say Lacanian theorists, who also say this is why all men feel castrated). While men with plus-sized penises may escape this penile neurosis, psychiatrist Gifford Chase, author of *Sex in the Fast Lane,* theorized that men with small and average-sized penises suffer from feelings of inadequacy all their lives. Says Chase:

> *A man's phallus is unquestionably his most prized possession. A small or short penis is more humiliating to a male than a Cyrano-sized nose or early baldness . . . an outsized organ is a badge of emotional merit, which, if absent, makes him feel he is somehow a failure as a man.*

These feelings of ineptitude help to explain somewhat the droves of men seeking the services of phallastic surgeons, hoping the nip and expand procedure will allow them, and their egos, a taste of big penis life.

Why Does a Guy Think His Own Penis Is Small and Where the Heck Does He See Other Guys' Penises, Anyway?

"The worst thing is to have a poor miserable pathetic little winkle; the best thing is to have a monstrous-looking creature . . . as big as a baby's fist with a crab apple in it. However big, the man wishes his penis were bigger."
—BRIAN RICHARDS, *THE PENIS*

A guy usually makes penile observations and comparisons in the locker room—where his is always smaller because he's looking down at it. Also, recent studies show that men almost always check out the neighbor while standing at the urinal in the men's room (where his is still smaller 'cause while he's looking sideways at Joe Bob he's still looking down at his—a phenomenon called the "foreshortening effect"). It's important to note that these situations generally feature flaccid penises, which are no indication of the size of a guy's erection. Insecure men would do well to remember this: the smaller the (flaccid) penis, the proportionally greater the erection and, more important, *there is relatively little variation among men in the size of their erections.* Honest.

"It is not basically a question of the size in repose, it is the size that it *becomes*."

—Ernest Hemingway, consoling F. Scott Fitzgerald.

Synonyms for Small Meat in the Gay Community:

Dinky, IBM (Itty Bitty Meat), Minnow, Peepee Meat, Pencil, Pinkie, Short Circuit, Wagette (Little Red Waggin'), Tad, Drip Dry (Too Short to Shake), Miss Rhode Island (the smallest state), Tiny Tot, Baby Huey, Pee Wee

Environmental Penis Hazard

Recent research has suggested that penises (attached to humans and animals alike) may be getting smaller. The reason? Lingering

SMALL MEAT:

a term used in the gay community to refer to a "little" penis (usu-ally under six inches) symbolized by holding the little finger erect. To a size queen,* anything under ten inches is small meat "Only nine inches? Sorry to hear about your deformity."

*Size queen: a homosexual man attracted solely by the penis length of his subject (although in recent years the term has been co-opted by women who prefer sexual partners who are considered "hung" as well).

effects of DDT in the environment. When the chemical breaks down, it decomposes into a number of estrogen-related com-pounds, which eventually enter the food and water supply. Ingestion of these substances during pregnancy affects hormon-al production—hormones influence phallic development in the fetus—and all of this results in a smaller penis. Yet *another* good reason to clean up the environment.

Small Penis "Virus"

In 1998, computer terminals belonging to selected members of the British House of Commons were dealt a special mock virus: when the user logged on, he was greeted with a computer error message that informed him he must answer a question to unlock the system. The question: "Do you have a small penis? Yes or no." The problem: Typing the word "no" would not get the befuddled user out. Only a "yes" answer yielded a response, which was then relayed around the system.

> "A faithful wife has no knowledge of big and little penises."
>
> —JAPANESE PROVERB

PENISES AND PARTNERS

"The arguments of women who say that it is performance,
not size that matters most are lost on the wind.
Nothing will ever convince the average man
that big is not best."
—BRIAN RICHARDS, *THE PENIS*

And that's such a shame too, because the fact of the matter is, *most* women aren't half as interested in penis size as men are. Not all, but definitely most. Surveys repeatedly show that the majority of women prefer average-size penises—conveniently, the size that most men have. In understanding and accepting why this is so, it's helpful to keep in mind some basic precepts regarding female anatomy and response: (1) the clitoris, not the vagina, is the primary organ of sexual pleasure, (2) friction to the outer third—the first one and a half inches of the vagina—is what counts, which means (3) thickness (girth) is more important than length, and finally, (4) they don't call the vagina the "accommodating organ" for nothing (this clever orifice adapts to fit snugly around almost any sized penis). Most women are all too aware that penile size is no prediction of the gentleness and skill (including touching, kissing, caressing, and tongue technique) of the owner. There is a great deal of truth and wisdom in the old saying: "It's not what you've got, it's what you do with what you've got that counts." Men are encouraged to "take a moment" over this one. . . .

The Penis Letters

While most men fervently believe that women want—in fact, need—a larger than average penis, *The New Kinsey Report on Human Sexuality* says "au contraire." Letters received by the Kinsey staff suggest that when women *are* concerned about penis size (not too often), it's because they think their partner's penis is *too big*. . . not too small. As one might guess, men who write to the Institute on this topic (many) worry their penis is too small. Once again, women who write, the penis is too big. Men who write, it's too small. Go figure . . .

Early Words of Wisdom

In 1687 French surgeon Dr. Nicholas Venette penned a wildly popular love and sex manual for married couples, *Tableau de l'Amour Conjugale,* ("The Mysteries of Conjugal Love Reveal'd") in which he provided this sage advice regarding "appropriate" size of male genitalia:

> *Penises that are too long or too fat are not the best, either for recreation or procreation. They irritate women and signify nothing special. If for no other reason than to make the sex act easier, the man's member should be medium sized. The thickness of a penis is not as annoying to a woman as excessive length.*

And the following from *The Perfumed Garden* by Shaykh Nefzawi:

If your member is short, lay the woman on her back and raise her legs in the air so that her toes touch her ears. Her buttocks being thus raised, the vulva is thrown forward. Now introduce your member.

Mark Twain Mocks the "Mammoth Cods"

Most people are well acquainted with the popular writings of humorist Mark Twain. Most people are *not,* however, acquainted with some of his more controversial works: privately printed essays and poems that reveal the literary master's penchant for bawdy humor. One such piece, *The Mammoth Cod Club,* was unveiled courtesy of the dogged sleuthing of erotic folklorist Gershon Legman, who found it in an unpublished anthology wrongly attributed to another humorist. Legman's detective work also uncovered the events that led Twain to pen the piece. In 1902, the novelist was invited on a sailing trip hosted by millionaire Henry H. Rogers, Twain's literary backer and investment counselor. Aboard Rogers's yacht would be an elitist group of high rollers devoted to drinking, gambling, ribald revelry . . . and cod fishing. In true "fish story" fashion, these gents had dubbed themselves "The Mammoth Cods" ("cod" being an old-fashioned euphemism for penis). Twain was unable to attend the event, but he did send along a poem (which he dubbed a "song") and a speech to be read after dinner . . . essentially a rousing spoof of the society's self-proclaimed "cod" superiority.

An excerpt from the "song" (which Twain imagined would

be "sung by hundreds of sweet, guileless children" in Sunday school):

> *Of beasts, man is the only one*
> *Created by our God*
> *Who purposely, and for mere fun*
> *Plays with his Mammoth Cod!*

And the following from Twain's cod-bashing essay:

> *I fail to see any special merit in penises of more than the usual size. What more can they achieve than the smaller ones? I have read history very carefully, and nowhere find it of record that the sires of Washington, Bonaparte, Franklin, Julius Caesar, or any of the other worthies whose names illuminate history, were especially developed; and as it is not a matter of history, it is fair to assume that they carried regular sizes. In this, as in everything else, quality is more to be considered than quantity. It is the searching, not the splitting weapon that is of use.*

The club Small, Etc. began in 1986 as a support service for men self-conscious about the size of their penis (even though most of its reported fifteen hundred members are said to actually fall within the normal range). This piffling penis club publishes a quarterly magazine called *Small Gazette: The Smaller Man's Forum*, where guys who feel small can chat with other small feeling guys about the benefits of, what else? Being small.

THE KING OF
SMALL PENISES

"How small is my penis? Well, flaccid, I'm in a sorry state. It's very small, tiny. I might be one of the smallest guys in the world. But when it's fully erect I'd say I'm at least average—five to six inches. . . . I would like to have a big penis. I'd be a different kind of guy if I had a big penis."
—HOWARD STERN, *COSMO* MAGAZINE, 1997

What chapter on small penises would be complete without a nod to the small Penis Meister himself, shock jock Howard Stern, whose ubiquitous use of the word penis on his daily radio show has elevated the part—especially small ones—to near celebrity status. Howard's notorious self-deprecating remarks about his sexual ineptitude and the lilliputian size of his own appendage has no doubt erased the angst of men who feel similarly afflicted (and according to studies, that would be, well, most of 'em). After all, Howard is a megastar, the "King of All Media," and a veritable sex icon among female fans. Status achieved in spite of his diminutive dick. What's not to like? Stern's phallic vulnerability is evident in his autobiography:

> *Having a small penis has haunted me throughout my life. Whenever I'm with a bunch of guys, like going to Atlantic City to gamble or stuff, and we have to make a stop on the way to urinate, I always make a beeline for the stalls. I can't do it at a*

urinal. God forbid someone should see my puny pecker. I bare-
ly clear the zipper.

When Roseanne accused her ex Tom Arnold of having a "wee willie," he shot back with "Even a 747 looks small landing in the Grand Canyon."

A Hard Man Is
Good to Find

*"At my age, I'm envious
of a stiff wind."*

—RODNEY DANGERFIELD

There was a time, not so very long ago, that impotence was thought to be a shameful indignity with which afflicted men suffered in silence. Whether a man believed the cause to be an untimely curse from the gods or an inevitable consequence of the aging process, it mattered not. No one spoke of it. Partners avoided it. And rarely did anyone do anything about it. But that was then. Today, many of the thirty-odd million men who experience difficulty getting it up and/or keeping it hard sing the praises and boost the financial portfolios of penis science—a brave new world replete with hydraulic engineers, mechanical marvels, and pharmacological wonder pills standing ready to the rescue. Before we delve into the specifics of such modern day miracles however, a little historical perspective regarding the many and varied methods devised by early man to erect an unwilling or unable member.

Ancient Secrets

In Babylonia during the eighth century B.C. (a time that knew not of managed care) physicians completely immersed themselves—some quite literally—in their attempts to cure a patient's impotency. The treatment regimen involved an elaborate ritual in which the physician beheaded a male partridge, after which he swallowed its heart, and then combined its blood with water. This concoction was set out overnight, and was then given to the patient to drink.

Ancient Roman physicians offered a multifaceted approach to men wishing to restore their erectile capabilities. The erect-wannabe was first advised to eat a specially selected erotic food—usually onions—followed by prayers for godly assistance. The next step involved smearing a phallic shaped object (think: dildo) with oil, pepper, and nettle seed, which was then shoved up the poor guy's rectum. With the object firmly in place, the final step required the hapless patient to rub his lower body with stinging nettles—a plant that earned its appropriately descriptive name given its stinging hairs, which cause itchy, painful blotches on the skin. What price, pleasure.

The ancient Romans were also early enthusiasts of "organo-therapy" as a means of treating sexual difficulties, including the erectile type. This type of therapy is predicated on the notion that eating select healthy animal organs will cure illnesses in the corresponding human organ. Thus, impotent Roman men ingested a variety of animal penises, including deer (a very popular appendage, as it was also said to be an effective antidote against snake bites) monkey, and cocks (the rooster variety).

Men Who Swallow

According to ancient Taoist sexology, a man who suffered from impotence could be cured by touching his tongue and lips to the vulva of a very passionate girl. He then was instructed to perform cunnilingus on her until she reached orgasm, after which it was deemed vitally important for the afflicted man to swallow all her orgasmic secretions. The rationale for this is found in the Taoist belief that yin essence, the feminine life force (found in female fluids) was infinitely stronger than any male power. Thus, men were encouraged to take in these fluids to obtain health, or in this case, a healthy erection.

"Break a Leg"

Penile fortifying methods involving potions, pastes, and passionate partners definitely beat the technique employed by the ancient tribe of female warriors known as the Amazons, who were said to capture male prisoners, not only to work as slaves, but also to satisfy sexual cravings. According to historical legend, the lusty Amazon warrior frequently broke or amputated the arms or legs of their male captives because they believed that "the genital member was strengthened by deprivation of one of the extremities."

WHAT'S IN A WORD?

The word "impotence" derives from the Latin *impotentia* meaning "lack of power." According to the *Book of Sexual*

Records, the word was first used in a poem titled "De Regimine Principum" by Thomas Hoccleve (1370–1454) to mean "want of strength" or "helplessness," ". . . Hir impotence, Strecchith naght so fer as his influence." But the use of the word to mean loss of sexual power first occurred in 1655 in *Church History of Britain* by Thomas Fuller (1608–1661) "Whilest Papists crie up this, his incredible Incontinency: others uneasily unwonder the same by imputing it partly to Impotence afflicted, by an infirmitie."

While many people continue to use the term "impotence" to refer to men who have trouble getting or keeping an erection (one capable of intercourse), political correctness and human kindness has fostered a name change in recent years. This is because the word impotence is just . . . bad. Mostly because it denotes a powerless, emasculated, feeble man. The term "erectile dysfunction," a.k.a. "E.D.," is less emotionally loaded, and is now the preferred choice among sexuality professionals (and gaining momentum among the populace).

DIVORCE, EUROPEAN STYLE

While most of the world considers the spectacle of "sexual matters made public" an offensive intrusion into people's private lives, the concept is by no means a new one. From the mid 1500s to the 1700s, impotence was one of the few means available (besides death) to dissolve a Catholic marriage, although anyone citing it as grounds for divorce had to prove it, *publicly.* Under the guidance of church officials, husbands underwent erection tests, and wives, virginity checks. Such exams were followed by a "trial by congress" (in effect, marital intercourse—or at least an attempt) for a select audience. After the petitioning participants were thoroughly inspected, they were placed in a designated bed with selected experts in attendance (the courtesy of bed curtains were generally provided). After a period of an hour or two—during which time those monitoring the event were treated to the auditory shenanigans of the trysting couple—the curtains were opened. The woman was then examined for signs of intromission and evidence of ejaculation, after which a written report was submitted to the ecclesiastical court on the events or lack of (quite possibly the origins of "performance anxiety").

OF HAIRY PALMS, BLINDNESS, DEMENTIA, AND IMPOTENCE

Throughout most of the nineteenth century, the medical community considered impotence to be just another of the many crippling diseases caused by the evils of masturbation. Conventional thinking held that the activity "used up" excessive amounts of energy and damaged the sexual system, and thus, anyone who sought treatment for sexual difficulties was tacitly admitting to acts of sexual perversion. While medical science has since changed its tune, shame and embarrassment continues today to prevent many impaired men from seeking professional help. Out of an estimated 30 million sufferers, only 2.7 million men pursued medical treatment options in 1997. It wasn't until the advent of Viagra in 1998 (see page 122) that bedroom doors began to swing open. . . .

Gross Anatomy

In 1877 America, Dr. Samuel W. Gross, the era's most renowned surgeon, made impotence the topic of a ground-breaking address before medical colleagues at the Philadelphia County Medical Society. Dr. Gross dutifully explained that "reduced sexual power, from whatever cause it may arise, is one of the most distressing of maladies, and is, therefore, entitled to the deepest sympathy and consideration on the part of the honest practitioner, by whom, unfortunately, it is rarely discussed." Citing his own observations and patient studies, Dr. Gross had come to the conclusion that impotence was "traceable, in the larger proportion of instances, to masturbation." His spellbound audience then learned the "scientific" details: "masturbation affects the sexual powers by inducing a state of constant congestion and undue excitability of the urethra." He theorized this excitability caused "internal strictures" to eventually form inside the urethra, which somehow "disabled" the ability of the penis to erect itself.

What to do? The good doctor advised his colleagues that there were essentially three ways to treat the malady: (1) give the patient bromide of potassium to "blunt the veneral appetite" hoping the patient wouldn't notice or care that he was impotent; (2) counsel the patient about the importance of "chastity in thought and action" (that always works); and (3) ream out the patient's urethra with a "steel bougie" or blunt instrument once each day. The suitably named Dr. Gross believed ramming a rod up and down the length of the urethra would break up the "strictures" that caused the impotence and thus alleviate the condition (an activity which no doubt elicited some booming variation of the word "Yeowie!!!").

Erectile difficulties clearly tormented beloved humorist Mark Twain, who penned the following *un*-humorous spoof of the Rubiáyát ("a loaf of bread, a jug of wine, and book of verse," etc.), as a lament on his own impotence (although line five is a delightful display of his infamous wit):

A Weaver's Beam

A Weaver's Beam—the Handle of a Hoe,
A Bowsprit once—now a thing of dough:
A sorry Change, lamented oft with Tears
At Midnight by the Master of the Show.

Behold—the Penis mightier than the Sword,
That leapt from Shealth at any heating Word
So long ago—now peaceful lies, and calm,
And dreams unmoved of ancient Conquests scored.

Sex researchers Masters and Johnson point out that most men experience their first failed erection while under the influence of alcohol. Of course, this "clinical" observation was noted by playwright extraordinaire William Shakespeare a few hundred years earlier, when he offered in the famous knocking scene of *Macbeth* "drink . . . provokes, and unprovokes. It provokes the desire, but it takes away the performance."

Hitting Below the Belt

Physiological factors are the cause of impotency in 90 percent of the cases involving men over the age of fifty. The *leading* cause of erectile difficulty is arteriosclerosis. Anything that wreaks havoc on the circulatory system: smoking, couch potato syndrome, or fat-laden diets, can cause penis problems.

C.O.D. (Condition of Dick)

To help distinguish whether or not an erection difficulty is physical or psychological in origin, professionals often recommend a self-test called the "Nocturnal Penile Tumescence (NPT)" stamp. This test is based on the finding that men with physiological erection difficulties usually have normal erections during sleep (which they are generally unaware of). By placing a ring of four to six stamps snugly around the base of the penis (don't lick 'em first—simply wet the overlapping stamp to seal the ring!) and checking to see if the perforations are torn in the morning, one can easily tell if an erection occurred in the night.

OPTIONS FOR THE ERECTION IMPAIRED

"We were born together. We grew up together. We got married together. Why, oh why did you have to die before me?"

SOLLY, SEVENTY-YEAR-OLD TAXI DRIVER,

MOURNING HIS PENIS IN JEFFREY BERNARD'S *LOW LIFE*

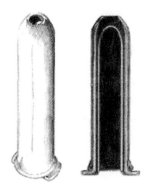

Early tubular penile stiffening device (1907) patent no. 844,778

In the early 1900s, men who were unable to get or maintain an erection were likely to turn to one of a number of mechanical penile splints that began flooding the country. In *American Sex Machines: The Hidden History of Sex at the U.S. Patent Office,* author Hoag Levins provides a delightful journey into the world of penis-stiffening gadgets. The first such patent was issued in 1906 for a tubular rubber splint that the would-be lover simply inserted his penis into, followed the next year by a metal frame gizmo that effectively stretched out the penis. These primitive models set the stage for many contraptions to follow, and of course, the mind continues its inventive churning. To date, close to forty inventors have submitted their erectile enhancing concoctions for patent scrutiny.

Early Implants

The first artificial prosthesis used to get the penis sufficiently stiff to undertake the task of sexual intercourse likely consisted of a rod or reed pushed into the urethra (obviously used only by highly motivated individuals). This primitive concept actually resurfaced in 1988 in a patent application filed by one John Friedman for a device lovingly called the "disposable internally applied penile erector." Shaped somewhat like a large plastic nail, it was designed to be inserted down the length of the penis to stiffen it from the inside (ooh, what guy wouldn't like that?). The historic first operation to restore an erection via surgically inserting something stiff into the penis was in 1936, using a piece of cartilage. Later, surgeons implanted pieces of bone, which proved problematic given their propensity to be absorbed by the body, causing the penis to deform. In the 60s doctors experimented with acrylic rods implanted along the full length of the shaft, which produced the ever difficult to disguise permanent erection.

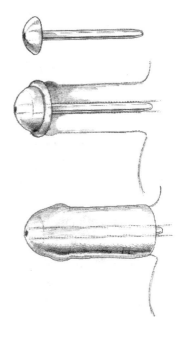

Internally applied erection device patent no. 4,869,241 (1988)

The first U.S. patent for a surgically implanted penis stiffening device was issued in 1974 in a technological coup to a citizen of what was then the Soviet Union. The penile implant race was on, and within just a few years, patents were obtained for implant models ranging from semirigid rods to double semirigid malleable rods to the multicomponent inflatable design to hydraulic inflatable implant systems.

Items Sure to
Raise More Than
a Few Eyebrows

Today's flaccid penis has a plethora of options (from temporary fixes to permanent prostheses) to choose from that afford the desired engorgement. These include constrictive devices (aka cock rings), vacuum pumps, medications (injectables and swallowables, and two types of surgical implants: 1) semirigid and 2) inflatable.

"Semi-rigid"

A pair of bendable silicon rods placed inside the penis, essentially creating an ever-present erection (fashioned in theory after man's canine best friend and the fail-proof bone in his penis)

The Bionic Penis (inflatable implants)

More aesthetically pleasing and more sexually satisfying than silicon rods . . . but also more likely to malfunction. There

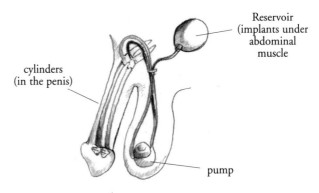

cylinders
(in the penis)

Reservoir
(implants under
abdominal
muscle

pump

The Bionic Penis Hydraulic Implant

are several models available, but all types essentially allow the owner to pump up an erection whenever needed and deflate it when it's not. A pair of hollow cylinders is placed inside the erectile tissue of the penis, and when the man is ready to have sex, he gently squeezes a pumping mechanism (usually implanted in the scrotum) to inflate the devices. These gadgets are still an evolving technology, however, and are not without risks (migration, gan-

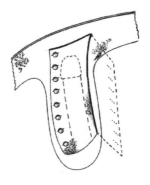

Special underwear (to conceal the perpetually shirft organ) patent no. 4,526,167 (1985)

grene, spontaneous inflation), although an estimated 24,000 men a year opt to take their chances.

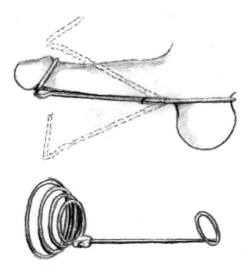

Early Spring design penile splint (1907) patent no. 867,340

The Devil Made Him Do It

The late comedian Flip Wilson (famous for his cross-dressing persona Geraldine) had the dubious distinction of being the first public human face of penis implant fame. Wilson sardonically remarked that his penis needed help because he had "worn it down" with overuse. Wanting to show off his new toy, Wilson unabashedly pulled out the surgically enhanced organ and showed it to the folks at Howard Stern's radio show while a guest of the Shock Meister.

THE MAGIC BULLET

"I've got four girlfriends. . . . It's the best legal recreational drug out there."
—HUGH HEFNER

In a world where impotent men nursing shattered egos routinely implored of their doctors "Can't you just give me a pill for this?" it was only a matter of time before the response would be "Yes!" That time arrived on March 27, 1998, and the world has not been the same since. From Wall Street to Wal-Mart, the now infamous impotence fighting juggernaut known as Viagra has changed the face of medicine and pop culture alike. Known genetically as *sildenafil citrate*, Viagra (a name which closely resembles the Latin *virga,* meaning a "new, young twig") was a failed heart drug that piqued pharmaceutical giant Pfizer's interest after several cardiac patients unexpectedly reported having erections. Discreetly swallowed an hour before sex, the drug works by enhancing the effect of nitric oxide in the penis. Once this happens, an enzyme is activated, which in turn relaxes the smooth muscle that allows blood to flow into the penis, and . . . bingo! an erection. **Note:** The little blue wonder pill does not work in the absence of *desire,* and only causes an erection when a man is already sexually aroused. Or so they say.

The Bad News

These drug-induced erections do not come without risk, nor is Viagra a panacea for an inept, insensitive lover. Common side effects include headaches, facial flushing, and indigestion, and rarely, vision changes (a sense of looking at the world through "blue colored glasses"). Men who take nitroglycerin or related heart drugs must *not* take Viagra because the drug mix can cause a deadly drop in blood pressure . . . and death. In verifying the long-held notion that men value sex over general health, urologists around the country reported many a patient plaintively uttering "If I have to go, that's the way I want to go out."

"I can't help wondering why we got a pill to help with performance instead of communication."

—ELLEN GOODMAN, *BOSTON GLOBE*

THE NATURAL WAY:
HERBAL ERECTION BOOSTERS

While frenzied scientists continue to pursue chemical erection preparations dutifully concocted in the tubes and coils of the laboratory, Mother Nature yields numerous offerings in her own abundant garden. Four of the most promising . . .

Ginkgo Biloba

Men in search of herbal erection boosters without pesky side effects may find the answer in ginkgo biloba, an extract from the world's oldest living species of tree. Ginkgo is a widely studied herb scientifically proven to boost the flow of blood throughout the body, and is particularly helpful as a memory aid. Good erections need good blood flow and thus, men who have iffy erections due to vascular problems may find this remedy useful. (Then he can not only get an erection, but *remember* having it, as well.)

Maca

Relatively unknown (for the moment) in North America, this Peruvian herb is rapidly gaining attention. Maca is a radishlike tuber, much like the potato, grown in the high Andes region of Peru. The plant was a staple of a sophisticated Incan empire, who recognized its fertility, virility, and strengthening properties some two thousand years ago. According to legend, the Incas ingested maca prior to battle in order to enhance their physical power, but prohibited warriors from using it *after* victory to protect the newly vanquished women from uncontrollable sexual advances. Animal research confirms maca increases reproductive rates, raises sperm counts, and increases semen volume. Numerous enthusiastic claims have surfaced in recent years touting maca's positive effect on erectile function. (Can *News at 11* be far behind?)

Muira Puama

If names were any indication of erection enhancing effectiveness, then "potency wood," alias "Muira Puama," would be a definite winner. Known for centuries as a powerful aphrodisiac and nerve stimulant in South American folk medicine, recent clinical studies show treatment with the natural extract to be highly effective *without* bothersome side effects (although as of yet, no one has figured out exactly how the stuff works).

Cautuaba

Likely to be unfamiliar to Westerners, this central nervous system stimulator is reportedly the most popular of all Brazilian herbal aphrodisiacs. Natives of the northern Amazon river basin have used cautuaba for centuries to improve sexual potency. Devoted users often combine the prized herb with muira puama to add extra zing to their already zippy sex lives.

We Want to Pump You Up!

Think "penis exercise" is nothing more than a sexual metaphor? Think again.

Penis Pull-Ups

For years, women have been encouraged to exercise a group of pelvic muscles called the pubococcygeal muscles (a mouthful conveniently shorted to "P.C. muscles") as a means of increasing urinary control, vaginal sensations, and strengthening orgasms. But women are not the only ones who possess P.C. muscles; men have 'em too, and by most reports, those who opt to exercise theirs are rewarded not only with increased urinary control, but *also*: Increased staying power (delaying the moment of ejaculation)! Longer and more intense orgasms! Sometimes, multiple orgasms! Decreased recovery time between orgasms! And, as a bonus, find they have firmer and more reliable erections!

To do the exercises (called "Kegels"), first get in touch with your own pelvic muscles. To do this, simply start and stop the flow of urine midstream. Once identified, squeeze and release these muscles (rapidly) twice each day (these can be done anywhere: at a computer, driving a car, channel surfing). Gradually increase the number of squeezes, working to about seventy-five, twice a day.

Note: Gentlemen, if your penis fails to become erect, or if you have trouble maintaining an erection, let it rest awhile. *Every* man will experience occasional erection problems. Chances are it's related to worry, anxiety, or fatigue.

VAGINA 101:

He Thought Her Name Was . . . "MULVA"

"He has endowed her with buttocks nobly planned, and has supported the whole on majestic thighs. Between these latter he has placed the field of strife which, when it abounds in flesh, resembles by its amplitude a lion's head. Its name among mankind is Vulva. Oh! how many men's deaths lie at her door? How many, alas, of the bravest! God has furnished this object with a mouth, a tongue, two lips; it is like the impression of the hoof of the gazelle in the sands of the desert."

—SHAYKH NEFZAWI, *THE PERFUMED GARDEN*

THE VULVA

When it comes to identifying women's genitalia, most people are guilty of referring to "everything between a woman's legs" as her "vagina." But the truth is, everything between a woman's legs is actually her *vulva*, of which the vagina is only a part (calling the entire area the "vagina" is akin to calling a person's entire face the "mouth"). The vulva consists of the outer, visible part of the female genitals, including the pubic hair, the labia majora and the labia minora, the clitoris, and the urinary and vaginal openings.

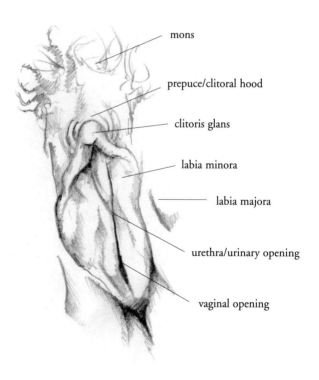

mons

prepuce/clitoral hood

clitoris glans

labia minora

labia majora

urethra/urinary opening

vaginal opening

> "Three things are insatiable: the desert, the grave, and a woman's vulva."
>
> —ARAB PROVERB

The word "vulva" derives from the Latin *volva,* meaning a "wrapper" or "covering." (Curiously, "Volva" is also the name for an ancient Scandinavian goddess who could turn into a mare and carry a man away to death.)

The vulva is also, unfortunately, sometimes called the "pudendum," derived from the Latin *pudendus,* meaning "shameful area" or "that which brings shame." Saint Augustine of Hippo (354–430), considered the most influential of the early Christian theologians, believed the genitals were labeled "pudenda" because Man was ashamed that these parts were the only ones he had no control over. (While the term pudenda originally referred to both sexes, it eventually came to be used only in reference to women's genitalia.)

Augustine was particularly disgusted by female genitalia, a sentiment evident in his much quoted phrase, *inter faeces et urinam nascimur,* "between shit and urine we are born." The revered theologian was among the early Christians repulsed by the idea that Jesus would have come into contact with the vile female orifice, and thus concocted a theory detailing an alternate route for His divine birth, a kind of miraculous "now you *don't* see him, now you *do*" entry that avoided the birth canal and genitals altogether. Other Christian genital-phobes suggested that Jesus made his way here through the navel or the breast. It should come as no surprise that Christian doctrine, at the time, held Satan responsible for fashioning the evil genital appendages.

Seinfeldian Slip

While still struggling to earn a degree of recognition respect, the vulva did get its fifteen minutes of fame during a classic episode of *Seinfeld,* in which Jerry (Seinfeld) could not recall the name of the woman he was dating, remembering only that it rhymed with a "female body part." Ultimately, Jerry is confronted by the woman to speak her name, and so he mutters with uncertainty ". . . *Mulva?*" (Seinfeld aficionados will recall her name, in fact, was Dolores).

You've Seen One, You've Seen 'Em All

An old ribald saying about the female genitals goes something like this: "Put a bag over a woman's head, turn her upside down, and you can't tell her apart from any other woman." A statement understood, perhaps even expected, from a society not given to appreciating the unique genital characteristics and qualities found among women. It is noteworthy, however, that many cultures in times past *did* take the time to notice, chronicling their observations in some of the most revered erotic works of all time.

The most extensive collection of "Genital Observances" are unquestionably those found in *The Perfumed Garden,* the sixteenth-century Arabic sex manual penned by Shaykh Omar en-Nefzawi. In this classic erotic text, the prolific sheik embarked upon a detailed "vulva journey," and meticulously cataloged the female genital parts into thirty-eight different types. A sampling of these, in Shaykh Nefzawi's own words:

- THE RESTLESS ONE—When this vulva has received the member it begins to move violently and without interruption, and knows no repose till it has hastened on the enjoyment and finished its work.
- THE BEAUTIFUL—This is the vulva which is white, plump, in form vaulted like a dome, firm and without any deformity. You cannot take your eyes off it, and to look at it changes a feeble erection into a strong one.
- THE CRUSHER—So called from its crushing movements upon the penis once he has entered. It takes him into her grip and would, if it could, absorb also the two testicles.
- THE EVER-READY—This name is given to the vulva of a woman passionately fond of the virile member. It is the one which, far from being intimidated by a hard and stiff penis, treats it with contempt and demands one harder.

Percentage of men who find an arched vulva sexy: 54

My World and Welcome to It . . .

In the late nineteenth century, an anonymous well-to-do English gentleman (surreptitiously known as "Walter") penned an eleven-volume, 4,235 page erotic memoir known today under the simplistic title *My Secret Life.* Essentially a sexual autobiography, the tome deals with nothing other than the sexual activities, proclivities, enjoyments, frustrations, and insights of the author. Whoever he was, one thing is clear: this man reveled in women's private parts (almost as much as he reveled in writing the word "cunt"), delightedly detailing his numerous astute "vulval" observations:

> *I have . . . seen them of all sizes and developments, and in color from pale coral to mulberry crimson. I have seen those bare of hair, those with but hairy stubble, those with bushes six inches long, and covering them from bum bone to navel.*

> *Out of a hundred cunts, not one is quite like to another, there is always some difference noticeable in them. In my belief, there is as much difference in the look of cunts as there is in noses. But sisters' cunts I think are generally somewhat alike.*

FRIENDS AND NEIGHBORS

Mons Pubis

The mons pubis (which is Latin for "fanny hill") refers to the hair-covered cushion of flesh that protects a woman's pubic bone. This part is also frequently referred to as the *mons veneris*, Latin for "mount of Venus," so named for the Roman goddess of Sexuality. Given an ample supply of nerve endings in the mons, caressing this area during sexual activity can be intensely pleasurable for many women.

Labia Majora

From Latin for "large lips" or "major lips," the labia majora are the larger folds of flesh around the vaginal opening. These lips—generally covered with pubic hair after puberty—contain oil-secreting scent glands as well as a small number of sweat glands. The labia majora are also home to a spongy mesh of erectile tissue that engorges with blood during sexual arousal. First-century Greek physician Rufus of Ephesus (believed by some to have been the personal physician to Cleopatra) referred to the labia majora as "lips of the myrtle" (myrtle, of course, was the sacred plant of Aphrodite, Greek goddess of love).

Labia Minora

From Latin for "small lips" or "minor lips," the labia minora are the smooth hairless folds of skin located inside the labia majora. These exquisitely sensitive lips contain sweat and scent glands, extensive blood vessels and nerve endings, and vary considerably in size, shape, length, and color from woman to woman. During sexual arousal, the labia minora swell with blood, becoming two to three times their usual dimensions. Generally pink in color when unstimulated, they undergo vivid color changes throughout the arousal process, including deep red/pink, bruised purple, or vampish maroon hues.

- In the seventeenth century, anatomists began referring to the inner lips as "nymphae," borrowing the term from the Greek mythological use of the word "nymph" to refer to water goddesses.

- Rufus of Ephesus labeled these sensuous flower-like lips "Fruit of the Myrtle."
- In the elegance of the Chinese language, the labia minora are known as "red pearls," their lower meeting point as "jade veins," and the point near the clitoral glans as "lute strings."

Other Labia Labels:

Two-Leafed Book, Hot Lips, Nether Lips, Feathers, Cookies, Bell Flaps, Columns of Venus, Garden Gate, Examination Hall

Perineum

The flesh and skin surface area between the vagina and anus (bordered on the sides by the thighs) is referred to as the *perineum*. The word comes from a Greek term meaning "to swim around something," and was used for the perineum because it is usually moist with perspiration. According to *Eve's Secrets* author Josephine Lowndes-Sevely, in some of the medical writings of the ancient Greeks, the *female* perineum (males also have one) was referred to as the "ejaculatory muscle," a term that suggests that even then, a sexual function was attributed to it (not to mention the fact that the ancient Greeks knew of and readily accepted the idea of female ejaculation). A word to the wise: The perineum is laden with nerve endings, and stimulation of the area is known to heighten sexual arousal in many women.

The Vagina Files

"Two lips and a clitoris
do not a vagina make."

—JOHN STEWART,
NAKED PICTURES OF FAMOUS PEOPLE

The female passageway. The female sex organ. The female organ of copulation. The birth canal. All polite conversational euphemisms for the *vagina*, a deeply folded muscular sheath extending approximately 3-and-a-half to 4 inches in length (in its unstimulated state) from the vaginal opening to the cervix. People often crudely compare the vagina to the likes of an empty toilet paper tube, but actually it's more like a drawstring purse than a tube, tunnel or a canal. When empty, it has no innerspace at all. The analgy of an empty glove serves as a much better illustration of the vagina as a *potential* rather than *actual* space—molding around whatever goes inside. And, except for the tiny cervical canal opening, the vagina is a dead-end passageway (meaning tampons, food delicacies, or small animals will not get lost).

The vagina contains three layers of tissue: (1) the inner lining, called the "vaginal mucosa," resembles the inside skin of the mouth, and has a soft, pliable surface, (2) underneath is the muscular layer, which can stretch considerably during intercourse, and especially during childbirth, and (3) fibrous tissue which is, well, fibrous, and connects the vagina to other pelvic structures.

Unlike most other primates, a woman's vagina tilts *forward* (at approximately a forty-five-degree angle), an evolutionary trait that makes face-to-face intercourse comfortable. A convenient—and important—evolutionary development according to anthropologist Helen Fisher. She says the ability of our human ancestors to look each other in the eye during sex encouraged intimacy and communication, strengthened the mom and pop pair-bond, and ultimately increased the likelihood that juniors and juniorettes would survive.

IF THESE WALLS COULD TALK

The walls of the vagina are lavishly supplied with blood vessels, but seriously lacking when it comes to nerve endings. In fact, the inner two-thirds of the human vagina are so insensitive that operations can sometimes be performed on it without anesthesia. Not so the outer third, however. The one inch (or so) at the lower end of the vaginal barrel is highly sensitive and extremely responsive to stimulation. Men reading this are advised to take note. Due to the fact that most of the muscle tissue in the vagina—along with a rich supply of nerve endings—is concentrated around the vaginal opening (Renaissance giant Leonardo da Vinci referred to this lower vaginal musculature as "the gatekeeper of the castle"), a woman's sexual pleasure via intercourse is much more dependent on the *girth* of a penis rather than the *length*.

FACIAL CLUES TO WHAT LIES BELOW

According to the ancient Taoist sex manual *Secret Instructions Concerning the Jade Girl* (*Yu Fang Pi Chueh,* thought to have been written in the fourth century), the characteristics of a woman's face artfully reveal the features of her sexual organs. According to the manual:

> *A woman with a small mouth and short fingers has a shallow porte feminine and she is easy to please.*

> *You can be sure that a woman must have big and thick labia if she has a big mouth and thick lips.*

> *If she has deep-set eyes, her porte feminine is bound to be deep too.*

> *If a woman has a pair of big sparkling eyes, her porte feminine is narrow at its entrance and yet roomy in the inner part.*

> *A woman with two dimples is tight and narrow down below.*

In *The Tao of Sexology,* Dr. Stephan Chang says the facial/vaginal clues provided by the ancient Taoists are about 90 percent accurate. Chang's text also includes the following facial tip-off to the vagina's texture and talents:

Puckered, protruding lips or protruding bone structure indicate an elastic vagina. It could be big or small, but it will be very wet, warm, and soft. It also vibrates and trembles, and it is considered by many men to be the most satisfying. Taoists refer to it as the "talking vagina" [while visions of pouty super-models danced in their heads].

A BALANCED ENVIRONMENT

The average pH of the robust vagina is 3.8 to 4.5 (compared to 6.0 to 7.0 of skin elsewhere on the body), which makes it fairly acidic. Vaginal secretions contain lactic acid which helps to maintain the lower pH. The low vaginal pH is optimally designed to eliminate unfriendly bacteria which give rise to the dreaded vaginal infection. Various factors can upset the delicate vaginal ecosystem (increasing the odds of the above-mentioned nasty infection), including:

- Antibiotics
- Douching
- Frequent bathing with unfriendly body soap
- Hormonal changes
- Diabetes
- Tampons or menstrual napkins containing deodorants
- Prolonged retention of a tampon, diaphragm, cervical cap, or sponge
- Synthetic underwear and/or panty hose (both retain heat and moisture)
- Chemical irritants, i.e., feminine hygiene sprays, colored toilet paper, bubble baths

- High carbohydrate and/or sugar diet
- Sexual intercourse without adequate lubrication

To Douche, or Not to Douche . . .
There Should Be No Question

Multitudes of women grow up believing the vagina to be a *dirty* area, harboring a host of nasty invaders that need to be routinely purged with a slew of douches, soaps, and deodorizing agents. Nothing could be further from the truth, nor more harmful to the female body. The truth is, the normal, healthy vagina is perhaps the cleanest space in the body—much cleaner than the mouth. It contains several beneficial life-forms specially designed to keep it that way. Douching and cleansing with assorted chemicals hoping to get fresh 'n' clean will more likely promote a down 'n' dirty environment by killing off the good guys. Infestation by hordes of unwelcome bacteria often follows, and chaos reigns: infection, foul discharge, and an odiferous smell that will never be deemed erotic. Save your vagina from this trauma: *don't* douche, *don't* spray, *don't* soap up. End of discussion.

DIAGNOSTIC DIGITS:

According to Traditional Chinese medicine, when a woman's finger tips are cool to cold, it is an indication that her genital area is "clean," meaning, free of vaginal infections and sexually transmitted diseases. Likewise, warm fingertips suggest the presence of infection or possible STD.

Is This What He Means by "Perfume"?

The Indian erotic classic *The Perfumed Garden* was written in the sixteenth century by Shaykh Omar en-Nefzawi. In addition to providing numerous coital techniques and positions, the good Shaykh apparently also felt duty bound to educate the Arabian masses on the delicate subject of feminine hygiene. "Know that bad exhalations from the vulva and the armpits are, as also a wide vagina, the greatest of evils," he proclaimed. His remedy?

Boil well in water carobs (fruit of the locust tree) freed from their kernals, and the bark of the pomegranate tree. The woman takes a sitz bath in the decoction thus obtained, and which must be as hot as she can bear. When the bath gets cold, it must be warmed and used again, to be repeated several times. The same result may be obtained by fumigating the vulva with cow dung.

Warning: No Huffing and Puffing. Blowing air into the vagina, either unwittingly or on purpose, is never, *ever,* a good idea. The activity can cause an air embolism, which in turn is quite likely to cause the receiver's death. This untimely demise can be remarkably rapid, occurring in a matter of seconds (not a good thing for a budding romance).

Who Varted?

Occasionally during sex (and sometimes during headstands or certain yoga positions), especially when the pelvis is elevated, gravity causes the inner two-thirds of the vagina to expand and draw in air. The outer muscles tighten, and when the penis is withdrawn or the position altered, the trapped air escapes with a "whoosh" (o.k., with a fartlike noise, sans the odor). Variously known as "queefing" or "varting," this phenomenon may be embarrassing to some, however, it is *not* harmful.

CAN YOU BELIEVE IT?

Items that have been retrieved by physicians from the vaginas of women (as documented in the medical literature):

Set of false teeth, pine cone,
rubber ball (discovered some twenty years later),
shot glass, highball glass,
flashlight bulb, cucumber,
onion, orange, hard-boiled egg,
the finger of a glove,
aerosol deodorant cap, leech,
dead mouse,
an iron handle (from forceps used as wire-cutters),
broken-off handle of a broom
(which remained undetected for three months).

Speaking of things in the vagina, in 1933, Denver gynecologist Dr. Earle Cleveland Haas obtained a patent for the internally worn tampon. He created his registered trademark Tampax from the words "tampon" and "vaginal pack."

SCENTS AND SECRETIONS

"The most prevalent basis for repulsion toward sex comes from the erroneous idea that women's genitals are disgusting and unclean and hence sex is disgusting and unclean."
—LONNIE BARBACH

About one in three women have vaginal secretions that contain certain types of scent producing compounds called "aliphatic acid chains." The scent of these women's vaginas varies with the phase of their menstrual cycle. There is no such vaginal scent in the other 66 percent of women; their vaginal aroma remains the same no matter what the day of the month.

Erotic Odor

The natural odor of the vulva, referred to as the "cassolette," contains various chemicals that, when whiffed by the male, are said to unleash his sexual response in a *big* way. Eastern love manuals sing the erotic praises of the cassolette, while Western women often perceive the odor to be a sign of uncleanliness and hasten to cover it up. Much of the cassolette undoubtedly emanates from the female labia, which contain scent glands and a number of eccrine sweat glands that add odorous molecules to the scent of the area. Among the various components identified thus far are pheromones (airborne sexual messengers), musk, and indole (the active chemical ingredient in scents with aphrodisiac properties).

Too Busy to Bathe?

The French remedy for the time impaired is called a "tart's wash." This quickie involves freshening only those "sweat-generating, scent-producing" (read: smelly) parts of the body: the armpits and the vulva. The name originated from early prostitutes, wishing to eliminate the rather pungent odor of sex in between clients.

At least one Frenchman would have nixed the idea of any sort of pubic hygiene ritual, however brief. The French emperor, Napoleon Bonaparte, apparently found the aroma of fetid genitalia to be an aphrodisiac of sorts (perhaps finding it a suitable adjunct to his rather notorious buttocks fetish). In the weeks prior to his return from the battlefield, he penned instructions to his wife, Josephine, not to bathe her intimate parts. *"Ne te laves pas, je reviens"* (Don't wash, I'm coming home) begged the little general.

Average daily amount of normal vaginal discharge for most women: about ONE TEASPOON (this may increase slightly around the time of ovulation).

Components of healthy vaginal discharge: Water, albumin, white blood cells, mucin (the oil substance that gives the vagina its slippery sheen).

Vaginal Sweat

When a woman is sexually excited the vagina produces extra lubrication, which comes directly from the vaginal walls (well, actually, the extra fluid seeps out of the tiny congested capillaries near the surface of the vaginal wall). The pressure caused by sexual engorgement forces drops of moisture out of the veins and through the wall. Masters and Johnson, studiously observing the event, thought it looked "like beads of sweat running down a hot forehead," and thus dubbed it the "sweating phenomenon" (although technically this is not a great analogy, since sweating of the *skin* is produced by sweat glands).

In the biblical "Song of Songs," female sexual fluids are referred to as "wine of the naval," or sometimes, "white wine" (naval is used to indicate vagina).

"Why trouble with the pill of immortality when one is welcome to drink from the jade fountain?"

—HSU HSIAO MU CHI

Among the Chinese, the "feminine life force," better known as "yin," is often represented as fluid coming from the "grotto of the white tiger" or the "palace of yin," a.k.a., the female genitals. According to Taoist beliefs, the power of yin was stronger than any male power, and thus, yin essence was considered one of the most beneficial substances a man could absorb. Ever concerned with longevity and virility, man considered it vital that he learn to take feminine fluids into himself.

Contemporary Euphemisms for Female Sexual Fluids:

Honey, divine nectar, clam juice, love juice, vaginal lube, groin gravy

Sickly Sweating

During the Victorian era, genital secretions were not considered a good thing, especially if a woman had the poor misfortune of suffering from the ubiquitous hysteria (as almost all women were apparently wont to do). Physicians of the time believed that as a woman's hysterical condition worsened, so did her genital secretions (a condition called "the whites"), and vice versa. To understand the psychology of this phenomenon, we turn to the self-anointed spokesman of the female psyche, Sigmund Freud:

> *The pride taken by women in the appearance of their genitals is quite a special feature of their vanity; and disorders of the genitals which they think calculated to inspire feelings of repugnance or even disgust have an incredible power of humiliating them, of lowering their self-esteem, and of making them irritable, sensitive, and distrustful. An abnormal secretion of the mucous membrane of the vagina is looked upon as a source of disgust.*

"G" Marks the Spot

The Grafenberg Spot, dubbed the "G-spot" (in honor of German gynecologist Ernst Grafenberg, who first "officially" identified it in 1944), is a controversial erotic hot spot, thought by some researchers to be a dime- or quarter-sized area on the upper vaginal wall, about halfway between the pubic bone and the cervix. While there is no *conclusive* evidence that it exists, some women enthusiastically report that stimulation of the G-spot area (either manually or by penile thrusting) can indeed trigger orgasm.

It is highly likely that the region identified as the G-spot is in actuality the urethral sponge, a distinct area of spongy erectile tissue that also contains clusters of nerve endings, blood vessels, and paraurethral glands (small glands that share common roots with the male prostate). In fact, the secretory glands that empty into the female urethra were actually known as "prostates" in *both* sexes until 1880, when they took the name of A.J.C. Skene. A number of researchers in Israel and the United States have discovered an enzyme in the tissues of the G-spot area that is also found in the male prostate gland, suggesting the urethral sponge may indeed be the female counterpart to this gland. This idea also offers a cogent explanation for the milky fluid expelled—the widely touted "female ejaculation"—from the urethra by some women after G-spot stimulation. While the experts are equally divided over the idea of female ejaculation, this phenomenon was matter-of-factly noted by the spot's namesake and "founder" Grafenberg:

> *Occasionally the production of fluids* [due to stimulation of the anterior wall] *is so profuse that a large towel has to be spread*

under the woman. . . . This convulsive expulsion of fluids occurs
always at the acme of the orgasm and simultaneously with it.

Okay, *If* She Ejaculates, What's in It?

While many practitioners continue to insist female ejaculation is
nothing more than uncontrolled urination, others not only vehe-
mently disagree, but have studied the orgasmic fluids sufficiently to
provide a biochemical makeup of sorts. According to *Eve's Secrets*
author Josephine Lowndes-Sevely, female ejaculate contains:

- Fluid from the paraurethral/prostatic glands (major
source)
- Cells from the upper lining of the vagina
- Mucous from the cervix
- Fluids from the lining of the uterus
- Fluid from the fallopian tubes
- Fluid from the bartholin glands
- Secretions from the sweat and sebaceous glands of the
vulva
- A minute amount of urine

Identified components include: glucose, prostatic acid phosphatase, urea, creatine, and fructose.

Locating the G-spot

Press one or two fingers gently but firmly into the front wall of
the vagina (the first one-and-a-half to two inches) making a

"come hither" motion. Initial stimulation may cause an urge to urinate, while continued stroking may lead to strong sensations of sexual pleasure and orgasm. Then again, it may just be annoying. Not all women will find it, and not all women will enjoy it if they do find it. That's because all women are blissfully different. And, aside from all the squabbling over what it is and where it comes from, it's safe to say that some women do in fact experience an expulsion of some type of fluid during heightened sexual arousal or orgasm. Not all. Not even most. But definitely *some*.

OFFICIAL RECOGNITION:

The word "G-spot" was inducted into the Oxford English Dictionary—the veritable gold standard of the English language—in 1997, some fifty-three years after Grafenberg claimed to have identified it.

Although modern researchers continue to this day to debate the existence of female ejaculation (along with the G-spot) the concept is by no means a new one. Indeed, across many cultures in centuries past, the phenomenon was considered an established piece of medical knowledge. In the ancient Taoist traditions, the term "palace of yin" specifically refers to the location in the body where the orgasmic secretion called "moon flower medicine" lies waiting to be released, and ancient pillow books proclaim "when she reaches the climax of pleasure, the moisture exudes, flowing freely downward." In the *Kama Sutra* (a fifteen-hundred-year-old tome) we read "the semen of women continues to fall from the beginning of the sexual union to the end, in the same way as that of the male." The Greek physician Galen wrote of female ejaculation in the second century A.D. And no less an authority than the "father of medicine," Hippocrates (460–370 B.C.) wrote these astute words of scientific orgasmic observation:

> *During intercourse, once a women is rubbed and her womb titillated, a lustful itch overwhelms her down by her clitoris, and pleasurable feelings and warmth expand out through the rest of her body. A woman also has an ejaculation, furnished by her body, occurring at the same time inside her womanly parts, which have become wet, as well as on the outside . . . If a woman feels an orgasm coming on, she will ejaculate with him . . .*

OF WOMEN AND THEIR VAGINAS

Unlike numerous sightings and statistics regarding the proportions of the penis, vaginal dimensions are rarely discussed in terms of size. But if they were, one would likely speculate the *largest vagina* honor would go to Scottish giantess Anna Swan (1846–1888), a woman who topped the height charts at 7' 8". Following her marriage to Cpt. Martin Bates (no slouch himself, although he was a good 8 inches shorter than his bumper bride), Anna gave birth on June 18, 1879 to the largest infant in history: a babe weighing in at 26 pounds, and measuring 34 inches in length. The child unfortunately did not survive the rigors of birth, but a cast made of the not-so-tiny tot remains on display at the Cleveland Museum of Health

Valleys of the Vagina

Chinese sexual adepts, ever mindful of the need to aid in matters of sexual instruction, divided the vagina into eight sections (cataloged according to the depth of the vagina from the opening). Each area is said to yield different sensations, and, the Chinese believe, is responsive to different styles of thrusting by the penis. They are fittingly called "the eight valleys" and each section has its own name:

The Eight Valleys
1. 0–2.5 cm: "Lute String" (about 1 inch)
2. 5 cm: "Water-chestnut Teeth" (2 inches)
3. 7.5 cm: "Peaceful Valley or "Little Stream" (3 inches)
4. 10 cm: "Mysterious Pearl" or "Dark Pearl" (4 inches)
5. 12.5 cm: "Valley Proper" or "Valley Seed" (5 inches)
6. 15 cm: "Deep Chamber" or "Palace of Delight" (6 inches)
7. 17.5 cm: "Gate of Posterity" or "Inner Door" (7 inches)
8. 20 cm: "North Pole" (8 inches)

The Sexually Aroused Vagina

The average measurement for a woman's vagina ranges from three to five inches in length when not sexually stimulated. *During* sexual arousal, however, things start to get busy . . . and bigger. The inner two-thirds of the vagina increases in length an additional two to three inches, while the walls widen, stretching a full two to three inches in diameter (vaginal diameter at full bloom is about three inches, a surprisingly uniform measurement in all women, regardless of body size or intensity of arousal). The uterus, along with its attached cervix, lifts up and out of the way. These vaginal maneuvers—labeled the "ballooning effect" by Masters and Johnson—allow for the comfortable presence and thrusting of the (whatever-sized) penis. At the same time, the outer third of the vagina (the first one and a half inches) undergoes its own scintillating transformation. A profuse engorgement of blood causes the vaginal opening to narrow and tighten around the incoming penis—a phenomenon known as the "gripping effect"—and grip it will, whether it be a cigar-slender pee-pee or a porn-star prize. These attributes serve to illustrate why the vagina is fittingly called the "accommodating organ."

In the infamous Victorian sexual memoir *My Secret Life,* the anonymous author, "Walter," candidly proffered his take on the "accommodating talents" of the female vagina:

> *I believe there never was a prick so big in any way that a cunt could not take it without pain, and even pleasurably. Its tip might perhaps knock at the portals of the womb too hard for some, but that is all. I have heard women say that the harder those knocks were, the more pleasure it gave them.*

> *All the talk I have heard of pricks being so large that women could not, or would not take them up is sheer nonsense. Several women have told me so. Some said they love to see and handle the big ones. None said that such stretches gave them more phys-*

ical pleasure than those of moderate size. . . . The elasticity and receptivity of a cunt is in fact as wonderful as its constrictive power.

MAYBE THEY COULD CALL IT "PURPLE PUSSY"?

Many women are familiar with the male condition popularly known as "blue balls"—an aching discomfort in the testicles that occurs when the blood-engorged genital area is not relieved by orgasm. But men are not alone in this type of sexual suffering; women have it too (although she lacks a "colorful" nickname for her discomfort). The blood engorged genitalia of the sexually aroused female also seeks orgasmic relief, and if none is forth-coming, she—like he—can experience dull pelvic heaviness and a lingering ache.

- Average length of time it takes for vaginal walls to lubricate following effective sexual stimulation: **1–30** seconds
- Average increase in length of vagina during sexual exci-tation: **2** inches
- Average speed of vaginal contractions during orgasm: **0.8** seconds
- Average number of vaginal contractions during orgasm: **9** (range: 3–15)
- Average length of time it takes the vagina to return to normal size following orgasm: **15** minutes

Masters and Johnson published a chart of one woman who experienced a 43-second orgasm . . . consisting of at least 25 successive contractions.

- Average length of time it takes the clitoris to return to normal size following orgasm: **15** seconds
- Percentage of women capable of consistently achieving vaginal orgasm: **30**
- Percentage of women who say they have never had a coital orgasm: **25**
- Intercourse position most likely to result in a female having a coital orgasm: woman-on-top

ANCIENT SEX RESEARCHERS

Physiological responses during sexual arousal—particularly those involving the genitals—are often thought to be the "discovery" of noted sex research pioneers William Masters and Virginia Johnson (a.k.a. Masters and Johnson). Wrong again, as they say. Lacking the benefits of modern technology and a lucrative book deal, the Taoist sex manual mentioned earlier, *Yu Fang Pi Chueh (Secret Instructions Concerning the Jade Chamber)* written almost two thousand years ago, preceded the dynamic duo with some remarkably astute observations of its own. In the manual, a mythical character known as the "Yellow Emperor" asks the question, "How can I become aware of the joyfulness of the woman?" Another character, called the "Plain Girl" (also variously known as the "Immaculate Girl" and the "Goddess of the Shell") responds: "There are five signs, five desires, and ten movements. By looking at these changes you will become aware of what is happening to the woman's body." The Plain Girl goes on to identify the five signs as:

(1) A flushing of the woman's face ("at this point the man should draw close to her").
(2) A hardening of her nipples ("then he should insert his love weapon").
(3) A growing dryness of her throat ("the man should begin slow movements of loving").
(4) A most and slippery vagina ("the man should plunge into her very deeply").
(5) Emissions of fluid through her vagina ("at this stage the man may move freely inside her body").

DESIGN-A-VAGINA

A common complaint—and source of sexual dissatisfaction—for many women is a vaginal condition in which the organ is described as "too-relaxed" or "overly-stretched." Usually these are women in their late thirties or early forties who have had at least two children (following childbirth, pelvic muscles tend to relax, and the internal and external diameter of the vagina increases). What to do? Many women immediately turn to surgery for a vaginal tune-up, but there are several non-invasive "tush-tightening" options to check out first.

To Enhance Pleasure During Intercourse, a Woman Should Begin With:

1. Changing Positions.
Some women find that bringing their legs together after inserting the penis does the trick—easily done if she lies on her back, while he (on top) places his legs outside of hers. Women who find a lax vagina interferes with indirect clitoral stimulation may find the woman-on-top position (which allows for more direct clitoral stimulation) effectively resolves the problem.

2. Exercise
Relaxed vaginas can be strengthened and toned the old-fashioned way—with exercise—specifically those designed for the pelvic muscles surrounding the vaginal canal (see pages 156 and 157 for details). In addition to manual exercises, industrious inventors have come up with various devices to assist the vagina in achieving a tighter status, including vaginal weights (little vaginal barbells, which generally weigh from twenty to seventy grams apiece) that are inserted into the vagina. The thinking here is that constant squeezing to keep the weights from spilling out (especially embarrassing when it happens in, say, the check-out line) will strengthen, and thus *tighten* the lax muscles.

And finally, if a relaxed vagina is beyond the scope of corrective exercises, a woman can always go under the knife and get . . .

3. Genital Plastic Surgery.

Using either conventional "nip and tuck" procedures or high tech lasers, "vaginal rejuvenation," as it's affectionately called, incorporates the tools of modern technology to tighten loose vaginal wall muscles by suturing them together, thus creating a smaller circumference. A woman can expect to shell out between $2,500 to $8,000 for a designer vagina, which is not likely to be covered by insurance. A skillful surgeon with a practiced touch is highly recommended, as too much tightening can result in painful sex.

Note: Be Advised that it takes more than a rejuvenated vagina to *rejuvenate* a bad relationship.

Workouts for the Vagina

In 1948, a University of Southern California gynecologist named Dr. Arnold Kegel developed a series of exercises designed to strengthen a muscle on the pelvic floor called the Pubococcygeus (pew-bo-cok-SIH-gee-us) or P.C. muscle. Affectionately called "Kegels" they were originally intended to help women achieve better bladder control, and were later found to also have a rather joyful side effect: increased awareness of vaginal sensations. Kegel reported that many exercising female patients either: (a) experienced orgasm for the first time; or (b) climaxed more easily and reliably than ever before. Today, thanks to meticulous research into female eroticism, we know that because these muscles contract during orgasm, strengthening them also makes a woman's orgasm stronger and more pleasurable, and enables her to create a wider variety of sensations for herself and her partner (what more could an orgasmically inclined gal hope for?).

To identify the P.C. muscle, squeeze the muscle used to stop the flow of urine, or contract the anal sphincter as if to hold back gas. **Note:** Inserting a finger into the vagina is an effective way to feel the muscle contracting.

The Basic Kegel Exercises: (for best results, do them for ten to fifteen minutes every day):

1. Contract and relax the muscle in time to a quick beat (like the beat of your heart), 10 to 25 times.
2. Contract the muscle, hold for a count of three, then relax. Repeat 10 times.
3. Bear down on the muscle as if pushing something out of the vagina. Relax. Squeeze the muscle tightly. Relax. Repeat 10 times.

While Dr. Kegel can claim credit for developing our present-day notions of "vaginal exercises," he was by no means the first to identify the value of such muscles. Eroticist and adventurer Sir Richard Burton made the following notation in his *Book of the Thousand Nights and a Night*:

> [there's] a peculiarity highly prized by the Egyptians; the use of the constrictor vaginae muscles, the sphincter for which Abyssinian women are famous. The "Kabazzah" [holder], as she is called, can sit astraddle upon a man and can provoke venereal orgasm, not by wriggling and moving but by tightening and loosing the male member with the muscles of her privities, milking it as it were. Consequently the "cassenoisette" [nutcracker] costs treble the money of other concubines.

Déjà Virgin

For many centuries, women of the Middle East used the powdered astringent alum to tighten vaginas perceived to be a tad wide. Said to be highly popular, primarily due to its reputed effectiveness, the powder was mixed with water and smeared around the vaginal opening. Once completely dissolved it was injected into the vaginal canal, amid claims that it "pleases the husband." Legend also has it that women in both Europe and the United States—especially those employed in houses of prostitution—turned to the powdered vagina-shrinking substance to appear inexperienced if not virginal, with many seeking to appear so several times a night.

Like a Virgin

"O, O, O to Touch and Feel
a Girl's Vagina and Hymen."

—TRADITIONAL MEDICAL STUDENT'S MNEMONIC
FOR THE TWELVE CRANIAL NERVES*

HYMEN

Few body parts have caused women as much grief as the hymen. It is a thin mucous membrane that surrounds the vaginal opening, although it does not, in most cases, completely block it. The actual appearance of the hymen varies from a single opening (annular hymen) to two (septate hymen) or more openings (cribiform hymen). Sometimes referred to as the "maidenhead," its presence has been thought by generations to provide ipso facto evidence of a woman's virginity. However, for this task it is a poor

---

*Olfactory, Optic, Oculomotor, Trochlear, Trigeminal, Abducens, Facial, Acoustic, Glossopharyngeal, Vagus, Accessory, and Hypoglossal

indicator at best. Hymens vary in size, shape and strength, and may remain intact, *even after repeated intercourse.* And at the other end of the why-it's-not-proof spectrum: the hymen may be totally absent at birth. And yes, virgins can, and *do* insert tampons with ease.

Studies show that only 42 percent of all women are born with a "normal" hymen that is likely to break and bleed when pressure is applied (and even then, the amount of blood is *very* slight); 47 percent of females possess a highly flexible hymen; and 11 percent have such a thin hymen that it breaks easily, most likely at an early age (and most likely through *nonsexual* activities like bike riding, gymnastics, horse-back riding, or strenuous exercise).

Feels Like the First Time

According to hymen folklore, first time intercourse hurts. A lot. Whispered horrors tell of an impenetrable wall that yields its hidden treasure only after brutal thrusts have left it ripped and shredded, amid spurting pools of cherry-red blood. It's not a pretty vision. It's also not an accurate one (although it is enduring enough to give more than a few virgins a bad case of the jitters). In truth, most girls don't even feel their hymen when it breaks, and blood, if there is any, is scant. A willing first time sexual encounter generally produces a stretched hymen rather than a torn one. Any pain or discomfort felt is usually due to a lack of sufficient vaginal lubrication and/or muscle tension, *not* an obliterated hymen.

Hymen hunters will find them in only two species: female horses and humans.

Hy'm in *Pain*

Sometimes, women who experience difficulty with intercourse are informed by their physicians that they have a "rigid hymen" that requires surgery to correct. This procedure, called a "hymenectomy," is actually rarely necessary. A woman can avoid the surgeon's knife by using her own fingers to gently and gradually stretch the hymen herself. This is accomplished by inserting one or two well lubricated fingers, and slowly exerting pressure against the resistant membrane. Repeat the process several times until the tissue has sufficiently relaxed. And if fingers leave you squeamish, a set of plastic dilators can accomplish the same thing.

Biological function of the hymen? None. Zip. Zero. Nada.

"You May Now Kiss the Bride"

The word hymen is from the Greek *humen,* meaning "veil" or "membrane," and is said to be named after Hymen/Hymena, the Greek god/goddess of marriage. Wedding trivia buffs may be interested to know that the rending of the veil (hymen) in the first act of sexual intercourse is still symbolically enacted by the blushing bride who lifts her bridal veil to receive her new husband's kiss following the marriage ceremony.

The Reborn Hymen

Traditions in many countries, particularly Mediterranean and African ones, as well as some parts of Asia, demand that brides display bloody sheets following the wedding night as proof of virginity. Failure to do so shames the family, and exposes them to the risk of violent reprisals that may include banishment, torture, or worse. Immigrants from these countries now living in western Europe have in recent years sought the help of surgeons to reconstruct the hymens of young girls who are no longer virgins—but wish to appear so. In its simplest form, the procedure utilizes catgut containing a bloodlike substance that bursts open during intercourse. This surgery—called "hymenorraphy" or "hymenoplasty"—is generally done a few days before a girl's planned nuptials, and is common in Japan (where it is known as "hymen rebirth"), and also in the Netherlands, where a patient has the legal option of removing any notes on the procedure from her medical records. Hymen reconstruction is also available in the

Although hymen reconstruction is illegal in most Arab countries, there are many sympathetic unofficial practitioners. The trade in Egypt alone has reduced revenge murders of women by 80 percent over the past ten years.

United States, where it is popular with Latin American women. Often referred to here as "revirginizing," clinics offering this surgery can be found on both the east and west coasts, and generally charge between $2,000 and $3,500.

Thrift Shop Hymens

Throughout the ages, women wishing to simulate virginity during a sexual encounter (as signified by "traces of hymen blood") without resorting to surgical techniques, accomplished the task by discreetly inserting various objects into their vaginas. These were generally small scraps of sponge soaked in blood or a small fish bladder filled with blood (the "evidence" was released by pressure during intercourse). Other less appealing options included blood-sucking leeches or fragments of broken glass placed in the vagina.

Cherry Pie

Since the nineteenth century, "cherry" has been a euphemism for hymen as well as for a female virgin, although the *Woman's Encyclopedia of Myths and Secrets* suggests the use of cherry for virginity may be traced to a mythic past, given the fact that cherry juice stains like blood: "Like other red fruits, such as the apple and pomegranate, the cherry symbolized the virgin Goddess: bearing her sacred blood color and bearing its seed within, like a womb." It's interesting to note that at the start of the twentieth century, the "virgin" status insinuated by the use of the term "cherry" applied to both males and females. But the advent of the phrase "popping (someone's) cherry" during the hippie reign of the 1960's returned sexism to the term (females are "cherries" and males are the ones "popping" them).

Flower Child

Defloration (from the Latin *deflorare* meaning "stripping of flowers" or "to remove the bloom") is, by definition, the stealing of a woman's prized "flower"—the tearing of her hymen. This act is usually accomplished through sexual intercourse, although in earlier times virgins were often ritually deflowered with sacred dildoes. While flowers may conjure associations of lightness and sensuality, the definition of "deflower" found in the Oxford English Dictionary underscores a darker imagery: "to violate, ravage, desecrate, to rob of its blood, chief beauty, or excellence (since 1486)."

Who Ya Gonna Call? Hymen-Busters!

• In primitive times, Man's abject fear of the demonic power of hymen blood gave rise to the custom of having the woman deflowered by slaves or strangers (their supposed "disinterest" left them immune to demonic possession). In central Africa, the bride-to-be's father paid a man to rupture the evil membrane, while in eastern Africa a husband could not have intercourse with his bride unless she had been deflowered by one of her admirers. And in Tibet, mothers would offer their virgin daughters to total strangers to complete the task.

Curiously, this type of defloration left a bride's prized "virginity" intact.

• In ancient Greece, aristocratic young girls were often ceremonially deflowered by having their hymens pierced with a stone penis of the god Priapus (whose generous endowment was associated with abundant fertility). By having Priapus as her first "lover," she was thought to be guaranteed a rich life filled with many children.

• In a ritual that continues today in parts of Nepal, young girls pay tribute to fertility gods by having their hymens broken using a piece of phallus-shaped fruit, hoping to win special favors and avoid sterility. (Gives new meaning to the phrase "be fruitful and multiply, doesn't it?)

The Black Rose

"Who has put this pubic hair on my coke?"

—CLARENCE THOMAS, ACCORDING
TO TESTIMONY BY ANITA HILL

PUBIC HAIR

In many a young lass, the first discernible sign of puberty (from Latin *pubescere,* "to be covered with hair," and *puber* "of ripe age") is the appearance of lightly colored, sparsely distributed strands of hair on the mons pubis. Within a few years, the hair spreads and grows darker, thicker, and coarser (but does not, in most cases take over the body). Much like eyebrows and underarm hair, pubic hair serves to absorb and divert moisture. It can be thick or scant, confined to areas covered by the briefest bikini, or spread up the abdomen toward the navel and down the inner thighs.

In *both* sexes, the appearance, amount, and distribution of pubic hair is due to the hormone testosterone (in boys, secreted from the testicles; in girls, from the adrenal gland). Too much testosterone in a woman often produces the typical male pubic pattern: a narrow band of hairs tapering up toward the navel. Likewise, too little of this all important masculinizing hormone in men yields an inverted triangle pattern generally seen in women.

Average age pubic hair begins to develop: 11 years

The primary function of pubic hair is to act as an odor trap for secretions released by the apocrine glands located in the pubic area. Once these secretions are unleashed, the hair traps the scent, enabling it to linger and act as an erotic stimulus to the opposite sex (an evolutionary thing). Curiously, women possess 75 percent more scent glands than men.

Pubic Ponderings

". . . it's like lettuce under the fruit,
it's only there for presentation."
—CHARACTER REFERRING TO PUBIC HAIR,
THE DREW CAREY SHOW

In earlier times, our scientific forefathers were puzzled by the presence of pubic hair. *Why Was It There? What Did It Do?* Opinions varied, from Greek anatomist Galen (130–200), who thought the pubic presence was simply ornamental, to Danish anatomist Kaspar Bartholin (1585–1629), who proffered the notion that the hairs were designed for "modest concealment" (a veritable covering for the "awakening genitals emerging from their chastity"). Other pontificating scholars suggested the hairs protected the sensitive mons area from the cold; from some unforeseen tragic accident; or appeared in order to relieve pressure during coitus by acting as "pads." Finally, it was widely held by most early anatomical investigators that profuse hair in the female pubic region was a sign of "strong sexual instincts and functions," while those women who lacked a triangular growth were surely doomed to be sterile.

Does She . . . or *Doesn't She?*

Pubic hair comes in various shades and colors, and, contrary to popular belief, is not always an accurate reflection of one's natural head hair color. In other words, one *can* be a true blonde up top and a brunette down below.

Jean Harlow, whose trademark white-blond hair and low-cut gowns made her the reigning sex queen of the 1930s (Harlow, of course, was the first to utter the infamous line, "Do you mind if I slip into something more comfortable?") routinely dyed her pubic hair platinum to match the hair on her head.

A Rose by Any Other Name . . .

The Chinese refer to pubic hair using various poetic terms, including "black rose," "fragrant grass," "sacred hair," or "moss." Women without any pubic hair are known as "white tigers"; black pubic hairs are said to indicate a strong and obstinate woman; brown with golden tints are the sign of an easy and generous woman; and fine, silky, short hair is said to mean quiet and retiring. In the Chinese culture, upward growth of a woman's pubic hair is considered a sign of beauty; and abundant hair is regarded as a sign of sensuality and passion.

In Japan, a woman with no pubic hair may also find herself without a husband, as the condition is considered grounds for divorce. A naked pubis is so unappealing, in fact, it's the focus of a popular Japanese insult, *kawarage*, which loosely translates to "with a vulva as bald and hard as a brick."

Not-So-Poetic Pubic Phrases:

Ace of Spades, Front Lawn, Front Door Mat, Bushy Park, Green Meadow, Fleece, Plush, Downy Bit, Muff, Bunny, Christmas Tree, Parsley, Cushion, Short Hairs, Nether Beard, Quim Beard

"Long Beautiful Hair—Shinin', Gleamin', Streamin' Flaxen Waxen"

Legend had it that Bilkese, the Queen of Sheba, had a silken pubic veil that extended *to her knees.* It's also been suggested that

Solomon refused to copulate with the hirsute queen until she had thoroughly removed all of said pubic veil.

Bismarck Archipelago women were known to have copious amounts of hair on their pubis and used it as a kind of "cloth" with which they wiped their hands.

Hair Today, Gone Tomorrow

You will find no pubic hair on the classic statues of women from ancient Greece and Rome for an obvious reason: the women of ancient Greece and Rome *had* no pubic hair. The downy mass was considered both ugly and unhygienic, and was routinely shaved or tweezed away (a practice that ceased after the fall of the Roman Empire).

In various provinces of India, women practice the ancient custom of removing their pubic hair, using special rings designed solely for this purpose. The rings, known as *arsi,* are worn on the thumb, and resemble an unusually large signet ring with flat, sharp-edged discs set with tiny mirrors (to reflect the area in question). The hairs are shaved with the ring's sharp edges.

Bridal Tradition

During the Ottoman Empire, young Moslem women typically had their veil of nature removed on the day of their wedding— considering it sinful to engage in sexual intercourse in a hirsute state. This prenuptial depilation was performed as part of an elaborate ritual at the baths in which all body hair was removed. A paste, a mixture of honey and turpentine, was applied to the entire body, allowed to dry, and then ripped off—causing all that unwanted hair to be yanked out by the roots. (Contemporary women will surely recognize the origins of—and no doubt empathize with—this early form of the bikini wax.)

Most painful time to have a bikini wax: Just before, during, or right after your period

Other painful time to have a bikini wax: Every other day

Slick

Slick is a contemporary slang term referring to genitals that have been shaven. Cultural rituals aside, it seems the look and feel of a bare pubis is a considerable sexual turn-on for many folks. In the interpretive realm, pubic hair is associated with adult sexuality, while bareness evokes images of childhood. Thus, those opting for the pubescent look may wish to hearken back to a time of sexual innocence. And men who request a partner to shave her pubes may feel safer with a woman who looks like an immature female (either that, or they simply consider the hair unaesthetic). Whatever the reason, shaving the pubic area requires an ample supply of anti-itch preparations to maintain one's sanity during the growing-in process. Consider yourself forewarned.

Take Two Pubic Hairs and Call Me in the Morning . . .

During the sixteenth century, French physicians often treated hysteria in women by pulling out clumps of pubic hair. According to Georges Valensin in *The French Art of Sex Manners*, this was done as a means of making the "suffocating humors of the brain flow to a place that was quick to receive them." Meanwhile, in other parts of sixteenth-century Europe, health workers prized the healing power of pubic hairs, and utilized the valuable strands for "pharmaceutical" purposes. A popular folk remedy for reviving comatose persons, as well as for disinfecting open wounds, was a concoction of burnt pubic hairs and other miscellaneous ingredients. However, the treatment only afforded relief to men if the hairs came from women, and vice versa.

GOOD GIRLS HAVE CURLS

In various parts of Europe during the Middle Ages, straight pubic hair was thought to be a sure sign of excessive masturbation. It's worth noting that miniature curling rods were also popular at that time.

Pubic Passions

"A thousand kisses to your neck, your breasts,
and lower down, much lower down,
that little black forest I love so well."

—NAPOLEON, IN A LETTER TO JOSEPHINE

In the late 1800s, velvet and fur became popular objects of desire among sexual fetishists—who were almost always male, by the by—and many a frenzied furrier reached orgasmic heights simply by caressing the soft silken materials (velvet underwear was a favored item). Eminent psychoanalyst Sigmund Freud (who else?) hypothesized that velvet and fur unconsciously symbolized female pubic hair (what else?).

Of course, female pubic hair—the real thing—also has a rich history as a fancied item of carnal lust among the fetish crowd. Men have long collected wisps of furry down from sexual conquests, treasures they often use to relive—or create anew—moments of sexual ecstasy. Many such cases are vividly described in *Psychopathia Sexualis,* a work which chronicles the writings of Baron Richard von Krafft-Ebing (1842–1902) the noted German physician who meticulously outlined the range of sexual deviance. One such entry describes a fetishist who delighted in tearing out female pubic hairs with his *teeth* (which he then stored and used for subsequent masturbation munchies). The gentleman in question had the audacity to bribe his way into newly vacated hotel rooms in order to retrieve the occasional stray pubic hair from the beds of female guests.

Nice Hat,
but Where's the Tassel?

In the eighteenth century, an exclusive men's club was formed in Scotland catering to the spirited and bawdy needs of the era's nobility. Convened twice a year as The Beggars Benison, the central feature of this gathering was a wig said to have been woven from the pubic hairs of King Charles II's many mistresses. Legend has it that newcomers were required to wear this unusual hairpiece during the initiation ceremony, which in and of itself was undeniably unique. After masturbating himself to erection, the member-wannabe situated his (hopefully) still firm organ upon a silver testing platter accompanied by approving blasts from a ceremonial trumpet. The erection was duly measured and the size noted in a logbook for posterity. Lodge members than shared a moment of mutual touching with their own erect organs, and later, all enjoyed a sumptuous banquet, replete with obligatory obscene toasts and lascivious songs. During the festivities, the beloved pubic wig was passed about the room, whereupon each member, no doubt giddy with glee, kissed the artifact and wore it atop his own head for a few glorious moments.

In a sophomoric coup, the wig was later snatched away by a group of lusty and fetishistic nobles from Edinburgh, and became the prized central feature of their notoriously erotic forum dubbed, appropriately, "The Wig Club." In its new home, the furry icon blossomed, as new members of the salacious society were required to make their own pubic offerings. In an attempt to replace their pilfered pubes, members of the now wig-less Beggars Benison turned to the mistresses of George IV, hoping to create a new pubic do. Alas, George was a bit more sedate than the frisky Charles. As a result, the beleaguered lads were able to gather no more than a few wisps, which they kept in a snuff box dutifully labeled "hair from the mons veneris of a royal courtesan of George IV."

Pubic du Pompadour

Before the bodacious Scots sported wigs made *from* pubic hair, seventeenth-century Englanders donned wigs made *for* the pubic region. At the time, fashion-forward Brits referred to their pubic wigs as "merkins," and later, in the nineteenth century, as "bowsers." And Wendy Cooper notes in her appropriately titled book, *Hair*, that in mid-sixteenth-century France, it was considered elegant in high society for a woman to pomade her pubic hair in order to encourage its growth and to then decorate the region with colored silk bows or ribbons.

I'm Ready For My Close-up, Mr. Demille

It wasn't until the year 1968 that pubic hair made its cinematic debut. In the pubic premiere, the heroine of Jonas Cornell's Swedish film *Hugs and Kisses* gets undressed in front of a mirror, wanders about the room, and looks at her reflection. As one might imagine, a bit of controversy surrounded this first female full frontal—in fact, the scene was originally cut from the flick but later reinstated due to popular demand.

Playboy's First Pubes

While Marilyn Monroe has the distinction of gracing the first centerfold pages of *Playboy* magazine for the 1953 debut issue, her pubic hair was nowhere to be seen. The honor of first appearing au natural—from boob to pube—goes to Paula Kelly, in the magazine's August 1969 issue.

ᵛ⃛

"Do you mind if I trim it?" he asked politely.

She smiled as she looked down at him. "Of course not. You can do what you like." Her eyelids fell to half mast as she gazed at him. "You do make me feel like a work of art."

"That's because you are one," he responded as he produced a small pair of scissors and began to trim the wispy edges.

Soon the thick mass of hair was transformed into a small circular tuft and he saw those vulnerable lips up close. He had never seen a woman's vulva so clearly. The love place. The cunt. The doorway to paradise. The come-to-me-and-lose-your-heart-and-soul place.

—LONNIE BARBACH, *50 WAYS TO PLEASE YOUR LOVER*

The Tender Button

*"Really that little dealybob
is too far away from the hole.
It should be built right in."*

—LORETTA LYNN

CLITORIS (CLIT uhr is): A small erectile organ at the front or top part of the vulva that is a center of sexual sensation in females (*Longman Dictionary of the English Language, 1984*).

THE NOT-SO-LITTLE DEALYBOB

To the naked eye, the clitoris *is* but a tiny part of a woman's genitalia, a protruding flesh button measuring a mere eighth of an inch to half an inch in diameter and a quarter of an inch to one inch in length. However, what you see is literally the *tip* of a clitoral iceberg, so to speak. While professional types have long known there was significantly more to the clitoris than its visible presentation, it wasn't until very recently that we learned just how much more. And the fact is, the clitoral organ is approximately ten times larger than the average person believes it to be. What the average person may not know is that most of the clitoris is hidden *inside* the body in a pyramid-shaped mass of erectile tissue, along with an impressive network of nerve channels and blood vessels traveling merrily alongside the walls of the uterus, vagina, bladder, and urethra. The full extent of the clitoral topography was newly uncovered courtesy of an exhaustive 1998 Australian research effort that utilized meticulous microdissection techniques along with high-tech 3-D photography.

The new and improved vision of the clitoris looks like so: the tip—technically referred to as the clitoral glans—is connected beneath the skin to the clitoral body, said to be about as big as the first joint of the thumb. The clitoral body, in turn, has two arms up to 9 centimeters long that flare backward high into the woman's pelvis. Also connected to the clitoral body are two bulbs,

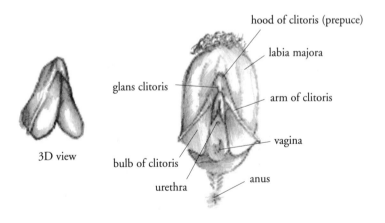

3D view

hood of clitoris (prepuce)

labia majora

glans clitoris

arm of clitoris

vagina

bulb of clitoris

urethra

anus

or crura (arms), that run downward and inward for about 3 inches along either side of the vaginal opening.

When all is said and in place, the clitoris surrounds the urethra on three sides while the fourth is embedded in the front wall of the vagina. During sexual excitement, *all* of the clitoral tissues become engorged with blood, thus increasing the erotic sensitivity of any tissues that happen to be nearby (think: vagina, labia, urethra, pubic mound). It's no exaggeration to say that where the clitoris is concerned, misguided experts throughout the ages made a molehill out of a veritable mountain.

WORD GAMES

According to Jane Mills in *Womanwords,* the word "clitoris" made its English debut in a 1615 anatomy book entitled *A Description of the Body of Man* (honest): "these ligaments . . . do degenerate into a broad and sinewy slenderness . . . upon which the Clitoris cleaveath and is tyed." By most accounts, the word itself originates from the Greek *kleitoris,* meaning . . . well, actually *what* it means depends on *where* you look. For example: *The Woman's Encyclopedia of Myths and Secrets* claims the Greek *kleitoris* meant "divine, famous, goddesslike" and that Greek mythology personified the clitoris as an Amazon queen named Kleite, ancestral mother of a tribe of warrior women who founded a city in Italy.

Whereas, *The Oxford Dictionary of Etymology,* along with the ever-popular Webster, says clitoris derives from the Greek *kleitoris* meaning "to shut."

Whereas, *The American Heritage Dictionary* maintains clitoris derives from the Greek *kleitoris* meaning "little hill" or "slope."

Whereas a nineteenth-century French medical dictionary says the word clitoris derives from the Greek Verb *kleitoriazein,* meaning "to touch or titillate lasciviously, to be inclined to pleasure."

Discuss amongst yourselves.

CLITORAL CURIOSITIES

"All our late discoveries in anatomy can find no use for the clitoris but to whet the female desire by its frequent erections."
—GEOFFREY DE MANDEVILLE, 1724

- Average clitoral size (visible glans) of a newborn baby: **0.345 cm**
- Average clitoral size (visible glans) of adult woman: ¼ to **1 inch**
- The clitoris is the most sensitive, nerve-filled part of a woman's body. The glans alone harbors over 8,000 nerve fibers (*twice* the number found in the penis). It is also the only human organ whose sole function is sexual sensation.
- Percentage of women who require some kind of clitoral stimulation in order to reach a sexual climax: **75**
- Intercourse position affording a woman maximum clitoral stimulation: woman-on-top
- During sleep, the clitoris appears to gain and lose an erection every 90 minutes, just like the penis.

• Some clitorises (glans) are *large* and some are *small,* (the size varies greatly among women, as does penis size among men) but there is no relationship between clitoral size and enjoyment of sexual activity or orgasmic ability. None. Zippo. Zilch. However, the farther away from the mouth of the vagina that the clitoral glans is located, the less stimulation it directly receives during intercourse, which accounts for the difficulty many women have achieving orgasm through intercourse alone. (Creative positioning and/or hand augmentation can be very useful here.)

• During sexual arousal, the blood engorged clitoral glans becomes exquisitely sensitive, ultimately reaching the point where it just can't stand any more direct stimulation. Seeking refuge, it pulls back and retires beneath its hood.

• Average *increase* in size of the clitoris during sexual arousal: **2 times**

• Average *length* of time it takes the clitoris to return to normal size following orgasm: **15 seconds**

• An uncommon condition called "clitoral priapism" causes a prolonged erection of the clitoral glans that is unrelated to sexual arousal and not relieved by orgasm. This unpleasant and painful reaction is usually associated with medication—those used to treat depression are the most likely culprits.

• If pleasing erotic stimulation of the clitoris lasts from 1 to 10 minutes, 40 percent of women will likely have an orgasm. If pleasing stimulation lasts for 20 minutes, 90 percent are likely to enjoy the pleasures of climax.

• According to Tantric teachings, a woman's *upper lip* is considered to be one of the most erogenous areas of her body, due to a special nerve channel that connects her palate and upper lip to her clitoris. Known as the "wisdom conchlike nerve" (named for its form, which at the lower end is encircled many times around, like a shell), it is said to channel orgasmic energy. Women are encouraged to visualize the nerve running from her clitoris to her upper lip in order to awaken it and consciously channel sexual energy through it, thus significantly enhancing her erotic pleasure.

- Reproductive function of the clitoris: none

TENDER EUPHEMISMS

"What's the matter, papa? Please don't stall.
Don't you know I love it and want it all?
I'm wild about that thing. Just give my bell a ring.
You pressed my button. I'm wild about that thing."

—*"I'M WILD ABOUT THAT THING"*
RECORDED BY BESSIE SMITH, 1929

While no match for the lengthy list of vaginal euphemisms, there are several well known clitoral aliases that have been coined throughout the ages. Including:

Clit, Jewel, Crown, Crown Jewel, Magic Jewel, Little Boat, Boy-in-the-Boat, Taste Bud, Rosebud, Buzzer, Button, Pearl, Golden Tongue, Bon-Bon of Love, Seat of Pleasure, Dolores

Another popular clitoral nom de plume actually originated as the title of a book, *Tender Buttons* (1914), an infamous work of abstract erotica penned by celebrated lesbian author, Gertrude Stein (1874–1946). A woman ahead of her time (and a good fifty years ahead of Masters and Johnson), Stein well understood the intricacies of the clitoral orgasm. She esoterically explored the title object, the clitoris, by touching on her subject in a way "tender buttons" would no doubt appreciate—from firm and flirty to soft and steady. (Although readers of the book would be excused for not getting it given her "coded" discussion of seltzer bottles, colored hats, rhubarb, and "sisters who aren't misters.")

WHO FOUND IT FIRST?

Many folks think the clitoris was the "discovery" of pioneering sex researchers William Masters and Virginia Johnson back in the 1960s, and applaud the St. Louis pair for identifying its crucial role in the female orgasm. The fact is, however, the tender button had been noticed long before the dynamic sex duo stepped into the so-called sex lab. Way long.

Hippocrates identified the clitoris as the seat of women's pleasure as far back as 500 B.C., and ancient Chinese pillow books suggest these folks were on to it many years earlier. But apparently no one noticed—or cared—because the organ continued to be "discovered" at various intervals throughout history. Finally, zealous work by Renaissance anatomists of the seventeenth century brought consensus within scientific circles as to the form and erotic function of the clitoris, and, given their superior scholarship and exacting scrutiny, these findings prevailed unchallenged over the next few hundred years. But then, *something happened*, and poof! the clitoris seemingly dropped off the anatomical radar screen at the dawn of the twentieth century.

In *Making Sex: Body and Gender from the Greeks to Freud*, Thomas Laquer sardonically points out that Masters and Johnson's "revelation" that female orgasm is almost entirely clitoral would have been "a commonplace to every seventeenth-century midwife, and had been documented in considerable detail by nineteenth-century investigators." In commenting on the mysterious absence and subsequent miraculous (re)discovery of clitoral phenomena, Laquer muses: "A great wave of amnesia descended on scientific circles around 1900, and hoary truths were hailed as earth-shattering in the second half of the twentieth century." The truth is out there—this might have the makings of good *X-Files* plot.

Eureka! I Found It!

In 1559, an anatomical explorer by the name of Columbus (Renaldus, not Christopher), while diligently searching the female body for signs of new life, chanced upon what he believed to be heretofore uncharted territory—the clitoris (apparently his *Hippocratic Classics* were on the shelf, gathering dust). Columbus described the spot as "preeminently the seat of a woman's delight," but clearly showed his Galenic leanings (i.e., the need to see female genitalia as defective penises) by continuing "if you touch it, you will find it rendered a little harder and oblong to such a degree that it shows itself as a sort of male member." Columbus duly anointed his discovery *mentula muliebris* (female penis), although he wisely decreed that it should be referred to as the "sweetness of Venus."

Eureka! Part 2

The nod for the first detailed description of the clitoris goes to the Italian Gabriel Fallopio, the gifted Renaissance scientist who first identified the uterine tubes that today bear his name. Fallopio was also the first to dissect the deeper internal structures of the clitoris, parts unknown to scientists before him. Embroiled in a bitter "me first" war, young Fallopio called Columbus a plagiarist, insisting that he (Fallopio) was the one who saw the clitoris first (although his work was not published until 1561, a good two years post-Columbus's "sightings"). At any rate, Fallopio deserves kudos for being among a small group of courageous scientists who dared to question Galen's (second century) assertion that the vagina was a penis turned inside out and instead jumped on (or started) the clitoris/penis bandwagon. Wrote a haughty Fallopio of the clitoris:

> *This small part corresponds to the male penis. . . . This very private part, small in size and hidden in the very fatty part of the pubis, has remained unknown to the anatomists, so that up to now from the preceding years I am the first to describe it, and if there have been others who have spoken of it or written about it, be known that they have not heard of it spoken of by me or by those who have heard me and, therefore, only for this reason there is not a good knowledge of it.*

Eureka, My Ass

Both Fallopio and Columbus were chided for their presumptuous claims of discovery by Kaspar Bartholin, the distinguished seventeenth-century anatomist who pointed out in *his* writings that the clitoris had been known to everyone since the second century.

The French Connection

"In French it is called temptation, the spur to sensual pleasure, the female rod and the scorner of men: and women who will admit their lewdness call it their "gaude mihi" [great joy]."
—JACQUES DUVAL, FRENCH PHYSICIAN, 1612

Well before Alex Comfort's classic sex manual *The Joy of Sex* hit the nation's bookshelves, renowned French surgeon Nicholas Venette penned *Tableau de l'Amour Conjugal,* an enthusiastic and graphic love and sex manual for couples (which went into a dozen editions and was translated into English, Dutch, and German). The year? 1687. Of the clitoris, Venette wrote:

> One sees above the inner labia an organ about half-a-finger's breadth tall, which the anatomist calls the "clitoris." I should call it the very passion and guide of Love. It is there that Nature has placed the throne of pleasures and sensuous joys. It is there that Nature has endowed excessive sensitivity and, too, has established the zone of wantonness for women. Thus, in the

action of Love, the clitoris fills itself with life forces and stiffens
like the penis of a man.

Venette should have stopped there, but alas, the thoughts, beliefs and mores of the times were just too darn powerful for this enlightened man. Thus, he goes on to say:

It is this organ that lewd women abuse. Sappho the Lesbian
never would have gained her notorious reputation if she had
had a smaller clitoris. . . . I once saw an eight-year-old girl who
had a clitoris half the length of a little finger; and if this organ
grows with age, as it appears it will, then I'm convinced it will
soon become as thick and as long as the one Platerus claimed to
have seen: which was as thick and as long as the neck of a goose.

Tsk Tsk, Venette.

WHERE'D IT GO?

"She showed me where that little button is . . .
now I can find that thing in the dark. And that
is a good thing for a guy to know."
—BRAD PITT, *JOHNNY SUEDE*

It may have piqued scientific curiosity, but as far as the rest of the world was concerned, the clitoris was neither seen nor heard of and definitely not felt throughout most of history. The organ's original disappearing act essentially occurred during medieval times, when the Christian church emphatically taught that women should not experience sexual pleasure, and that intercourse, a necessary evil, should be tolerated only for the sake of procreation. From that time onward, both men and women were kept in the proverbial dark (the condition under which they usually fumbled with each others' genitals) about female sexuality. This included any knowledge of what it was that girls actually had down there. At some point, even physicians came to believe that no clitoris would be found on a virtuous woman, ensuring that she would remain pure and faithful.

The Clitoris Witch Project

In her book *Witchcraft,* Barbara Rosen mentions a 1593 witch trial in which the investigator—a married man—discovered a clitoris for the first time. The bewildered and distraught gent concluded that this "little limp of flesh, in a manner sticking out as if it had been a teat, to the length of half an inch" could only be a devil's teat (where Satan supposedly got his nourishment). So amazed was he by his discovery, that although at first he determined not to show it to anyone "because it was adjoining to so secret a place which was not decent to be seen; yet in the end, not willing to conceal so strange a matter," he exposed the woman's genitals to others, who, likewise, were astounded. On the strength of this evidence the witch was ultimately convicted.

THE GREAT VAGINA/CLITORIS DEBATE

Few people are aware that up until the dawn of the twentieth century, there was no such thing as a vaginal orgasm.

Hundreds of medical texts and generations of anatomists had clearly and thoroughly documented the erotic superiority of the clitoris and its key role in female orgasms. In fact, a clitoral orgasm was the *only* kind of orgasm anybody knew or cared about. Vaginal sensitivity in the sexual milieu had long since been discussed and dismissed. As Thomas Laquer writes in *Making Sex*, "the abundance of specialized nerves in the clitoris and the relative impoverishment of the vagina" had been known for hundreds of years, stretching back to the seventeenth century. Apparently someone forgot to tell this to a man named Sigmund Freud. For reasons difficult to fathom, in 1905 Freud took it upon himself to rewrite anatomical science. First, he "rediscovered" the clitoris, giving new meaning to the organ, and then he singlehandedly invented the vaginal orgasm. Influential guy that he was, folks bought into it, and orgasmic chaos has reigned ever since.

He Said . . .

Freud declared that all mature, adult women should expect vaginal orgasm as the normal sexual response, proclaiming:

> *In the phallic phase of girls the clitoris is the leading erotogenic zone. But it is not, of course, going to remain so. With the change to femininity the clitoris should wholly or in part hand over its sensitivity, and at the same time its importance, to the vagina.* (New Introductory Lectures on Psychoanalysis)

She Said . . .

We have bought the idea that the vagina is the primary sex organ and that therefore, the only real way to have a "mature" orgasm is through the thrusting of the penis in and out of the vagina. In reality . . . the clitoris is the female sex organ. Roughly comparable in sensitivity to the penis, the clitoris serves no other function than that of providing sexual pleasure. The vagina is comparable in sensitivity to the male testicles. Therefore, if instead of sexual intercourse, which directly stimulates the male's most sensitive organ, and only indirectly stimulates the female's most sexually sensitive organ, love-making were practiced by a male rubbing the clitoris with his testicles—then women would be orgasmic and men would be in groups for pre-orgasmic "treatment." (Lonnie Barbach, For Yourself: The Fulfillment of Female Sexuality)

Misbehaving Vaginas

"If there was anything I hated,
it was investigating the organs
of the female pelvis."

—JAMES MARION SIMS, *GYNECOLOGIST,* 1884,
INVENTOR OF THE VAGINAL SPECULUM

The carnal mysteries that lie within the hallowed walls of the vagina have long been a source of both marvel and muddle. At times yielding and cooperative, and the purveyor of unparalleled pleasure, the vagina (and her associates) also frequently behaves like an insolent adolescent; it won't do what it's supposed to do, it won't respond to or participate in activities, it refuses to come when called, and it can be the cause of endless pain and misery. Scientific attempts to understand and tame these rebellious vaginal antics have been historically sparse and, for the most part, disappointing. However, recent pharmaceutical successes with penile difficulties have revved up researchers (and giddy investors) and spawned a frenzied search among lab wizards to unlock and similarly conquer the fickle female pleasuredome.

Twenty-first-century innovations for treating what vaginally ails her run the gamut from Viagra-like pills to topical love creams to tiny vacuum cleaner gizmos the likes of which June Cleaver could never have imagined. Most treatments are designed to boost blood flow to the vagina and clitoris in order to increase a woman's sexual sensitivity. Some of these vaginal fixes are enticing and promising, and are briefly discussed on pages 198 to 200. But first, a detour.

PANDORA'S BOX

Before curious minds turned their attention to the all-important vaginal questions "How does it work?," "Why *doesn't* it work sometimes?," and "How do you fix it?," there was yet another vexing anatomical query which demanded serious deliberation: "Just what the heck was in there, anyway?"

As told by Sir Richard Burton in *Book of the Thousand Nights* it was standard Middle Eastern belief that nymphomania was caused by worms in the Vagina.

The Toothed Vagina

The Vagina:

a. Sometimes has teeth

b. Is somewhat inflexible and will only comfortably accommodate a penis 4–5 inches in length

c. Has a rich supply of nerve endings extending up to the cervix, but not beyond

d. Is a "self-cleansing" organ which does not require the assistance of feminine hygiene agents, soaps, or douches

—HUMAN SEXUALITY EXAM QUESTION

FROM AUTHOR'S FILES

While the above question was designed to bring a momentary smile to anxious test-taking students, once upon a long time ago the concept of teeth-bearing vaginas was anything but funny. Ancient mythology is rich with horror stories of vaginas that contain teeth, glass, or other sharp objects that can cut the penis or worse, bite it off. Medieval Christian authorities (who likened the vagina to the gate of hell) taught that certain witches, with the help of magic spells, could grow fangs in their vaginas. And the concept of devouring female genitals resurfaced yet again early in the twentieth century when many of psychoanalyst Sigmund Freud's patients recounted similar macabre stories.

Today, the so-called **vagina dentata,** or "toothed vagina" (the vulva has labia, "lips," and many men have believed that behind the lips lie teeth) is widely considered to be the classic symbol of man's fear of sex, expressing the unconscious belief that a woman may eat or castrate her partner during intercourse. This subliminal fear is fueled when the once erect penis goes limp and "dies" inside the voracious vagina.

The Mudurucu', an Amazonian tribe, refer to sexual intercourse as "eating penises."

Freud's "Castration Anxiety"
Revisited

In formulating one of his now infamous developmental theories, Freud righteously informed his minions: "Probably no male human being is spared the terrifying shock of threatened castration at the sight of the female genitals." The Bearded One opined that the boy believed the penisless girl once had such an organ as his own beloved member but that—horror of horrors— it was somehow taken away from her.

However, in the *Woman's Encyclopedia of Myths and Secrets*, Barbara Walker suggests Freud had the *reason* for the boy's terror of threatened castration and female genitals all wrong. The real reason for the terrifying shock, says Walker, likes in mouth/vulva symbolism—that creepy toothed vagina. In other words, instead of fearing women's genitals because she lost hers, the male's fear is based on the notion that she (and her drooling vagina) might *take his*. Simply put, his fear is one of being devoured.

❧
DID YOU KNOW?

The original promotional poster for the big screen adaptation of Peter Benchley's ocean thriller *Jaws* had to be slightly modified before acceptance. Studio heads thought the gaping carnivorous mouth of the star looked a bit too much like a tooth-bearing vagina.

How's This One Grab Ya?

"When I arrived, I found the man standing up and supporting the woman in his arms, and it was quite evident that his penis was tightly locked in her vagina."
—EGERTON Y. DAVIS, EX. U.S. ARMY

In addition to his fear of the dreaded "toothed vagina" is Man's longstanding fear of "penis captivus," better known as the "I'm stuck and I can't get out" phenomenon. In this scenario, a man's penis gets stuck inside a woman when her vaginal muscles go berserk and suddenly clamp down inexplicably. Whispered accounts of lovers' loins mercilessly stuck together have filtered out of brothels and emergency rooms alike, and even into the pages of respected medical journals. In the December 4, 1884 edition of the *Philadelphia Medical News,* a juicy account of penis captivus appeared under the pen name of Egerton Y. Davis, purportedly hailing from Pentonville, England. Egerton Y. Davis turned out to be the fanciful pseudonym of the mischievous Sir William Osler, a member of the *Medical News*'s editorial board, and the captivus story turned out to be a hoax arising from a sophomoric attempt to embarrass a pompous colleague.

Regrettably, the notion that a penis can become "trapped" inside the vagina is not limited to the curious imagination of the Western world. Natives of the Marshall Islands in the Pacific believe that incestuous relations lead to vaginal spasms which trap the penis. Various other cultures fear that an episode of "penile entrapment" will surely lead to the discovery of an illicit relationship (being those countries without the services of a Special Prosecutor). The misconception of a trapped penis undoubtedly arose from studious observation of our canine friends, who do indeed suffer from this phenomenon. But *human* penises do not, repeat, *do not* get stuck.

Do Not Enter

Although vaginas do not inexplicably clamp down on unsuspecting penises, sometimes they do inexplicably spasm, causing the muscles surrounding the vaginal opening to tighten. This condition, called "vaginismus," either: (a) prevents the penis (or finger or tampon) from entering; or, if it does manage to wriggle in, it (b) makes sex excruciatingly painful. Women generally describe the discomfort as an intense tearing or burning sensation. Either scenario is not good. Curiously, a woman may nonetheless be capable of sexual arousal, and may even have orgasms in spite of her uncooperative vagina.

Why Does This Happen?

Vaginismus, which affects about 2 percent of women, is generally triggered by a fear of penetration, with the vagina involuntarily responding much like the eye does when threatened by a finger. Although physical factors may be involved, the cause is usually psychological. Traumatic sexual experiences such as rape or sexual abuse can produce vaginismus, but more commonly therapists encounter factors such as shame or guilt about the genitals (from early childhood messages like "Don't touch down there! That's nasty!") and fear, often caused by the faulty belief that sex will be horribly painful.

The Good News

Vaginismus is 100 percent reversible, using a combination of psychotherapy, desensitization exercises, and vaginal dilators in graduated sizes.

Talk About Being Henpecked . . .

If a woman of the Ganda of Uganda should suffer from a dysfunction known as *olwazi* ("Tight Vagina"), which inhibits her participation in sexual intercourse, she will likely undergo a treatment regimen that involves pouring grain into the vagina and letting a rooster peck it out.

Let It Flow, Let It Flow, Let It Flow

"When a woman inclines to learning, there is usually something wrong with her sex apparatus."
—F.W. NIETZSCHE

According to recent figures, 43 percent of women are said to experience some form of Female Sexual Dysfunction (F.S.D.), a rather broad term that includes:

1. lack of sexual desire
2. the inability to be sufficiently aroused (which includes a lack of lubrication and sensation)
3. the inability to orgasm
4. pain during sex (including involuntary vaginal spasms)

While the causes of F.S.D. are many and varied, most researchers have chosen to focus their remedial efforts on the vagina and clitoris, having apparently adopted the mantra "increase genital blood flow" (in spite of the fact that women's *biggest* sexual complaint is low libido). Without adequate blood flow, sex is a limp and vacuous affair. Get enough, and the cosmos of sexual ecstasy is but a few sighs away. Or so it is with men. But what of women? Does the same paradigm apply to their fleshly feelings? Maybe, somewhat, and no.

As with men, a woman's genitals also fill with blood during sexual arousal, resulting in engorgement of the clitoris and lubrication of the vagina. While insufficient amounts of the red stuff can lead to vaginal dryness—which in turn may make intercourse painful, and orgasm difficult to contemplate, much less achieve—increased blood flow enhances lubrication. But lubrication alone does not make sex satisfying. As medical researchers are discovering (and others have long known), women's satisfactions and sensual pleasures are far more complex (in other words, good blood flow may be worthless without self-esteem, good body image, or a partner who does the dishes).

Nevertheless, the race for a female flow fix is on.

Hydraulics to the Rescue . . .

In May of 2000, the FDA entered the female orgasm arena and put their seal of approval on a "medical device" intended to help women along the climactic journey. Borrowing from the knowledge that blood flow to the penis was central to sexual arousal, researchers applied a bit of goose-and-gander logic and developed a gadget to pump blood into the homologous clitoris. Available by prescription only, the newly christened "Eros CTD" (Clitoral Therapy Device) is a small, soft, oval funnel (1.25 inches long and .75 of an inch across) with a tube attached to a handheld, battery-operated vacuum apparatus. To work the device, the cup is placed over the clitoral glans for a few minutes (but no more than 4.4!) until it feels engorged. Medically approved clitoral vacuuming doesn't come cheap. Expect to shell out around $360.

Steals and Deals

Financially strapped orgasm-less women may want to bypass the medical establishment and consider the Honeysuckle Vibe, a quivering soft pink cup made of jelly rubber (2 inches long and 1 inch in diameter) which fits over the clitoris, softly vibrating along with gentle vacuuming. This battery-operated carnal goody is available sans prescription from the cheerful folks at Good Vibrations (goodvibes.com) for around $20 bucks. Happy shopping.

Pharmacology to the Rescue

Note: None of the following have FDA approval (yet) for use in the treatment of female sexual dysfunction. However, all are legal and available for off-label use.

Edibles

• *Viagra (sildenafil):* as with men, Viagra allows more blood to flow into the genitals. But unlike men, most women do not seem to be miraculously cured by the little blue wonder pill. In fact, studies show it to be no more effective than a placebo. Individual women may experience erotic benefits, however, and Viagra appears especially promising for older females and those who have undergone a hysterectomy.

• *Apomorphine:* this drug's foray into the role of genital blood flow enhancer comes after years of use as a treatment for Parkinson's disease. Its sexual side effects were altogether unexpected. Essentially, apomorphine targets mental processes leading to arousal, and works by stimulating the brain's center for sexual response.

Spreadables . . .

• *Aprostadil (also known as Prostaglandin E1):* a naturally occurring potent vasodilator found in the skin as well as in semen. Long used as a penile injection agent to treat impotence, the female version utilizes a kinder and gentler suppository or rub-on cream. Alprostadil directly affects the tissues it comes in contact with, and thus, once the libidinous goo is placed in or around the vaginal opening, blood vessels dilate, tissues swell, and lubrication begins, all in as little as five minutes.

• *Dr. K's Dream cream:* a topically applied lust lotion, made of two blood-flow enhancing compounds, Aminophylline (commonly used to treat asthma) and the amino acid L-Arginine. For reasons unknown, slathering this experimental sex cream on the clitoris and surrounding tissues has boosted lubrication, arousal, and sensation in many an excited user. And, while long-term safety also remains unknown, dedicated fans nonetheless flock to www.loveenhancement.com for the stuff.

Herbs to the Rescue

Herbs with either a folk tradition or a bit of research evidence (or both) . . . to back up claims they work as Genital Blood Flow Enhancers in Women:

Gingko Biloba, Ginger, Cayenne, Avena Sativa, Kava Kava, L-Arginine (amino acid), Gotu Kola, Parsley

Damiana
With an erotic botanical name like *Turnera aphrodosoaca,* it's not surprising that the herb Damiana has been touted as a love tonic

since ancient times, having been used as such by the Mayan civilization. For the last few centuries it has been an extremely popular passion potion among Mexican women. Research shows it contains an essential oil that stimulates the genital tract, and alkaloids similar to caffeine that can increase the sensitivity of sexual organs.

Scents That Cause a Significant Increase in the Flow of Blood to the Vaginal Area:

Substance	Flow Increase
Good and Plenty candy and Cucumber	**13** %
Baby Powder	**13** %
Pumpkin Pie and Lavender	**11** %
Baby Powder and Chocolate	**4** %

How Dry I Am . . .

If vaginal dryness is a woman's only problem, be aware it can be treated with a lubricant rather than a pricey (and potentially hazardous) medication. User-friendly sexual lubricants (water-based is the safest type) can be purchased in both drug stores and sex boutiques. Brands like Astroglide, Probe, Slippery Stuff, and K-Y Liquid (better for sex than jelly) are *very* popular. Organically inclined folks may want to try uncooked egg whites.

Note to Women: The experience of sexual intercourse should be a painless one. This means no pain at all. Not even a little bit. If it hurts, you and your body are not doing it right. Get some help.

WHAT ABOUT THE BIRDS AND THE BEES?

Q: "How do porcupines do it?"
A: "Very carefully."

—CLASSIC ANIMAL JOKE

While "the birds and the bees" may be a classic metaphor for human procreation—used in The Talk by countless generations of moms and dads—the fact of the matter is, birds, bees, and their collective kinfolk have their own compelling reproductive story to tell.

As with humans, in order to get lucky many of God's creatures engage in courtship rituals that include a variety of seduction activities: they dance, they romance, and they display the wonder that is them (their power, their plumage, their penises). Unlike humans, however, it is here that we discover all penises and vaginas are *not* alike. From organs that gobble up the body to those that spiral like a corkscrew, the sexual appendages gracing the inhabitants of the wild kingdom are as varied as the species they adorn, similar only in the job they do: ensuring the continued presence of their kind along the cycle of life.

THE BIRDS . . .

Once upon a time, most species of male birds had penises. Today, however, all but about 3 percent of the world's avian population have lost the organ. Why did this happen? Well, according to those in the bird-know, the organ was apparently abandoned because *female* birds didn't like it. No need to worry about future generations, however, because penis-less birds have been provided with an alternative method of reproduction known as the "cloacal kiss," in which the male deposits sperm from his cloaca at the opening of his partner's cloaca. She then draws up the sperm for storage, content to let 'em wait until she's good and ready to release her eggs, at which time they'll be fertilized. Since Ms. Bird actively draws in the sperm—as opposed to passively receiving them—she is in complete control over whose sperm among her fine feathered friends will reach her eggs. And, of course, being in control is something she *does* like.

. . . AND THE BEES

A new queen bee leaving the hive to start one of her own will be followed by some two hundred eager males. While in flight, one of the bunch will successfully mount Her Royal Highness and copulate, only to have his penis remain embedded in her vagina when he attempts to pull away (which effectively disembowels him as he falls to his death). His severed penis now acts as a plug to hold in the sperm, which will fertilize some two million eggs over the next five years.

Can Batman Do This?

If one has to mate while hanging upside down by the toes, it's helpful to have a penis like the bat. This curved appendage pivots at the base, and is able to move to and fro all by itself, eliminating the need for precarious thrusting by the male.

The *Other* White Meat

The tip of the pig's generous eighteen-inch penis is twisted into a kind of corkscrew. During copulation, frenzied pig thrusting causes the organ to rotate up the vagina until the coiled tip becomes lodged in the folds of the female's cervix. In other words, he quite literally screws her. Once firmly stuck in place, Mrs. Pig's vagina begins to rhythmically contract against the shaft of Mr. Pig's penis, bringing on his ejaculation and with it up to a generous pint of semen.

Itsie Bitsie Teenie Weenie

The huge male gorilla, exuding power and virility and weighing in at over five hundred pounds, has an erect penis of about . . . two (count 'em, two) inches. Gorillas are said to have small phalluses because they do not compete with their genitals. They live with stable harems, impress their rivals with their large body size, and never felt the evolutionary need to develop large organs.

Monkey See, Monkey Do

A male chimpanzee solicits a female by opening his legs, displaying an erect penis and flicking his phallus with a finger while gazing at his potential partner. And when not interested in mating, the limber mammal is likely to perform fellatio on himself . . . because he can.

- When the male ostrich is sexually aroused, his penis protrudes stiffly from his anus.
- The female howler monkey has a very large clitoris—about the same size as the male monkey's penis—causing her to sometimes be mistaken for a he. This gender confusion has spurred several erroneous reports of homosexual monkey activity.

Boning Up on History

The human penis has no bone, but the raccoon penis *does* (as do dogs, seals, walruses, and whales). Unique among the penis bone crowd, raccoon bones have a whole language and cultural history unto themselves. Known by various colloquial terms that include "pecker bone," "coon dong," "love bone," "Texas toothpick," and "mountain man toothpick." In earlier times 'coon bones were frequently used as love tokens and gambling charms, and even now are often worn as necklaces in parts of the Midwest and southern states. They even had a practical use aside from their biological one. In colonial times, sharpened "pecker bones" were used by tailors to rip seams. (How long before Martha Stewart suggests they might lend a festive touch to a tray of hors d'oeuvres?)

Woof!

The long, pointed penis of a dog is composed of tissue, along with a handy bone which aids in the stiffening of an erection, putting man's best friend in the enviable position of never having to say "I'm sorry." Once the penis enters the female, its tip fills with blood, swelling until it resembles a bulb. At the same time, the muscles of the female's vagina begin to close behind said bulb, locking the two animals firmly together (a sight many are familiar with). Following his ejaculation—which occurs *very* slowly—Fido is unable to remove his penis, and thus is forced to remain locked in a doggy embrace for anywhere from a few minutes up to an hour.

And the Winner Is . . .

The average African bull elephant penis weighs a whopping 60 pounds, with an erection that extends over 6 feet. Add to that testes that weigh about 4.4 pounds (encompassing a volume of 184 cubic inches—about the size of a large football) and you have one *very* generously endowed creature garnering top honors in the land animal category.

CREEPY CRAWLERS

• The female bristle worm, whipped into a sexual worm frenzy after watching a tantalizing courtship dance, will bite off her partner's genitals and swallow the enclosed sperm. This savory appetizer effectively fertilizes her eggs as the sperm passes through her digestive tract.

• In the not-wanting-to-go-where-others-have-gone-before category, a male damselfly uses his penis to scoop out the sperm of previous suitors before he himself ejaculates.

• In the invertebrate version of anonymous sex, the female threadworm simply pokes her vagina through the skin of her host vegetable when she is ready for copulation. The males, in turn, crawl around the vegetable's surface until they find a hole that appeals to them, which they then nonchalantly proceed to fill with sperm.

• The male land snail has an enormous penis (by snail standards)—about as long as the snail itself—that is conveniently located on his head.

• Topping the snail in the category of penis size (and quite possibly all others, especially if you measure it as a percentage of body length) is the alpine banana slug. Measuring in at about six inches of slime, these creatures boast a penis over thirty-two inches . . . 542 percent times their body length!

• Once the female bumblebee eelworm has become impregnated, she crawls through the earth seeking the hibernating body of her namesake host—a queen bumblebee. Once nestled comfortably inside, she begins a macabre transformation. Her vagina begins to expand

and continues to grow until it has literally gobbled up the *entire body* surrounding it. Now an organ some twenty thousand times the size of the worm itself, the *"vagina formerly known as eelworm"* blissfully leads its own life until the young worms inside have hatched.

Kato Kaelin of the Fish World

The male starworm may be the ultimate live-in lover. This diminutive dwarf sets up permanent residence inside the female starworm's vagina, with nothing to do all day but fertilize her eggs as they're released.

Pregnant Fathers

The male seahorse has no penis, and if that wasn't bad enough, he's also the one who ends up pregnant. During copulation, the flamboyant female (in appearance and behavior) presses *her* tiny "penis" into a special pouch in the male's stomach, passing along about six hundred eggs to be fertilized. She then swims happily away, with no babies, no worries, and no stretch marks.

Fish for the White House Aquarium

The female African mouthbrooder deposits her unfertilized eggs in the water and then catches them in her mouth, while the wily male waits nearby. He has red spots on his anal fin that look like eggs, which the female naively attempts to gather. However, when she opens her mouth, she is instead greeted with sperm ejaculated by the male. Fertilization takes place inside her mouth. She never gets to use her sex organs.

Eight is *Not* Enough

The male octopus has no penis, an inconvenience he gets around by using one of his arms. The female octopus has her vagina in her nose and is not always interested in having anything stuck up inside it. This temperamental creature has been known to bite off the arm-used-as-a-penis of the male and swim away with it.

One final word on the octopus and perhaps the ultimate example of the inimitable penis acting independently of its owner. Some species of octopi possess a penis arm that occasionally breaks away from his body, wandering aimlessly through the water as an autonomous animal in search of a female to impregnate . . . usually somehow managing to find one. After faithfully depositing its sperm, the penis arm dies, strangely left to dangle from the female's body.

Grand Champion

Topping the penis size chart in *all* categories is the blue whale, who measures in (make that *out*) at an impressive ten feet. Mr. Whale even has a name for his gargantuan penis: it's called a "dork."

How the Wild Kingdom Is Hung

Animal	Erect Length
Blue whale	10 ft.
Elephant	6 ft.
Bull	3 ft.
Stallion	2½ ft.
Wild Boar	18 in.
Tiger	11 in.
Man	5.4 in.
Chimpanzee	3 in.
Gorilla	2 in.
Cat	¾ in.
Mosquito	$\frac{1}{100}$ in.

SACRED PARTS

"I cannot imagine God as anything other
than a hard penis raised high, seated on
the base of its two testicles as a monument
erected to virility, the creative principle,
the Holy Trinity, an idol of horn hanging
at the exact center of the human body . . .
trifoliate flower that is the emblem
of the passionate life, I will never be
done singing your praises."

—THE ALEXANDER OF MICHEL TOURNIER'S
LES METEORES

Long ago . . . and far away, ancient man turned a curious eye up
toward the heavens, beheld a radiant sphere of light, and knew it
was good. Under the watchful gaze of this flaming red ball, crops
grew from the earth, and children sprang forth from human and

211

beast alike. What magic! What power! What energy! (Masculine forces, all.) Awed by its magnificence, man knew this was an entity to be worshipped to ensure its daily return from the mysteries of night. And so was born the Sun myth, the universal religion of mankind. Grateful species that he was, man diligently searched the land for some earthly object to properly honor the regenerative disk but lo and behold, found what he was after dangling between his own legs. An object filled with its own potent magic. An object of unmitigated power. An object teeming with masculine energy. In the tangible phallus, man found the perfect symbol of creative and fertile energy (the sun). Thus, the ubiquitous practice of phallic worship was born. Or something like that.

In the Name of the Father, the Son, and the Holy Dick

Throughout most of the history of the world (in most parts of the world) worship of the male phallus was a somber, reverent, and pervasive tradition. Serious historians and researchers have expressed concern that present-day preoccupation with the physical/sexual nature of the male organ interferes with the study of the sacred and spiritual elements underlying the origins of the practice. Among the adoring ancients, the sight of the phallus awakened no obscene, lascivious, or sophomoric ideas. Quite the contrary (remember, it was the symbol of the earth's—and its inhabitants—creative and fertile energy). Phallic scholars caution titterers against confusing *symbol* with *content,* and assert that considering phallic worship in the literal sense is akin to accepting Christianity as cross worship or Judaism as worship of a six-pointed star.

With that thought in mind, intrepid explorers of Man's sacred beginnings invariably discovered that you cannot delve into the fundamentals of *any* religion without discovering phallic roots. In *Taboo No More,* author Mark Thorn maintains that phallic images, in one form or another, have been the seeds of all deities over the course of human history. He points out that St. Hippolytus, the authoritative third-century Christian theologian and martyr asserted that *all* the sacred mysteries of religion originally sprang from a "fascination with the male sexual organ."

Well . . . maybe not *all.* Abundant archeological evidence reveals that female genitalia (often called the "yoni") actually preceded the phallus (or the "lingam") as an object of worship and reverence, most likely due to their magical power to give life (and because men, at that time, were clueless about their own contribution to conception). Our earliest ancestors were awed by the wonder and mystery of creation and by a woman's power of reproduction, which was associated, somehow, with the genitalia. What Man could not understand, he worshipped. (Even today, the yoni continues to be the foundation for a myriad of religious cults and sacred rituals in various parts of the world.) The female genitals are seen by most experts as sacred symbols of the great goddess, and, in a more cosmic sense, the "Universal Mother" or "Source of All." There is ample evidence to suggest that in past civilizations, given her unique powers, woman was regarded as *superior to man.*

The Magical Yoni

Begetting babies wasn't the only trick attributed to woman's fleshy folds. Indeed, throughout the centuries and across the cultures, the vulva was thought to possess numerous magical qualities—early primitives believed that simply exposing these parts could heal the sick and scare away storms. Ancient civilizations, including the Romans and the Greeks, believed the sight of a naked vulva could cause gods to flee. In India, the sight of the exposed vulva handily warded off evil spirits. Early Egyptian women exposed their vulvas to drive evil spirits from the fields. And early Europeans believed flashing the vulva at the devil would cause him to retreat in abject fear.

THE PHALLUS ASCENDS THE THRONE

Some historians believe that the shift from vulva worship to phallic worship occurred with man's discovery of his part in procreation (likely sometime after 10,000 B.C.). Over the span of a few millennia the world was turned around, *and never looked back.* As with yoni worship, phallic worship derived as an expression of man's desire for children, for the perpetuation of the race.

> *"I hope to know no other temple than nature,*
> *to adore naught but the sun, to worship*
> *only the radiant member that creates man."*
> —MAURICE SACHS, *LE SABBAT*

It's Alive, It's Alive!

The ancient Egyptians originally idolized the phallus as a separate living entity, a veritable deity of celestial origin (worshipped for its godlike ability to create life), rather than as part of another living thing. It was only later that human or animal bodies were attached to the oversized phalli and worshipped as icons (the further one goes back in antiquity, the more frequently one finds the phallus represented as unattached). This practice was elucidated by Herodotus, the fifth-Century B.C. historian, who wrote that the Egyptians "have invented human figures the height of an arm's length, to which they attach genital parts almost as long as the rest of the body." The early Romans also embraced the body-less penis concept, and actually named the isolated phallus "Mutinus" or "Tutinus" (and sometimes the combined "Mutinus Tutinus").

Shiva's Lingam

Perhaps the most famous of all sacred penises and the premier example of phallic worship is that of the Indian god Shiva, the "male creative principle" said to be found within *both* man and woman. Shiva's symbol is the erect phallus, called the "lingam," which represents the Great Spirit in a state of excitement. Shiva is worshipped all over the Indian subcontinent, as well as in neighboring countries. Throughout the nation's cities, towns, and villages, one finds small and large statues of Shiva's lingam, adorned daily with fresh flowers and other gift offerings.

Why the Lingam?

As to the question "How exactly did the Hindus come to worship Shiva's Lingam?" Who knows? Apparently there are many legends regarding the origins of the practice. In the version told by Sarah Denig in *The Mythology of Sex*, Shiva and his consort, Parvati, "were visited in their paradise by other gods, who found them enjoying sexual intercourse. Ignoring their visitors, they continued their lovemaking. Several of the gods became extremely angry and cursed the pair, who, as a result, died still entwined in sexual union. As he died, Shiva declared his shape from now on would be the lingam, so that in order to worship him, men must make models of it as objects of veneration." And there you go.

> "The phallus functions as an all embracing symbol in the Hindu religion, but if a street urchin draws one on the wall, it just reflects an interest in his penis."
>
> —CARL JUNG, *MAN AND HIS SYMBOLS*

The Blissful Yoni

Among the early Hindus, the female yoni ("holder") was also the object of veneration. According to Benjamin Walker's *The Hindu World*, the yoni, like the lingam, was also believed to have a life of its own, and was regarded as "a sacred area, an occult region worthy of reverence, and a symbol of the cosmic mysteries." The yoni is variously described as "the abode of pleasure, the source of great bliss, and the delight of delights," and is said to have been created specifically

> *As honey to attract the male organ. It is likened to the second mouth of the creator, and it continually sends out a silent command to man to come and sip. It is the chief ruler of the universe, for it brings men in all walks of life under its control and subjection.*

(And all this time women were thinking it was the Wonderbra . . .)

ABOUT THOSE SACRED SYMBOLS YOU'RE WEARING . . .

The Cross

Contrary to what you may have learned in Sunday school, the Latin or "passion" cross was not a Christian symbol from the beginning. Phallic historian Richard Payne Knight relates that the cross served as the emblem of "creation and generation" (i.e., the phallus) well before the church adopted it as the sign of salvation, a fact which he believes actually facilitated its reception among the faithful. According to Barbara Walker's *Woman's Dictionary of Sacred Symbols and Objects,* the Latin cross was not assimilated into the Christian religion until the seventh century A.D., and was not fully authorized until the ninth century. Walker sardonically points out that choosing this symbol was not inappropriate for a church composed entirely of men, and reminds us that its mythological alter ego, the Tree of Life is still a metaphor for male genitals among the Arabs.

The Ankh

The Egyptian ankh—a widely popular pendant, ring, or bracelet accessory—is thought to be the probable precursor to the Christian cross. Most often explained as a "symbol of life," the ankh represents the union of the yoni and lingam—of both female and male energies that combine to create all things. The ankh is also said to represent the mythological union of the Egyptian gods Isis and Osiris—apparently a very steamy one, given this cosmic merger purportedly caused the waters of the Nile to flood every year, ensuring the fertility of Egyptian lands. Thus dubbing this symbol "The Key to the Nile," reflects its early fertility symbolism.

The Celtic Cross

Today's Celtic cross was actually known to the early Hindus as the *kiakra,* a sign of sexual union; the cross (lingam) within the circle (yoni). Following its adoption by Christianity, it retained some of its original symbolism and today, as part of the clergy's vestment, the Celtic cross is frequently worn close to the priest's genitals.

The Six-Pointed Star

The hexagram, representing the Jewish faith as the Star of David, was not, in fact, adopted as an emblem of Judaism until the seventeenth century. Long before stories about David and Solomon showed up in the Bible, the intertwining triangles were considered sacred fertility icons among the Hindus, depicting a union of the sexes (Shakti and Shiva, the male and female divinities). The downward-pointing triangle (Shakti) was considered a female symbol that corresponded to the yoni, whereas the upward pointing triangle (Shiva) was supposed to represent the male lingam.

Penis Amulets

Ancient Romans commonly carried (or wore about the neck) amulets of penises, much in the same way we today wear religious crosses or stars. These sacred amulets were believed to guard against the loss of power, as well as providing an effective means to ward off bad luck and the universally dreaded evil eye. Essentially, they represented a kind of magical, multipurpose charm. (The ever-popular gesture of giving someone the finger is actually a remnant of this early tradition.) The custom of wearing or carrying small phalluses as protection against bad luck continued throughout the Middle Ages and has not altogether been abandoned. It continues today to be a practice among the Gypsies.

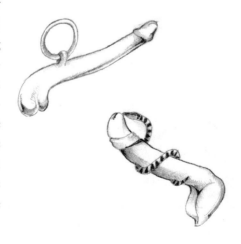

The Evil Eye

Carrying around penis amulets designed to ward off the evil eye naturally begs the question: "what the heck is an 'evil eye' and where did it come from?" Present day definitions of the term liken it to "a look or stare" with the power to harm others by magic or supernatural means. No surprise there. But many folks might be surprised to learn that this magically charged look actually originated from the male fear of women's power over men, and in particular, *her power over the male organ.* In *The Mushroom and the Cross,* John Allegro says that ancient Man was mystified and troubled by woman's seeming ability to arouse his passions and "stir his member to life" beyond the owner's control—simply by her physical presence—and attributed these powers to a type of magic or sorcery. These women were thought to possess telepathic control over people's minds, which became known as the evil eye. The concept was later extended to any form of mental dominance.

Penis From Heaven

During the late Roman era, small handheld penis amulets were often used as devotional offerings, and were tossed into holy wells or springs much in the same way a penny is tossed into a wishing well.

Vulva Amulets

Roman women were also known to wear amulets about the neck, although the ladies commonly chose to wear carvings of female genitals (representing the sacred vulva of the goddess). Seeking protection for more than just their bodies, the women also placed vulva amulets on the entrances of temples. The talismans were thought to guard against evil influences, in particular the dreaded evil eye. These symbols later came to resemble an unfinished ring or open circle, looking a bit like the crude form of a horseshoe. Yep, the upside-down horseshoe—commonly found above or next to doorways for good luck—is a surviving remnant of this "genital" tradition.

FOODS AND FESTIVALS AND PHALLUSES, OH MY!

• The custom of shaping bread in the form of the male sex organ was a common religious ritual among the early Romans (honoring and celebrating fertility of crops and themselves), who in turn passed it on to the Christians. While perusing Old French cookbooks, one can still find recipes for such shapely breads and cakes, referred to as *des cones sucrés* (sweet penises), or, if blessed by a priest, *du pain bénit* (blessed bread).

• Like the Greeks and Romans before them, the medieval Christians incorporated phallic worship into their religious rites to assure an abundant harvest. On Palm Sunday, the village priest would lead a long procession featuring a giant phallus carried on a decorated chariot, attended by groups of men called *phallophori*. Women and children held palm branches with loaves of phallus-shaped bread suspended from them. These processions generally ended at the village square where naked women would place garlands of flowers atop the huge phallus, followed by festivities of singing and dancing.

• With the advent of Christianity, the church officially frowned on rituals featuring phallic imagery, viewing them as immoral and depraved, and attempted to dissuade the masses from engaging in the pagan activities. But the early Christians were reluctant to give up their worship of the phallus, which they viewed as sacred and essential to survival. While some villages continued to carry the penis in religious processions, others, bowing to cleric pressure, simply baked breads in the shape of sex organs. The Church finally relented on the bread issue, perhaps feeling some small victory by ordaining that these buns could be accepted in Christian holidays—but only by marking them with a cross. Thus evolved the *hot cross bun*.

Pagan Rebellion

By the twelfth century, most parts of Europe had embraced Christianity and abandoned the pagan tradition of overt phallic worship. Most . . . but not *all*. Some inhabitants clung tenaciously to the practices of paganism, although their allegiance to the phallic deities underwent a barbaric transformation. One such ancient cult abhorred all things Christian, especially the people who practiced the faith, and worshipped a totemic variation of Priapus (the phallus) they called *Pripe-Gala*. Followers of *Pripe-*

Gala frequently invaded surrounding territories, inflicting heinous torture on the vanquished. Later, during religious ceremonies, worshippers of *Pripe-Gala* sacrificed the heads of the conquered Christians at the altar of their phallus god, a ceremony that was accompanied by grotesque howling and chants: "Let us rejoice today: Christ is vanquished; and our invincible *Pripe-Gala* is his vanquisher." (Needless to say, the original phallic gods, presiding over the prosperity of all living things, would not have been pleased.)

Present-Day Fertility Festivals

Japan is one of the few countries where overt phallic worship presently continues to be a part of public religious celebrations. In the *Hounen Matsuri* fertility festival held each March in Komaki, all participants, including women and children, carry phalluses as good luck charms. At the height of the celebration, each person touches and kisses a huge carved wooden phallus while praying for bountiful harvests and for his or her wishes to be fulfilled. And at the *Tashiro Jinja* festival at Nagoya, a large wooden phallus is paraded down the streets, and at the end of the procession is ritually thrust into a straw "vagina," followed by a sake bath poured over the union. The penises are then taken to a sacred shrine, where women visitors stroke the wooden shaft to increase their chances of meeting the "perfect partner."

Roman men had their gravestones carved with the likeness of only their head and their genitals.

CIRCUMCISION

Foreskin . . . or *Against* It?

"The human male is cursed with a super abundance of foreskin over the penis. Circumcision remedies the fault by removing the excess of foreskin."

—S. I. MCMILLEN, M.D., *NONE OF THESE DISEASES*

The word "circumcision" hails from the Latin *circumcidere*, to "cut around," and is most commonly used in reference to the removal of the *penile foreskin* in the male. However, the term may also refer to the removal of the *clitoral hood*, or sometimes—albeit inappropriately—the entire *clitoris* in the female.

Historical, as well as present day, reasons for subjecting a male (usually an infant) to circumcision are many and varied, but generally fall under the following categories: religion, puberty rites, sacrificial offerings, fertility offerings, medicine, hygiene, sexual pleasure (more or/*and* less), and aesthetics.

THE FIRST CUT

The origins of this rather curious ritual have been discussed and debated for centuries, but to this day, no one can say with absolute certainty where, when, or *why* it began. Ancient Hebrew writers assert the practice was instituted by Jehovah as a sign of the covenant between Himself and Abraham, but they would be wrong because the rite of circumcision was practiced by the Egyptians and Phoenicians long *before* the birth of Abraham. In fact, according to Greek Historian Herodotus (fifth century B.C.), people were snipping foreskins some 2,400 years before our Common Era, and even *then* the ritual was an ancient custom.

In the beginning, Man believed he had to *give* something in order *get* something. Thus, it's believed prehistoric farmers offered their foreskins (part of the most cherished and valued member of the body) to fertility gods in the fields, hoping to ensure more plentiful crops. In fact, some anthropologists think circumcision was originally performed as a sacrifice to a *female goddess*—likely the goddess of fertility—to place children under her protection and consecrate their reproductive powers to her service.

LEGENDS AND FOLKLORE

Oh, Sister . . .

The people of Vanatau (formerly New Hebrides, an island in the South Pacific), explicitly assert that *women* instigated the practice of male circumcision. Ancient legend has it that one day a young man went into the jungle with his sister, whereupon the girl climbed a breadfruit tree and, using her trusty bamboo spear, began to cut down a few pieces of ripe fruit. Somehow, she also managed to accidentally cut off her brother's foreskin (most likely the origin of sibling rivalry, as well). After the young man recovered, he had sex with a woman who found the encounter so enjoyable she excitedly told another woman, who in turn spread the news to all her friends. Needless to say, the man was soon in great demand, much to the chagrin of the other male villagers, who now found themselves mocked and sneered at by their womenfolk for their sexual inadequacies. Amid growing anxiety, the men finally decided to pay the foreskin-less man to reveal the secret to his success ". . . and they have wisely cut their children ever after."

His Boomerang *Did* Come Back

Among the Adnjamatana tribe of southern Australia, the originator of circumcision rites was said to be neither male nor female, god nor goddess. It was a bird. Actually, a semihuman bird, called *"Jurijurilja,"* considered one of the totemic ancestors. According to the legend, *Jurijurilja* was out and about one day, and chanced upon a boomerang which he proceeded to throw. Upon returning, the boomerang circumcised him (imagine his surprise) and then entered the vulva of his wives, cutting them internally so that they bled, and thus, began their monthly menstrual periods.

His Feminine Side

The ancient Egyptians believed that humans came into this world with both a feminine and a masculine soul, with the male's *feminine* soul residing in the foreskin, and the female's *masculine* soul hiding out in the clitoris. As a part of puberty rites, these tissues were removed to make the boy *fully male* and the girl *fully female* (similar beliefs and accompanying rituals continue today among some primitive cultures, including the Dogon of Africa). Following removal, the male's foreskin was generally burned as an offering to the fertility gods to ensure sexual prowess and fatherhood. Curiously, the practice of burning foreskins continues today in many parts of the world, although now done generally as a token of good luck.

The Untold Story of the Fragrance Industry

When burning the above-mentioned offerings, as one might imagine, the resulting aroma was less than pleasant. No slouches in the discovery department (especially when motivated by the fetid odor of burnt flesh), the ancients concocted a novel remedy to stem the stench. According to Panati's *Sexy Origins and Intimate Things*, incense (such as frankincense and myrrh), were tossed into the flames, resulting in (drum roll) . . . perfume! The origins of the word perfume are from Latin *Per* + *Fumus*, meaning "through smoke," and perfume itself originated to mask the scent of burned foreskins. Something to think about the next time you reach for that favorite eau du toilette. . . .

Sign Here Before Entering . . .

Some historians believe that among the ancient Egyptians, circumcision came to represent a sign of affiliation by the people in the service of their god. Apparently, the Egyptians also felt outsiders joining in the service of their god should have this sign as well. When the Greek philosopher Pythogoras visited Egypt in the fifth century (B.C.) he was obliged to submit to circumcision before being allowed to study in the temples.

Perhaps You'd Like That with Chianti and Fava Beans

It's said that King John of Abyssinia, a descendant of Solomon and the Queen of Sheba, was a notoriously cruel and macabre host who forced guests not of his faith to change their religion— a conversion which required they undergo circumcision. The procedure was carried out with a sharp stone or piece of flint (in accordance with the book of Genesis), following which the victim was made to swallow his own prepuce.

THE JUDAIC COVENANT . . .

According to the Bible, circumcision is said to have passed into the Jewish tradition with Abraham, who, at God's request, circumcised himself at age ninety-nine and relieved his sons of their foreskins as well. The procedure was required for all Jewish males as a sign of the covenant between the Jews and God:

> *"You Shall be circumcised in the flesh of your foreskins, and it shall be a sign of the covenant between me and you. He that is eight days old among you shall be circumcised; every male throughout your generations, whether born in your house or bought with your money from any foreigner who is not of your offspring . . ."* (Genesis 17:11–12)

The circumcision initiation of a newborn male into Judaism—which takes place on the eighth day after his birth—is referred to as *b'rith/bris* (or *brith milah/bris milah*) "covenant of the penis."

Did You Know?

For some two thousand years, from 1700 B.C. until about 140 A.D., Jews practiced "biblical circumcision," where they did not, in fact, cut off the male's entire foreskin, but instead removed only the tip of it, as an act of faith. A cursory glance at Michelangelo's sculpted masterpiece *David* would seem to show an uncircumcised lad, but the future king of course was, and the statue factually presents circumcision the way it used to look. Around 140 A.D., biblical circumcision was modified to make it impossible for a Jew to appear to be a gentile by stretching forward his remaining tissue, as many were apparently wont to do (see "Uncircumcising" on page 240). The "new and improved" procedure, called *Peri'ah* ("laying bare the glans")—which essentially stripped the foreskin away from the glans—was at this time adopted by the priests and rabbis, and continues to be the model for today's procedures. According to original Talmudic law, it was the responsibility of the father, as the priest of the family, to perform the circumcision himself. The *mohel* (a professional circumcisor) was a later invention. Because the procedure was (is) painful, some historians have suggested the duty changed hands out of a fear of future retaliation. (An interesting note on the origins of *mohel:* The Hebrew word for circumcisor is thought to have an archaic meaning that refers to "father-in-law.")

Did You Also Know?

Some Orthodox Jews include the rite of sucking, or *metizah* (a.k.a., *messisa, mizziza,* and *mizizah*), "sucking the blood" during the circumcision ceremony, a practice which has curious beginnings. In 168 B.C., Judaism was declared illegal by Emperor Antiochus IV Epiphanes. As such, ritual circumcision was made a crime, and those who defied the law were ordered to suffer death by crucifixion, flogging, stoning, or devourment by wild dogs. Understandably, the practice of snipping foreskins was driven to secrecy, and resulted in difficult-to-verify results. (Some historians have suggested the *metizah* practice was introduced in the Talmudic period, 500–526 C.E.) To make sure that the operation was indeed performed, then, as now in some ultraorthodox groups, either the *mohel* or an honored guest applies his lips to the baby's penis, to draw off blood by sucking. (**Note:** There are some scholars, including Alfred Kinsey, who have suggested that the sucking ritual was a survival of an ancient phallic cult—involving the use of sacred prostitutes—that required ritual fellation.)

The practice of orally sucking the newly circumcised infant penis was not limited to the Jewish faith. For many years, Roman Catholic priests also routinely performed the ritual, although the reasons for doing so are not clear. It *is* clear, however, why the Catholics halted the practice. According to Allen Edwardes and R.E.L. Masters in *The Cradle of Erotica*, the French emperor Napoleon Bonaparte ordered an end to the sucking ritual, primarily because the attending priests were often syphilitic and frequently infected the infants while performing the rite.

The Holy Relic: "We Have It!" "No, We Have It!"

In the early twelfth century, a bitter battle raged within dozens of churches across Europe. The focus? Who (what or where) was actually in possession of the alleged holy foreskin of Christ Himself. No less than thirteen churches claimed to be in simultaneous possession of the precious relic, including the Charroux Abbey in France, a medieval village church north of Rome, the Abbey at Coulombs, and the Church of Notre-Dame-en-Vaux, among others. Believing his to be the real McCoy, Henry V of Agincourt reportedly borrowed the foreskin housed in the Abbey at Coulombs, when his wife, Catherine of France, was about to give birth in order to ensure an easy delivery. (Henry was so pleased with the result, he later built a special sanctuary for the sacred relic.) When asked to pick a winner, Pope Innocent III, lacking any DNA evidence to consult, flatly refused declaring "only God could know the truth." The foreskin at Charroux finally got the holy nod in the 1500s, and (supposedly) has since bestowed thousands of pregnancies upon grateful viewers.

The *Real* Reason Men Developed Fear for the "M" Word

In earlier times, Arabic Bedouin tribes would circumcise the male the day *before* he was to marry, as a ritual offering to ensure fatherhood. During the procedure, the groom was required to sing, thus proving his conquest over pain to the surrounding crowd. A boy incapable of holding back tears was sometimes killed by his father for having shamed the family (one fifth would die anyway from resulting infections).

Meanwhile, in other Arab tribes, circumcision was often performed *during* the actual marriage ceremony, with the new bride executing the honor. The ritual required removal of not only the foreskin, but also skin from the *shaft of the penis*. Once peeled off, blood from the wound was sprinkled on the bride's clothes as a means of blessing the union (the original meaning of "blessed" was "to be bled upon"). Throughout the proceedings, the hapless young groom expressed nothing but a stoic face, since any evidence of discomfort might have raised doubts about his masculinity. Of course, the *real* test occurred later in the evening, when the new groom—accompanied by his raw penis—was expected to perform his sexual responsibilities in a "vigorous and passionate" manner.

Chatan, the Arabic term for "Bridegroom," is supposedly derived from an ancient expression for "a husband is cut (circumcised)."

RITES OF PASSAGE

Legend has it that the Poro people of Liberia practiced elaborate puberty rites in which the circumcised foreskin of the boy was exchanged for the excised clitoris and labia minora of the girl. *Then*, as part of the ceremony of initiation, the exchanged parts are cooked . . . and eaten (yum).

Maybe the Poro were inspired by tales of a pubertal ceremony held in the seventeenth century in Madagascar. In this somewhat bizarre ritual, the resident holy man cut off the boy's foreskin with sharpened fingernails, following which the severed piece of flesh was dipped in egg yolk, then swallowed by the boy's godfather.

Royal Influence

The French King Louis XIV, known for his licentious nature and vigorous sexual appetite, was said to have suffered from phimosis, a condition that prevents the retraction of the foreskin over the glans, making erections difficult and painful. To relieve the condition, the royal penis was reportedly circumcised at age twenty-two, following which the procedure became fashionable among European aristocracy for generations.

Following the preference of Queen Victoria, male members of the royal family tend to be circumcised.

CUTTING IN AMERICA

"A remedy which is almost always successful in small boys is circumcision. . . . The operation should be performed by a surgeon without administering an anesthetic, as the brief pain attending the operation will have a salutary effect upon the mind, especially if it be connected with the idea of punishment."

—DR. JOHN HARVEY KELLOGG (OF CORN FLAKE FAME)
ON TREATMENTS FOR SELF-ABUSE

Prior to 1870, Christian babies were *not* circumcised. Period. The practice owes its popularity in America to Dr. Lewis Sayre, a physician often referred to as the "Columbus of the Prepuce," who claimed to have cured a young boy of paralysis by simply stretching out the child's foreskin and snipping it off. Dr. Sayre, and his merry band of circumcision-crusading colleagues, determined that a range of diseases, including epilepsy, convulsions, paralysis, tuberculosis, hip-joint disease, hernias, eczema, poor eyesight, elephantiasis, idiocy, and insanity could be cured by the procedure. (Circumcision has the dubious distinction of being the "cure" for more diseases than any other procedure in the history of medicine.) Much to their foreskin clipping dismay, this later proved to be untrue.

Undaunted, the Victorian physicians successfully convinced Christian parents and religious leaders that tight foreskins put young males in a continual state of *sexual arousal*, leading them to commit that most heinous of sins: masturbation (which many believed was the primary cause of the aforementioned diseases). The best way to save the poor youth from the ravages of this self-polluting menace was, of course, circumcision. And that, as the cliché aptly states, was all she wrote. For decades, parents dutifully had their sons' penises snipped and clipped to control masturbatory insanity. And once the anti-masturbation theory was discredited, (which took some time—as late as the 1970s leading American medical textbooks still advocated routine circumcision as a way to prevent masturbation), circumcision advocates continued to support the practice as necessary for hygienic purposes; to control the spread of STD's; and to prevent penile cancer.

"The argument is also put forth that the circumcised organ is more hygienic, for the prepuce collects nasty secretions. So does the ear, but the removal of this rather ugly appendage is frowned upon."

—WILLIAM KEITH MORGAN,
MEDICAL JOURNAL OF AUSTRALIA

Today, of course, most disease prevention claims have been discredited and dismissed. In 1971, the American Academy of Pediatrics *reversed* its pro-circumcision stance, stating there is no absolute medical justification for it. In 1989, the group back-pedaled a bit by saying there were "some benefits and some drawbacks," but in 1999, they wisely reaffirmed that the procedure should *not* be routinely done on all boys. The 1999 policy also stated *for the first time*, that baby boys who were circumcised should be given some kind of pain relief during the procedure. Duh.

A LITTLE PIECE OF USELESS SKIN?

Circumcision advocates often argue that the foreskin is nothing more than a useless piece of superfluous skin. Maybe they don't know the following:

Circumcision cuts off more than 3 feet of veins, arteries, and cap-illaries; 240 feet of nerves; and more than 20,000 nerve endings.

• The average size of the adult prepuce (foreskin) is about 15 square inches, or roughly the size of a 3 X 5 index card.
• After infant circumcision, the average male, when grown, has lost 51 percent of his penile skin. In some men, the number may be as high as 80 percent.
• The glans/head of the penis is actually covered by a mucous membrane. Removal of the foreskin effectively leaves the area exposed, resulting, essentially, in scar tissue.
• The male foreskin has a richer variety and greater concentration of nerve receptors than any other area of the penis, making it the *most erotically sensitive* part of the organ.

Oops . . .

First Thought . . .

I think circumcision is a fine idea, especially if most of the boys in the neighborhood are circumcised—then a boy feels "regular." Dr. Benjamin Spock *Common Sense Book of Baby and Child Care,* 1945)

On Second Thought

My own preference, if I had the good fortune to have another son, would be to leave his little penis alone. (Dr. Benjamin Spock, revising his stance on circumcision in *Redbook* magazine, 1989)

TO CUT . . . OR NOT TO CUT

Over the years, spirited coffeehouse debates on the sexual merits of circumcised vs. intact penises have passed more than a few idle moments, while the attempts of researchers to *scientifically* declare a winner have been received less enthusiastically. Suffice it to say clinical findings remain murky at best, and subject to biased interpretation. Long thought to be the gold standard, the 60s research of Masters and Johnson found no difference between circumcised and uncircumcised males in regard to the sexual pleasure they experience (findings which did little to stem the controversy). In 1997, University of Chicago sociologist Edward O. Laumann and colleagues published a much anticipated report in the *Journal of the American Medical Association*. On the sexual front, the trio of researchers found that circumcised men are more likely to masturbate and engage in oral and anal sex than their intact brethren. What to make of this? Sensing victory, the pro-circ enthusiasts gleefully chirped it meant that "circumcised men have more fun," are more creative, and have a more expansive libido. "Nay," say the leave-it-aloners, who, of course, offer a different spin on the data. Pro-prepuce folks feel that coital sex sans-foreskin may be *less* satisfactory, forcing a trimmed man to seek out other forms of stimulation. And the beat goes on. . . .

He Sheds, She Says . . .

And what of *women*'s penile preferences? Are they for skin or against it? The miniscule amount of clinical research and only slightly more abundant anecdotal evidence on the topic seems to indicate the fair sex favors the trimmed version, a predilection based primarily on aesthetic appeal and a real or imagined belief that clipped is cleaner. However, when her *sexual* satisfaction is the focus, the tables turn a bit. According to a 1999 study, women with *un*circumcised partners are *more* likely to have multiple orgasms during sexual intercourse and are *less* likely to experience sexual discomfort during prolonged coitus than women whose partners have been cut.

Dockers

Enterprising sexual thrill seekers sometimes engage in a form of masturbation called "docking," in which the foreskin of partner

A is pulled back, whereupon partner B's foreskin is stretched over the tip of partner A's penis (take a moment to conjure the imagery). The two penises, after being locked into place, are then stroked so that the skin is moved back and forth over the glans (head). Men without foreskins can't do this. . . .

Born in the USA

- Approximately 64 percent of newborn males in the United States are circumcised each year (although the numbers are steadily decreasing).
- A baby boy's chances of being circumcised in the United States varies according to region. Born in the Midwest? 75.9 percent of newborns are snipped. The South? 57.1 percent. Best chances to avoid it are in the West, where "only" 42.3 percent get clipped.
- Circumcision is the most common surgical procedure in America. In the United States, 3,300 baby boys are circumcised each day; one every 26 seconds.

A MEDICAL COMMODITY

The abundant availability of foreskins in the United States led to its prominent appearance in the world of artificial skin technology. It became the darling of the field once lab wizards discovered the genetic material gleaned from one prepuce alone yields about 250,000 square feet skin. Burn victims are the most frequent beneficiaries of transplanted skin. Not only that, multipurpose tissue that it is, biomedical and pharmaceutical companies also use recycled infant foreskins in the manufacture of insulin.

- One in 5,000 babies suffers acute complications arising from circumcision, which range from uncontrollable bleeding to fatal infections. The procedure has a death rate of one in 500,000.
- Circumcised boys have a lower pain threshold than girls or intact boys.
- Approximately 85 percent of newborn males born outside the United States are left intact. In Canada, less than 30 percent of males are circumcised while in Great Britain, West Germany and Scandinavia, only about 1 percent undergoes the procedure.

UNCIRCUMCISING

"They also hid the circumcision of their genitals, that even when they were naked they might appear to be Greeks."
—JOSEPHUS, *HISTORY OF THE JEWISH WAR*

Stretching the Truth

Many Hellenized Jews living in ancient Greece utilized a technique known as "stretching" in an attempt to restore their severed foreskins. It seems that exercising in the customary nude state with their uncircumcised Greek friends apparently caused them to feel less manly and subjected them to ridiculing taunts, likely because the Greeks considered the exposed glans of the penis offensive. This moderately painful procedure involved pulling the residual skin up over the glans and tying it. Additionally, many Jews wore a bronze weight called a *Pondus Judeaus* on the remaining foreskin to stretch it. The restorative procedure was known by the Greek word *epispasm.*

Aesthetically speaking, only the ancient Greeks considered the uncircumcised penis an object of beauty.

Lost, But Not Forgotten . . .

A variation of the ancient foreskin-stretching practice has been recently revived by contemporary circumcised men also wishing to restore their lost (but not forgotten) foreskins. Estimates by restoration groups suggest that upward of 18,000 Americans are, as we speak, in the process of "putting it back." By methodically stretching the remaining penile skin using strategically placed surgical tape, elastic, and eventually attaching graduated weights to the contraption (a procedure fondly referred to as "tugging"), many have obtained impressive results. Although, according to Jim Bigelow, author of *The Joy of Uncircumcising!* what you actually get depends on how much tissue is left and how much elasticity it has. It should be noted that the new skin is not a foreskin per se, since it lacks the nerve endings lost through circumcision, but does create an envelope that keeps the glans moist and sexually sensitive. And aesthetically speaking, many claim the faux foreskin looks like the real thing. So while Mother Nature may not be fooled, many doctors *are*.

FAMOUS HOTRODS

Not Circumcised? Neither Are These Hardtops:

Johnny Carson, Liam Neeson, Hugh Hefner,
Ron Howard, Don Johnson, Eddie Murphy, Elvis Presley,
Frank Sinatra, Robert Redford, William Hurt,
Jesse Jackson, Magic Johnson, Tom Selleck,
Arnold Schwartzenegger, Tony Danza, Prince William

Circumcised? The Following Convertibles Are, Too:

Tom Cruise, Mel Gibson, David Letterman, Clint
Eastwood, John F. Kennedy, Kirk Douglas, Tom Berenger,
Phil Donahue, Wayne Gretsky, Warren Beatty, Rob Lowe,
Matt Dillon, Donny Osmond, Sylvester Stallone,
Prince Charles, Billy Hamilton

F.G.M.: They *Call* It "Circumcision"

"In some countries they only cut out the clitoris, but here we do it properly. We scrape our girls clean. If it is properly done, nothing is left, other than a scar. Everything has to be cut away."

—SUDANESE GRANDMOTHER FROM
HANNY LIGHTFOOT-KLEIN'S *PRISONERS OF RITUAL*

Female Genital Mutilation (F.G.M.), is a cultural practice which involves the removal of some or all of a woman's external genitalia—a procedure said to have been inflicted upon one hundred thirty million girls and women around the globe. Approximately six thousand females are mutilated *each day* (mostly by illiterate old women with no knowledge of anatomy) in twenty-eight African countries, as well as the Middle East, Indonesia, and Malaysia. The purpose? To sexually desensitize the female, in the hopes of preserving her virginity for marriage.

How It's Done

There are three basic varieties of this custom, and the severity of the mutilation is dependent upon the culture in which it is practiced. In each case the procedure is generally performed on a terrified young girl between the ages of five and seven—held down with her legs forced apart—with the consent, and in the presence, of those she would usually turn to for help. No anesthetics are used in any of the following procedures:

Circumcision

Also known as *Sunna* (Arabic meaning "tradition"), circumcision is the removal of the prepuce and/or tip of the clitoris. Considered the "mildest" form of F.G.M., this operation nevertheless requires great skill, surgical tools, and knowledge of anatomy—conditions typically not available in the primitive areas where the procedure is performed. To that end, it is not uncommon for the entire clitoris along with a large portion of the external genitalia to be mutilated, as well. This type of mutilation affects only a small proportion of women.

Clitoridectomy or Excision

In this disturbing procedure, the entire external clitoris—with or without the labia minora—is amputated, usually with nothing more sophisticated than scissors, a razor blade, or broken glass, (sharpened fingernails are sometimes used to pry out the clitoris of a baby). This form of mutilation is inflicted upon approximately 80 percent of affected women.

Infibulation or Pharaonic Circumcision

So called because it was supposedly known to the ancient Egyptians, this is the most drastic variation of F.G.M., in which the clitoris and inner and outer labia are sliced off, and the raw, cut edges of the vagina are then tightly stitched together with catgut, thread, or thorns. A pinhole-sized opening is preserved by inserting a sliver of wood (usually a matchstick or small reed) into the wound during the healing process to allow passage of urine and menstrual blood. Usually, the legs are bound together for several weeks while the vagina closes, and the immobilized victim receives little or no food and only sips of water.

Infibulation is performed to guarantee that a bride is a virgin—and the smaller her vaginal opening, the higher the bride price. In most cultures that practice infibulation, a woman is cut open with a knife by her husband on her wedding night to allow sexual intercourse, and cut further to permit childbirth. Reinfibulation occurs once the baby is born.

Mutilation Name Game

Collectively, the aforementioned practices are sometimes referred to as "female circumcision," but the term is a gross misrepresentation. Clitoridectomy is more analogous to "penisectomy" than to male circumcision; a comparable procedure would range from amputation of most of the penis, to removal of all of the penis, including its roots of soft tissue and part of the scrotal sac. All done, of course, *without* anesthesia.

LEGENDARY ORIGINS

Within some cultures, ritual genital mutilation is firmly tied to myths and legends passed down through the generations. Among these are the Dogon people of Africa, who adhere to the belief that the Earth's creation occurred in a very sexual manner. According to Sarah Dening's *Mythology of Sex*, the Dogon believe that *Amma*, the creator god, made the earth out of clay so that it lay flat like a female's body. An anthill represented the earth's vulva, and a termite hill marked her clitoris. The story tells how *Amma*, being lonely, decided to have sexual intercourse with his new creation. However, as he approached her, the termite hill rose up, making it impossible for him to penetrate her. *Amma*'s response was to cut it down, and then proceeded to fulfill his desires. Dening relates that this myth is held to be one of the reasons for the custom of clitoridectomy among the Dogon women.

Men Behaving Badly

Other theorists have turned to the primitive exercise of power and control in attempting to explain the origins of FGM. In *Sacred Wounds*, Bruno Bettleheim suggested the practice was born of early man's envy of woman's powers of procreation, and his desire to acquire power over the vagina. By forcing women to bleed from their genitals, Bettleheim believes awestruck men may have been making an attempt to gain understanding of and power over the woman's "secret process" of giving life.

F.G.M. in America

Ritual genital mutilation is not confined to the boundaries of African and Middle Eastern countries. It is heartbreakingly evident in Western countries as well. Investigations reveal that when immigrants from Africa and the Middle East settle elsewhere (Europe and North America), they bring along this unsavory operation with them. In 1997, a federal law took effect which criminalizes female genital mutilation in the United States. The law requires new immigrants (from countries where the practice is widespread) to be informed that they face up to five years in prison for performing the procedure and/or arranging it for their daughters. The Centers for Disease Control and Prevention estimates more than 150,000 girls residing in the U.S. have experienced F.G.M. while living in this country.

Mutilation and Masturbation

The Victorians

Unbeknownst to many, female genital mutilation was not confined to the likes of primitive cultural traditions. In nineteenth-century England, one of the most tragic chapters in the history of medicine ensued with an orchestrated surgical assault on female sexuality. The target? The clitoris. The goal? It's removal. The reason? Treatment of various psychological disorders, commonly thought to be caused by that vile self-polluter, *masturbation*. Although the procedure was *first* used in Berlin in 1822, it wasn't until 1858 that it gained widespread popularity under the influence of prominent London obstetrician Isaac Baker Brown, credited with developing the modern-day *clitoridectomy*. In 1866, the year Baker Brown was elected President of the Medical Society of London, he published a book called the *Curability of Certain Forms of Insanity, Epilepsy, Catalepsy and Hysteria in Females*. Although masturbation was considered degenerate and dangerous in both sexes, Brown claimed that in women, the activity was a form of "moral leprosy" leading to hysteria, sterility, and convulsive diseases, and thus advocated the removal of the clitoris (using his preferred surgical instrument, scissors) to cure a woman suffering from any of these. Among symptoms that suggested to him that an operation was in order were "distaste for marital intercourse" and "a tendency to walk in the country alone" and to "come back exhausted." Brown was later forced to resign from the Medical Society, curiously, *not* because of his reprehensible operations, but rather due to his shameless self-promotion, and more specifically, because he dared to discuss the dirty subject of female masturbation.

While there was uniform consensus among Victorian physicians regarding the moral and physical evils of masturbation, many physicians were nonetheless reluctant to perform the radical clitoridectomy. A "less invasive" procedure recommended to prevent the wicked behavior that endangered the purity of nineteenth-century girls involved sewing the vaginal lips together to put the clitoris out of reach.

American Kids Are Told:
"Play with Something Else"

The scourge of female masturbation was not unique to Europe, and the clitoridectomy cure soon found its way across the ocean. The procedure was first performed in America in the late 1860s, continuing unabated until the late 1930s. The last recorded clitoridectomy for curing masturbation in the U.S. was in 1948, on a five-year-old girl.

If Cornflakes Don't Work . . .

The dangers of masturbation were also a focus of Victorian do-gooder Dr. John Harvey Kellogg (1852–1943), best known for developing a bland breakfast cereal dubbed "Corn Flakes" (1896) as a dietary alternative to help patients keep their hands off their genitals (if the product failed to work when taken orally Dr. Kellogg recommended it could also be given as an enema). Prior to the creation of his cereal empire, the Battle Creek, Michigan doctor had offered forth his esteemed medical wisdom in the *Ladies Guide to Health and Disease.* (1883). While discussing treatment for particularly obstinate cases of self abuse, Dr. Kellogg intoned the periodic need for more drastic measures than his cereal concoction could provide:

> *Treatment: Cool sitz baths; the cool enema; a spare diet; the application of blisters and other irritants to the sensitive parts of the sexual organs, the removal of the clitoris and nymphae, constitute the most proper treatment.*

Can This Marriage Be Saved?

An early English publication called *The Gentlemen's Magazine and Historical Chronicle* reported in 1737 that one George Baggerly was sentenced to two years imprisonment as he:

> *Wickedly, barbarously and inhumanly did force . . . needle and thread into the private parts of Dorothy Baggerly . . . and did then and there sew her up to the great damage of said Dorothy and against the Peace of our Sovereign Lord the King, his Crown and Dignity.*

It seems that Mr. Baggerly, who had to go to work five miles from home, "was afraid to leave his wife to her inclinations." She told her mother. And some friends. Mr. Baggerly pleaded guilty.

Ancient Tailors

Sewing the labia together to inhibit sexual activity actually harkens back to ancient times. Early Romans routinely stitched the major lips of talented female singers in the hopes of preserving their voices (they took needle and thread to male singers, as well, stitching together the foreskin of the penis). The Romans believed sexual activity would negatively affect the ability to produce a pleasing vocal sound and thus sought to discourage coital encounters. Apparently "Just say 'No'" was out of the question.

In the nineteenth century, primitive sex-inhibiting instruments—like needle and thread—gave way to the strength and technology afforded by steel. No, *not* a return to medieval chastity belts—these women should have been so lucky. Men determined to prevent sexual access to a woman's genitals at this time frequently opted for rings and padlocks inserted through the labia majora—a practice routinely found in countries such as Italy, Germany, France, England, Czechoslovakia, and India.

The Cutters Club

In *A Historical Perspective on Women's Health Care*, G. J. Barker-Benefield presents a chilling report on the origin of the "Orificial Surgical Society," founded in America in the 1890s by Dr. D.E.H. Pratt, a surgeon at the Cook County Hospital in Chicago. The official stance of this obsessed group of cutters was that any deviation in the normal clitoris required "surgical attention." Case histories of clitoridectomies and vaginal operations documented their repeated use to "cure" a variety of ailments, including measles, melancholia, kleptomania, and the dreaded hiccups. Dr. Pratt wrote these telling words in 1898 in the Society's official Journal:

> *If one were to choose the most important spot in point of influence over the entire (female) system, it would have to be the clitoris and its hood. When it becomes . . . appreciated that the clitoris and its hood constitute the most sensitive electrical button, which can be pressed to arouse this entire sympathetic nervous system to increased activity, the importance of proper treatment of this delicate and influential anatomical spot will be more thoroughly established.*

Long Before the Stepford Wives

The physicians of the exclusively male orificial society explained to patients' husbands that the operation would save men from their wives' "demanding explosive sexuality," and it was sold to husbands as a means to secure sexual control over their wives, assuring the women's subordination.

SHAVE AND A HAIRCUT

"Since this happened all anybody
wants to see is my penis."

—JOHN WAYNE BOBBITT

JOHN WAYNE BOBBITT

The word "penis" (let alone one separated from its body) was largely verboten on nightly television news and rarely discussed in everyday polite conversation. Until, that is, June 23, 1993. In the early morning hours of that fateful day, Virginia manicurist Lorena Bobbitt fulfilled the surname destiny when she took an eight-inch kitchen knife and sliced off her sleeping husband's penis. She later claimed that the ex-marine had come home after a night of barhopping and raped her, and that her actions ultimately were the result of years of abuse by her domineering mate. While fleeing their apartment in the family car—still clinging to the bloody organ—Lorena tossed it out the window where it landed in a grassy lot in front of a 7-Eleven store.

She later stopped at a pay phone to call police and tell them where to look and the wayward penis, amazingly, was found. In good condition no less. Over nine hours and $50,000 later, John Wayne Bobbitt emerged from the operating room, and one week later walked out of the hospital a complete and functional man. To prove just how functional, a year later he starred in a hard-core porn video, *John Wayne Bobbitt, Uncut,* which featured close-ups of his now infamous reattached organ (both limp and erect), as well as scenes of Bobbitt engaging in sexual intercourse with several naughty nurse starlets. He made a follow-up flick following penile enlargement surgery fittingly titled *Frankenpenis.* In 1996, following a short stint as a stripper, John Wayne left the porn industry to become a minister after he "found God" at a Spago restaurant in Las Vegas . . . apparently lost Him (but not before the Reverend Bobbitt pondered calling his own congregation the "John Wayne Bobbitt Church Without an Organ") . . . and got a job as a bartender/limo driver/handyman at the Moonlight Bunny Ranch, a Mound House, Nevada, brothel. He was fired three months later for his overzealous "hands-on" interest in his colleagues. John Wayne Bobbitt was last seen driving across the Arizona desert in the company of a Bunny Ranch prostitute, no doubt looking for a peaceful (or is it *pieceful*?) place to live.

Names given to John Wayne Bobbitt's penis in the June 27, 1993 *Washington Post* (which never once used the word "penis"): Alistair, King Gustaf V, Mr. Belvedere, and Kornheiser

The first reported penile transplant surgery in medical history was allegedly performed in 1987 in Thailand. The unfortunate pioneering recipient was a philandering soldier whose unrecovered appendage was sliced off and tossed out by his jealous wife, while the donor was a Thai man (of similar tissue type) undergoing a sex change operation. The success or failure of the outcome was not revealed.

"If the penis is accidentally amputated, stay alert. Wrap it in a bag to prevent freezer burn, and place it in the fridge. Total replant surgery is possible by highly skilled microsurgeons . . . the time lapse between injury and re-attachment should be less than six hours. Any later, and the ability to urinate, experience penile sensations, erect and ejaculate may be lost."
—DOROTHY BALDWIN, *MALE SEXUAL HEALTH*

AN ANCIENT WHODUNNIT

While modern American cities often adorn their streets and parks with decorative fountains, clocks, and the occasional historical figure (usually atop a horse of some type), ancient Athens found itself dotted with decorative monuments of a different sort. As a tribute to the mythical god Hermes (god of travelers, trickery, and luck) Athenians erected peculiar half-statues which they fondly dubbed "Hermeses." Found in the courtyard and doorways of private homes, on street corners, in public arenas,

and scattered along the road, these curiosities had the shape of plain rectangular stone columns except for two distinguishing carved features: a bearded head and, at groin level, an erect penis. And that's all. As with most revered icons, these statues were frequently gifted with food items and flowers (usually hung on the conveniently erect penis, which, by the way, was frequently touched, stroked and kissed by passing women in hopes of becoming more sexually desirable) and widely adored by the cities' masses. Or so they thought. One summer's eve in 415 B.C., just as the Athenian men were preparing to launch a bold military coup against Sicily and the rival Spartans, a group of conspirators stole through the night, performing a bit of "plaster surgery" on the lucky herms. When Athenians rolled out of bed the next morning, much to their shock and crotch-clutching horror, almost all the Hermeses had been dutifully castrated.

And just who was it that committed the heinous crime? Curiously, despite extreme measures to find the herm-choppers, no one really knows. History reveals that officials quickly eliminated the possibility of a harmless prank, and charged numerous prominent citizens . . . many of whom were executed, while the others fled before they could be. The favored theory of modern historians indicts young males engaging in political protest, but in 1985, author Eva Keuls offered an intriguing alternative in her treatise *The Reign of the Phallus*. She points her finger at none other than the *women* of Athens. Keuls suggests that Greek women—forced by husbands, priests, physicians, and soothsayers into daily worship of the protruding member— were "mad as hell and weren't gonna take it any more" (or something like that) and thus exhibited one of history's earliest expressions of feminist protest by symbolically hitting phallocratic Athenian men where it hurt most.

OTHER NOTEWORTHY SEVERED PENISES

Le Petit Corporal

At the time of his death in 1821, Napoleon Bonaparte's penis had shrunk to an inch in length, with corresponding miniscule testicles. An autopsy revealed that France's first emperor suffered from massive endocrine failure, which apparently was also the cause of his alleged impotence in the last years of his life. Following his death, "The Little Corporal's" penis was removed, although questions remain as to who actually did the removing. Some have speculated the Italian pathologist who performed the dictator's autopsy plucked the part. But according to the memoirs of Napoleon's valet, Ari, the pilfered penis was actually the work of Abbé Vignali, the cleric who administered the last rites (and whom Napoleon reportedly insulted prior to doing so). The "Bonapart" is said to have remained in Vignali's family until 1916, when his descendants sold it to a British rare book firm. After a series of sales and trades, the private piece eventually ended up at Christie's auction house in London some fifty years later. Tagged as a "small dried up object," the Imperial penis failed to obtain a sufficient bid. It was later sold to Dr. John Lattimer, a urologist at Columbia

Presbyterian hospital in New York for $3,000 (although various others periodically claim to be in possession of the royal relic).

The Mad Monk

In the early 1900s, Siberian mystic Grigori Rasputin was known across Russia for his incredible healing powers, his political influence as an adviser to the imperial family, his lustful relationships with women, and perhaps most notably, for his thirteen-inch penis. In 1916, conservative Russian aristocrats led by Prince Felix Yussupov—jealous of all his powers—plotted his assassination. After being poisoned, shot, sexually assaulted, shot again, and beaten, the attackers sliced off Rasputin's penis, flinging it defiantly across the room (they later threw Rasputin into the icy waters of the Neva River where he finally drowned). The infamous penis was quickly recovered by a servant who reportedly passed it on to one of his former lovers. Faithfully preserved in a polished wooden box kept by her bedside, the organ was described in daughter Maria Rasputin's biography of her father as looking "like a blackened, overripe banana, about a foot long."

DID YOU KNOW?

The word "sex" derives from *seco*—meaning to amputate or cut off.

Do You Call It "Dad"?

According to her various myths, Aphrodite (Greek goddess of love) was born from the severed phallus of the dying god Uranos—castrated with a sickle by his son Cronos, the youngest and strongest of the Titans—who then threw the organ into the sea. As the story goes, Aphrodite then emerged from the white sea foam, said to be semen of the heavens, that surrounded the severed member (that's right, bleeding to death, the dude still had the strength to copulate with the sea and beget Aphrodite). The name Aphrodite means "foam" or "foam born."

The Mister Is a Sister

In 1952, Dr. Christian Hamburger, a Danish Surgeon, amputated the penis of an American ex-GI named George Jorgensen—thus completing a process that resulted in one of the earliest and first "successful" sex change surgery. A few weeks later a stunned world was introduced to Christine Jorgensen, a woman who now had the body she believed nature had erroneously deprived her of at birth (although doctors did not construct a vagina). Since that time over 6,000 Americans have undergone the gender switching knife.

Before the world was introduced to Christine Jorgensen, however, Lili Elbe, who was born Einar Wegener in 1886, quietly paved the phallus-shedding he-to-she way. In early 1930, Wegener, a well-known Danish painter, went to Berlin to have his

259

penis and testicles removed. After a series of surgical procedures, Lili attempted to have a vagina constructed in the hopes of having intercourse with her soon-to-be husband. Sadly, Lili never realized the joys of being a "complete" woman, as she died during her "recuperation."

PRESTO-CHANGO!

Penis to Vagina

Utilizing the skin of a castrated penis is preferred for the creation of an artificial vagina (a procedure referred to as a "vaginoplasty"), primarily because skin grafts from other areas of the body are likely to produce hair. After the organ has been removed, the skin of the penis is stripped off and turned inside out like the finger of a glove and inserted into a surgically created opening. The tip end—the glans—becomes the roof of the vagina because "inside out and upside down" it is a remarkable look-alike for a genetic female's cervix. This procedure is so successful that more than a few gynecologists have performed exams on artificial vaginas without knowing they were artificial.

Vagina to Penis

To construct an artificial penis (referred to as a "phalloplasty") reconstructive surgeons generally fashion the organ from abdominal skin or tissue from the labia and perineum (using the latter two in the case of female to male gender reassignment surgery, in which case they will also use the labia majora to construct the scrotum). In a more recently developed technique, surgeons remove a flap of skin from the underside of the recipient's non-dominant forearm (along with its sensory nerves, muscles, veins, and arteries), to construct the urethra, glans, and penis shaft. Blood vessels and nerve endings are connected using microscopic surgical techniques, and once the pudendal nerve grows into the nerve ending present in the new phallus (about three months) the organ becomes sensitive to touch. Doctors say organs fashioned from forearm skin are more sensitive and tend to function better than those constructed with other tissues. Some patients (males who lost their penis via accidental means) are eventually able to ejaculate.

Why'd They Do That?

Leave It to Beaver

The word castrate, which specifically refers to the removal of the testicles, is believed to come from the Latin word for "beaver," *castor*. The animal's unusual behavior was described in the fifteenth century work *Hortus Sanitatis*, which claimed that when under attack, the toothy beaver would chew off and leave behind his testicles, making his escape while his predator pondered the curious remains. Thus inspired, the Romans created the word *castrare*, which essentially means to "act like a beaver and chew someone's balls off."

Use It, Lose It

• Although contemporary jurists have recently favored the practice of punishing convicted sex offenders by rendering their testicles useless, the procedure is by no means a twentieth-century innovation. It was the Egyptians, some six thousand years ago who first punished individuals found guilty of sex crimes with castration (which could include removing the testicles, the penis, or both). During that time, a man convicted of rape suffered complete removal of his genitals. A woman guilty of adultery suffered the highly visible loss of her nose. (While public humiliation might be seen as one rationale for this procedure, one is tempted to consider a Freudian explanation: cutting off a woman's nose—a popular phallic symbol—can be seen as the equivalent of castration. Nose cutting was a common punishment for adulteresses in many cultures throughout history.)

• According to various historical accounts, after having spent the night in the arms of a lover, legendary Syrian queen Semiramis would have her paramour castrated to prevent him from giving the same pleasure to any other woman.

You and Your Little Dog, Too

In the tenth century, Althelstan, King of Wessex, devised a unique extended punishment for rapists who dared to assault young virgins from powerful families. First, the man was beaten, then castrated, and then he was killed. But wait, there's more. Following his execution, the law of the Anglo-Saxon Kingdom decreed that the rapist's horse and dog *also* be punished: "scrotum and tail . . . shall be cut off as close as possible to the buttocks."

Dragging Out the Punishment

While numerous societies routinely relieved a man of his genitalia for committing various infractions of the law, the ancient Greeks were the only culture to use castration for one purpose alone: to punish rapists. This is largely due to the high esteem in which the Greeks held manhood. According to Panati's *Extraordinary Endings of Practically Everything and Everybody*, offenders subjected to this form of punishment were called a *spados*, or *spadone*, meaning "to draw out" or "drag," an apt description of how the testes were removed from the scrotum, leaving a trail of blood. Panati says these men were despised in Greek society, subjected to cruel jokes and denied employment. To minimize social scorn, they often spent their remaining days masquerading as women, and thus, believe some linguists, we find the origin of the slang expression "drag" for a man in women's attire.

MORE WHY'D THEY DO THAT?

Other reasons for cutting off a man's balls or penis . . . or both:

Alternative Medicine

British physicians of the Victorian era believed that epilepsy was due to masturbation triggered by a continual state of sexual arousal and therefore the obvious cure was genital castration. Obviously, it stopped the masturbation. Electrical brain seizures, on the other hand, continued unabated. And believe it or not, in New Jersey and Wisconsin, a law allowing the castration of epileptics remained on the books well into the twentieth century.

And then there was sixth-century Empress Theodora, a former prostitute turned royal wife (of Byzantine Emperor Justinian I, 527–565 B.C.), who was reported to enjoy masturbating while *watching* men being castrated.

It's Not "Pat"

Eunuchs (castrated men) tended to have a very *androgynous* (from Greek *andros* "man" and *gynos* "woman") appearance—they were smooth-skinned and hairless, with a soft (one might say "pleasingly plump"), feminine distribution of body fat, often bearing breasts to rival a woman's. The Romans referred to the tempting penis/ball-less variety as a *voluptas*—Latin for "pleasure" and the origin of the word "voluptuous."

The men of ancient Rome were erotically fond of the feminine-looking eunuchs, particularly the powerful men who ruled the city: the reigning emperors. Augustus Caesar (27 B.C.–A.D. 14) publicly indulged his penchant for castrated men, as did Caligula (12–42 A.D.) a debauched ruler who openly copulated with a favored eunuch priest. But the most flagrant eunuch exploiter was surely Nero (37–68 A.D.), who married his favorite eunuch, Sporus, in a public ceremony, claiming the youth looked like his deceased pregnant wife Poppea (whom he was said to have conveniently murdered with a kick to the stomach).

SINGING WONDERS

• In Italy, during the seventeenth and especially the eighteenth century, it was common practice to castrate gifted prepubescent (i.e., pre-voice-deepening) boy singers, thus preventing the onset of the dreaded boys-to-men phenomenon (the procedure effectively preserved a singer's precious soprano voice throughout his entire career). In the mid-1700s as many as two thousand young Italian boys were castrated every year. Referred to as "castrato" (from the Latin *castrare,* "to castrate") these singing wonders retained their penis, and still managed to grow to manly proportions—indeed, often exhibiting a greater development than found in ordinary men. Due to physiological changes resulting from the operation, a castrato's lung capacity would expand, his diaphragm muscles strengthened, and the result was a unique, unnatural voice—clear and piercing like a choirboy's, booming and powerful like a man's.

• The practice of castrating young boys for the sake of the musical arts may have arisen unintentionally from the emphatic writings of St. Paul, who expressly forbade women from singing in church ("Let your women keep silent in the churches." 1 Corinthians, 14:35). Singing itself, however, was not only encouraged, it was a musical artform in great demand within the hallowed cathedrals; thus, when innovative composers scored a piece requiring pure and angelic voices, allowing males to be castrated seemed to be a much lesser evil than allowing women themselves to appear onstage. (Undaunted, some women nevertheless prevailed. In his memoirs, Giacomo Casanova recounted the story of a talented woman singer, frustrated by the ban forbidding females to perform on stage. Disguising herself as a castrato, the woman was able to pass the required male exam by taping a sausage to her thigh, successfully fooling the inspecting priest.)

• Legend has it that castrati skirted the biblical injunction that clearly forbids a man ("wounded in his stones or hath his privy member cut off," Deuteronomy) from "entering the congregation of the Lord." In order to continue singing in church after having his parts severed from his body, he was adominished to "ever after carry it in his pocket."

• While castrated men were staples in Rome's coveted church choirs, the Vatican forbade castrated men from marrying, since they could not procreate (why else get married?) nor would they accept mutilated men into the priesthood. The Catholic church also has a law stating that no pope may rule who has been castrated or whose genitals are otherwise deformed. Cardinals at one time acted as inspectors, and would walk past the pope-elect, who sat in a special chair—called the "porphyry chair"— which exposed his genitals to the groping hand of the youngest deacon situated underneath. Assuming everything was in place, the cardinals confirmed their approval by chanting *"testiculos habet et bene pendentes"* (loosely translated, "That's one fine set of holy balls you got there."). And why'd they do that? To prevent any *woman* usurper from ascending to the throne. According to the religious history rumor mill, one of the church's ninth-century popes was said to be a woman (Joan) masquerading as a man (John), discovered only when she had the poor sense to get pregnant, delivering the baby while on her way to church one day. She died, the event was hushed up, and the exposure ritual introduced to prevent future travesties.

• Italian castrati are widely regarded by historians to be not only the music industry's first bona fide superstars but the performing world's first sex symbols as well. Wildly adored by audiences, they were greeted by frenzied fans at city gates, cheered and engulfed when out in public and much sought after by enthusiastic women as safe sex partners. The vast majority of singing castrati were heterosexual men who, despite the loss of sperm producing testicles were more than capable of getting and maintaining erections. In fact, rumored to possess extraordinary sexual gifts, it was said that once a woman had known a eunuch, no "complete" man could satisfy her.

GUARDIANS OF THE FLOCK

The word EUNUCH, from the Latin *eunuchus* and Greek *eunouchos*, literally means "guardian of the bed" or "keeper of the bedchamber" and aptly describes the men chosen as protectors of royal concubines and harems. It was believed that the eunuchs, having been shorn of all their external sexual organs, were equally shorn of their capacity to take advantage of the opportunities offered by service in the harem.

In ancient Rome and Athens, as well as in Persia and China, removal of the testicles, scrotum and/or penis was referred to as "shaving" and men who experienced complete removal of all their genitalia were said to be "fully shaved."

During the Ottoman Empire, guards of concubines in Turkish harems were exclusively "fully shaved" black eunuchs . . . purposely chosen for their ugliness. White eunuchs, with penis intact (or any other white man, for that matter, with the exception of the Sultan) were not permitted to touch, or even to look at the women of the Harem (a nasty death awaited those who did) and generally served in the sultan's own quarters (this was because no one was sure the eunuchs were genuinely impotent . . . and of course, we now know they weren't). Curiously, intact men who managed to elude the guards and infiltrate the harem were often punished anyway, forced to endure the misfortune of harem castration. While deep in the embrace of a concubine, she would rip out her disloyal lover's testicles with her fingernails.

DID YOU KNOW?

The inventor of paper was a Chinese eunuch.

In China's Forbidden City, Tz'u Hsi, the "Dowager Empress of China" (1861–1908) required eunuchs to carry their pickled genitals in jars that hung around their necks, (which they referred to as "the precious"), to be readily available for court inspection. Most Chinese eunuchs chose to have their preserved organs buried with them upon their death, believing they would then be reincarnated as a "full" man. And optimistic eunuchs, hoping for regeneration of their lost sexual organs while still inhabiting the "fleshly world" would often eat the warm brains of newly decapitated criminals.

TROPHIES OF WAR

Castration was common military sport among the Egyptians, Assyrians, and Israelites, where genitals of prisoners were triumphantly brandished as "trophies of war" after defeat. But the *main* purpose for the castration of the vanquished was to gain, for the victor, the masculine power of the victim. On a related note, prior to ascending the throne, sacred kings had to *eat* the genitals of the deposed predecessor, in order to absorb their holy power.

In 1200 B.C., Pharaoh Merneptah of Egypt defeated the Libyans and their allies and cut off more than 13,000 of their phalli as souvenirs. The inscription found on an ancient victory monument at Karnak gives the following trophy tally:

Phalluses of Libyan Generals	6
Libyan Phalluses cut off	6,359
Sicilian Phalluses cut off	222
Etruscan Phalluses cut off	542
Greek Phalluses presented to King	6,111

Genitals gathered as trophies of war even make an appearance in the Bible. In the eleventh century B.C., as the price for marriage to his daughter Michal, King Saul assigned David the formidable task of securing the foreskins of one hundred dead Philistines. In proving he was indeed worthy, David returned with not one, but two hundred foreskins, all still conveniently attached to their penises.

> *He took their foreskins to the king and counted them all out to him, so that he might become his son-in-law.* (1 Samuel 18:24–27)

To Save the Soul

Some religious zealots gladly undertook self-castration in order to restrain themselves from erotic temptation and the commission of sin. Origen (185–254 A.D.), a Greek Christian philosopher and church father was said to have castrated himself in order to preach and teach in the presence of women—and avoid the potential sins of man's natural (think: carnal) tendencies toward them.

WHADDAYA DO WITH LEFTOVER PENISES?

During the course of certain Athenian festivals, women planted castrated male sex organs, as if they were sowing seed, to insure fertility of the fields (perhaps next to the black-eyed peas?).

Russian Roulette

In 1774, a fanatical Christian group called the Skoptzies, "The Russian Sect of the Castrated," was founded by Andrei Ivanov, a Russian peasant. Members of the Skopzi sect believed the only way to become pure and chaste enough for heaven was through castration, and they traveled around the Russian empire propagating the message "Everyone can be the Tsar with this conversion," while attempting to woo converts by quoting the New Testament "And there be eunuchs which have made themselves for the Kingdom of Heaven's sake (Matthew 19:12)." After two children, a couple's marriage was officially declared over and the men sacrificed their testicles, the women their clitorises. Initially, the "Baptism of Fire" (castration) was performed by burning the testicles with a red-hot iron (no doubt related to one of their favorite sayings: "Sin is so profound that the only way to Heaven is through iron and fire." The technique was later abandoned for the more civilized knife or razor (apparently they figured an alternate route to the holy gate could be achieved through steel and aluminum). The purest of the sect, referred to as "Bearers of the Imperial Seal," amputated their penises a few months later. Up until the 1970s, a hundred members of this community could still be found.

SELF-MUTILATORS

While historical accounts of men removing their own genitalia usually involved a religious affiliation of sorts, such was not always the case. Greek Satirist Lucien related the following account of self-mutilation in one of his "Dialogues": A young Syrian Nobleman, named Combabus, was ordered by the king to accompany Stratonike, the royal queen, on an extended journey. Fearing lustful impulses during the long voyage, Combabus secretly castrated himself, and had his genitals placed in an ornate casket, which he secured with a royal seal and presented to the king. While on their trek the queen did fall in love with the handsome Combabus, and indeed tried to seduce him, to no avail. Nevertheless, various rumors got back to the king, who had the young man arrested upon his return, charged with adultery, and thrown into prison. Of course, on the day of the trial, Combabus played his trump card and asked the King to unseal the box, at which time the King saw for himself that the lad was, in fact, innocent.

In spite of those sensational MACHETE WIELDING MISTRESS MUTILATES LOVER'S MANHOOD! tabloid stories, the fact is, the greatest penis peril lies in the owner's own hand. In other words: modern day severed penises are most commonly the result of self-mutilation or accidental trauma.

SOMETIMES A CIGAR . . .

"Sometimes a cigar is just a cigar."

—SIGMUND FREUD

Imagine, if you will, the following settings: the vegetable aisle of the local market; the launchpad at Kennedy Space Center; fishing on a mountain lake; gazing at the spectacular Chicago skyline; your closet. Whether you're aware of them or not, genital symbols are there. In fact, as you're about to discover, they're *everywhere*. Inside. Outside. Above and Below. Even elsewhere on your own body. The simple fact is, no other earthly object can claim as many stand-ins as human genitalia.

SYMBOLISM À LA FREUD

Whereas early Man applied the name of everything tall, hard, and penetrating to the male organ, Sigmund Freud (1856–1939) *reversed* the process and called all these objects "phallic symbols." The penis, of course, was the axis of Freud's universe, and its presence, or lack thereof, formed the basis of many of his theories. It's been said that some psychiatrists observed the penis attached to the boy, while the eminent founder of psychoanalysis found the boy attached to the penis.

Widely considered one of the most influential thinkers of Western civilization, Freud expanded the meaning of sexuality beyond mere genital activities such as sexual intercourse, and included many things the average person wouldn't ordinarily think of as sexual, like a baby sucking its thumb. Freud had a knack for transforming even simple objects into symbols filled with previously hidden sexual meaning, often related to the genitals. To that end, here is a sampling of Dr. Freud's take on disguised genital symbolism:

> *[The] penis . . . is symbolized primarily by objects which resemble it in form, being long and upstanding, such as sticks, umbrellas, poles, trees and the like; also by objects which, like the thing symbolized, have the property of penetrating, and consequently injuring the body, . . . that is to say, pointed weapons of all sorts: knives, daggers, lances, sabres. Firearms are similarly used: guns, pistols and revolvers, these last being a very appropriate symbol on account of their shape.*

> *The female genitalia are symbolically represented by all such objects as share with them the property of enclosing a space or are capable of acting as receptacles: such as pits, hollows and caves, and also jars and bottles and boxes of all sorts and sizes, chests, coffers, pockets, and so forth.*

Ironically, genital association became such a popular pastime that Freud uttered his famous "Sometimes a cigar is just a cigar" line as a caution against overuse of phallic imagery. (Presidential cigar peccadilloes might have caused him to rethink that one. . . .)

Freud's Penis de Resistance

Perhaps the most well known of Freud's many constructs, "penis envy" was unquestionably the heart and soul of his theory on the psychology of women—the veritable symbol of his ideology on the gender order of the universe. Freud postulated that somewhere between the ages of three and seven, every little girl discovers—much to her shock and horror—that she does *not* *have* a penis. After that, essentially, all psychic hell breaks loose. She now feels different. She feels handicapped. She feels ill-treated. She feels inferior. She becomes *envious* . . . hoping someday to have one. Blaming her mother for all of this loss/chaos (she must have been the one who took her penis, after all) the young girl eventually decides the only way to compensate for her penis deficiency is by having children. With this thought in mind, she comes to view her father (whose penis is supposedly intact) as a love object, while harboring jealous antipathy toward Mom. Unfortunately, there is no happily-ever-after epilogue for the penis-less woman. In Freud's view, she was forever doomed to be inferior to man—given her state of sexual inequality—and achieving the status of beloved wife was the best she could ever hope for. (This insipid little theory huddles right up there with Freud's blunderous take on the vaginal orgasm.)

"I HAD A DREAM . . ."

Carl Jung (1875–1961), the creator and father of analytical psychology (and a student and contemporary of Freud's) reported in his autobiography his first remembered dream (around the age of three or four—a "grand dream"—that was to him the Basic Material and perpetual source of his life and scientific work. For most of his life, Jung kept the dream a secret, finally revealing the visceral contents at age sixty-five. The dream, as recounted by Jung:

I was in this meadow. Suddenly I discovered a dark, rectangular, stone-lined hole in the ground . . . I ran forward curiously and peered down into it. Then I saw a stone stairway leading down. Hesitantly and fearfully, I descended . . . I saw before me in the dim light a rectangular chamber about thirty feet long . . . and in the center a red carpet ran from the entrance to a low platform. On this platform stood a wonderfully rich golden throne . . . Something was standing on it which I thought was a tree trunk twelve to fifteen feet high and about one and a half to two feet thick. It was a huge thing, reaching almost to the ceiling . . . it was made of skin and naked flesh, and on top there was something like a rounded head with no face and no hair. On the very top of the head was a single eye, gazing motionless upward . . . The thing did not move, yet I had the feeling that it might at any moment crawl off the throne like a worm and creep toward me. I was paralyzed with terror . . . and I awoke sweating and scared to death.

It wasn't until many years later that Jung realized he had seen a phallus, which he determined was characteristic of a "universal subterranean god." Initially, Jung decided the dream represented his ambivalence toward Jesus Christ, i.e., as a reassuring figure of love vs. a fearful figure who called adults and children to the grave. He later tossed that theory out and instead opted to believe his subterranean phallic god stood for both a symbol of spiritual birth as well as a symbol of continued spiritual existence and after-death resurrection. (A pretty heavy interpretation for a dream about a big dick in a hole).

PARTS IS PARTS (AND *THEN* Some)

Fingers . . .

The Bird

Across the continents and through the generations, most people are keenly aware that the middle finger, known in Greek mythology as the Jupiter/Saturn finger, symbolizes a phallus. We know it today, just as folks in ancient Rome knew it when male prostitutes stuck their middle digit into the hair of their heads to signal potential customers. The phallic symbolism was also clear in medieval times, when the church, who associated it with the devil, labeled the finger *digitus infamis* or *obscenus,* a.k.a. "The Obscene Finger." (Early Christian authorities considered it evil to wear a ring on the middle finger given its sexual significance.)

The early bird finger, as it is fondly referred to in this day and age, was also looked upon as an amulet against magical influences, and early Romans often carried finger replicas in much the same way they carried phallic totems for protection against the evil eye.

"I Do"

In the ancient Eastern world, the wedding ring placed on any finger symbolized the yoni (vagina) and the lingam (penis), and the act of putting a wedding ring on the bride's finger was—and still is—considered an act of sexual union. During the wedding ceremony, the ring was often shifted from one finger to another, a symbolic enactment of sexual intercourse.

Peace

In the 60s, forming the letter "V" with the index and middle finger was widely meant as a peace sign. Prior to that, World War II soldiers flashed the same fingers to signal "victory." However, to the early Europeans, the action symbolized a double phallus, and was used to suggest infidelity. When displayed in the presence of the cuckholded husband, it meant "your wife has been cheating on you."

O.K.

Contemporary folks often press the thumb and forefinger together at the tips while extending the other three fingers, a symbol generally meant to signify "o.k." But to the early Hindus, this was considered a revered *mudra* (sacred gesture), meaning "infinity" or "perfection" and was a sign most generally associated with female genitals. A similar gesture was also popular among early Roman prostitutes. While waiting at their windows, these ancient ladies of the evening would solicit potential customers strolling past by forming a vagina ring with their thumb and index finger. Willing clients on the street would signify their acceptance by holding up a finger, the equivalent of an erection.

I Got Your Nose

In Mediterranean lands, especially Italian ones, a symbol of the vulva known as the *mano in fica,* "fig-hand," is made by pressing the thumb between the adjoining index finger and the middle finger (picture the childhood favorite "I got your nose" maneuver). This gesture was used by the early Romans primarily as a defense against the proverbial evil eye (although the sign is actually thought to have Asian origins, representing a Lingam/Yoni).

The fig-hand is also common in Greece—particularly among members of the underworld—but the Greeks refer to it as a "fist-phallus" and its exhibition represents a

The Fighand or Mano en Fica

showing of the penis. The fig was (and still is) made and displayed to an opponent while uttering some variation of the words "You've had it, Bucko." To up the insult ante, the aggressor may extend the right arm—with fig-hand firmly in place—and simultaneously clasp the left hand under the right armpit. The intended message? "I shove my whole prick up you."

One final fig-hand note: Sixteenth-century Satirist, philologist, and benedictine monk Francois Rabelais suggested the symbol represented a fig in a donkey's Anus (which the insulted is being invited to "seize with his teeth").

And while we're talking fig and fuck, some linguists believe the Anglo-Saxon word "fuck" may have derived from *ficus,* or "fig."

Finally, early Christians called the gesture *manus obscenus,* "the obscene hand," and it would appear theirs is the legacy that endures. Today the fig sign is used as a derogatory sexual display, much like the raised middle finger, intended to convey the message "fuck you."

Hair . . .

The link between hair and sexual power and fertility is a long and established one, stemming from the close association of hair with puberty, along with hair's own magical powers of regeneration. On the other head, the symbolic union of the genitals and hair is a diverse and speculative one, and a rich source of anthropological and analytical musings. In *Hair: Sex, Society, Symbolism,* author Wendy Cooper says "given the links between pubic hair and the genitals, and by 'displacement' between head hair and sexual power, the cutting off of a man's hair is a symbolic castration."

It is supposedly for this reason that a shaven head is adopted by religious ascetics who renounce their sexuality. The equation of hair with sexual power, fertility, and virility, and its loss with "impotence" or weakness, as it were, is vividly illustrated in the biblical story of Samson and Delilah.

It has also been argued in the analytical realm that hair represents man's "public phallus," one that he can exhibit unabashedly to the masses. This supposedly accounts for the pride, mirror time, and hairspray spent perfecting his do. Unruly locks, on the other hand, are said to portray the erect penis (they don't call it "bed hair" for nothing).

Mouth . . .

Zoologist Desmond Morris, an astute observer of the species, has said that any part of the body that looks even a tad like the genitals may also elicit genitally oriented thoughts. And thus, the imposters are deemed to be genital echoes. It should come as no surprise that as echoes go, the mouth is considered a veritable vagina wannabe. Think about it: a moist, slit-like opening, surrounded by plush lips that swell and redden during sexual arousal. Indeed, symbolically viewing the female mouth as a vulva is a tradition that governs the behavior of many cultures throughout the world.

- Some societies—partriarchal Moslems, for example—require that the mouth be covered by veils (theirs being a culture that equated women's mouths with the notoriously feared vagina dentata, or "toothed vagina," discussed in Chapter 5).
- Other societies equate copulation with female eating (in some languages they are actually the same word) and thus will prohibit women from eating anything where they could be seen by men.

Tongue . . .

In many Eastern cultures, the tongue between the lips is said to represent the sacred lingam-yoni (penis-vagina): male genital with female genital (note that the Latin *lingus*, "tongue," is related to lingam, and the vulva contains labia meaning "lips"). In some Asiatic countries, the tongue protruding from the mouth is seen as life-giving, and thus is regarded as a sign of potency. In Western tradition, however, sticking out your tongue is viewed as an insulting gesture, a "showing of the phallus" equivalent to extending the middle finger.

Ear . . .

The relationship between the ear and the female genitals has a far-reaching and eclectic history. As early as 4,000 years ago, the Egyptians cut the ears off adulteresses as punishment, while in Burma young girls entering puberty were initiated by having their ears bored, signifying their entry into womanhood. Buddha was said to have been *born* through the ear, and some Early Christian writers believed the Virgin Mary was impregnated through the ear by the angel Gabriel. Early psychoanalytical writings on dream interpretation substitute the ear for the vagina in masturbation.

Belly Button . . .

This one seems to push the edges of the genital envelope, but, according to Kate and Douglas Botting in *Sex Appeal,* the belly button is also an effective genital echo, even though, as the Bottings point out, "it's tiny . . . it goes nowhere, does nothing, and permits little to be done to it." As an attractant of male sexual interest, however, the belly button yields significant power. Much of this is attributed not only to its vaginal shape, but more important, to its location: smack dab in the middle of a woman's naked belly.

Knee . . .

A Middle Eastern euphemism for penis was "knee" (*genu*), which was mentioned so often that many people believed the knee was the source of semen. A father used to establish paternal rights to a child by setting the infant on his knee, which is why "genuine" (of the knee) came to mean "legitimate."

And Toes

The masculine big toe has long been considered a universal phallic symbol. As such, Hindu love rituals, past and present, frequently involve a toe kiss, a powerful and erotic practice in which a woman sensually kisses the big toe of the man to arouse him. This activity is considered a symbolic form of fellatio.

ALL THINGS WISE AND WONDERFUL . . .

While Freud viewed almost all things as phallic symbols, some pre-Christian thinkers viewed the penis as symbolic of almost all things. The litany of phallic allegory is thoughtfully paraded in the writings of second century (A.D.) Greek soothsayer and rhetoric teacher Artemidorus Daldianus, who wrote:

> *The penis corresponds to one's parents, on the one hand, because it is itself the cause of children . . . it signifies a wife or mistress, since it is made for sexual intercourse . . . It indicates brothers and all blood relatives . . . It is a symbol of strength and physical vigor . . . It corresponds to speech and education . . . The penis is also a sign of wealth and possessions . . . it also indicates the respect that is inspired by high rank."*

(Apparently the only thing not linked to the penis was PMS.)

SIX ASSORTED PHALLIC SYMBOLS

Shoes

In the eleventh century, savvy European men initiated a fashion trend that begat a three-hundred-year love affair with a long, phallus-shaped shoe known as the "poulaine." William Rossi's *Sex Life of the Foot and the Shoe* relates that the purpose of the poulaine was to simulate an erect penis. As such, the shoe had a stuffed toe which grew from a couple of inches, to four, to eight, and finally to fourteen (the toe eventually had to be stuffed with moss or wool to keep it erect!). The poulaine ignited a storm of controversy among conservative-minded folks, and thus, under intense pressure, Charles V of France condemned the phallic shoe as "an exaggeration against good manners, a scoffing against God and the

Church, a worldly vanity and a mad presumption." Wearers pooh-poohed the diatribe, and the vogue blossomed under the royal attack. Over in England, under the rule of Edward IV, Parliament eventually prohibited phallic extensions more than two inches beyond the toe, but again, nobody paid any attention. Undaunted, poulaine protesters took their case to the pope, who obliged them in 1468 by cursing the practice. However, the people (again) prevailed, and the poulaine persevered.

∿⳨

EQUAL OPPORTUNITY NOTE:

While most cultures viewed the shoe strictly in phallic terms, Freud maintained that while the toe (and heel) was indeed a phallic symbol, the inside of the shoe symbolized the vagina.

The poulaine was reportedly a popular guest at aristocratic dinner parties where it was commonly used for under-the-table titillation. The man's erect poulaine would reach across to lift the skirt of the lady seated opposite him, making its way up as high as she would permit. Orgasms were said to be a fairly common "between-course appetizer." Rossi also writes that it was common for a wife or mistress to remark sarcastically to a husband or lover who was unable to achieve an erection "your poulaine is more man than you."

A shoe style commonly found today in countries such as Turkey, Greece, and Bulgaria features a turned-up toe with a large furry pompon either on the toe tip or farther behind on the vamp area. According to Rossi, the furry ball symbolized the female genital area while the extended toe style was clearly phallic in nature.

"The erect, turned up toe curves around to direct its tip at the pompom, and signifies male-female mating."

Rabbit's Foot

Celtic tribes living in Western Europe some 2,500 years ago noticed the amazing breeding capacity of the fruitful rabbit. Thus, wishing for a bit of fertility luck of their own, legend has it they took to carrying around its foot—a symbol of its seemingly tireless penis.

The Necktie

Ah, the necktie, a length of cloth tied about the (usually) male neck and allowed to hang loosely, with no purpose other than to call attention to itself. The phallic symbolism here would be hard to miss. Men fiddle with it, straighten it, stroke it, and have their confidence bolstered when wearing a "lucky one." A woman in the throes of flirtation will caress a man's tie, coyly tugging on its tip, and walk her fingers up its length. And

Former presidential aide George Stephanopolus revealed that when President Bill Clinton remarked "Nice tie" upon shaking someone's hand, he really meant "Screw you" (apparently a comment made frequently to journalists).

numerous are the symbolic emasculation scenes in film whereby the woman—in a fit of fury— will cut it off (the tie) with a large pair of scissors.

The Serpent

Male or Female? Maybe both. On the one hand, the serpent was associated with worship of the goddess, and, as one of the oldest symbols of female power, was considered holy in preclassic Aegean civilization since it embodied the power of life. Historians remind us the early Hebrews were intent upon stamping out goddess worship, which is probably why the Serpent is shown in such unfavorable light in the book of Genesis.

On the other hand, the serpent also has obvious masculine symbolism. According to Mark Thorn's *Taboo No More*, when it twines around a rod it stands for the erect organ "under the spell of sexual passion." In fact, this is the configuration in which the serpent appears on the staff originally held by Christian bishops and called "The Staff of Life."

But perhaps the ultimate symbolism is found in the story of the original Eve, who had no spouse except the serpent, a "living phallus" she is said to have created for her own sexual pleasure.

The Rocket

Quite possibly the epitome of classic phallic imagery and symbolism, one that loudly proclaims in both shape and thrusting function (not to mention the cosmic orgasm) to—borrowing from the audacious Capt. James T. Kirk—"boldly go where no man has gone before."

Phallic Architecture

The Space Needle, Eiffel Tower, Washington's Monument, Big Ben, Empire State Building, Cleopatra's Needle, Leaning Tower of Pisa

In *Building Sex: Men, Women, Architecture and the Construction of Sexuality,* author Aaron Betsky opines that phallic symbols dominate building design for a reason—the imposing skyward structures represent male domination in society. Betsky writes that men have created a world which represents their bodies in general, and their sexuality in particular. Women, on the other hand, are relegated to having influence over the less visible interior. In the world of buildings, as with the presentation of their (sexual) bodies, "Men rule the outside. Women, the inside."

HER TURN: SIX CLASSIC SYMBOLS OF THE VAGINA/VULVA

Triangle

The great Paleolithic Caves contain hundreds of drawings and carvings of down-facing triangles with vertical clefts bisecting their bottom angles. During the prudish days of prehistoric scholarship, several ideas were advanced regarding their interpretation—none of which could obscure the obvious reference to female genitals. Most ancient symbol systems recognized the triangle as a sign of the goddess's genital "holy place," the source of all life. In very early times, the triangle was worshipped much in the same way modern Christians worship the cross.

᭣᭣

Greek Mathematician Pythagoras considered the triangle sacred, not because of its perfect shape, but because as a symbol of the "Holy Door"—vulva of the "Mother Delta," it represented universal fertility.

Yoni Sign

A hand gesture made by placing the thumb tips together and the forefinger tips of both hands together (with all remaining fingers extended, facing downward) to form a triangle is a yoga sign. The *Women's Encyclopedia of Myths and Secrets* says the yoni sign was an occult secret for many years, although today it represents a symbolic invocation of female power. This gesture is sometimes used as a token of greeting or benediction among feminists.

Dove

Although the dove was transformed by the Christians into a symbol of the Holy Ghost, in its previous incarnation this angelic bird was primarily a symbol of female sexuality, and was frequently associated with female genitals. In fact, in some Eastern languages, the word "dove" is synonymous with "yoni." The dove represented the specifically sexual aspects of the goddess, and was universally recognized as a sacred symbol of Aphrodite or Venus.

Cowrie Shell

Given its deeply involuted pinkish mouth, it's easy to understand why this shell has been considered among many cultures to be a symbol of the vagina (said to represent "the divine yoni"). Prized for tens of thousands of years, the cowrie shell was frequently used as a sacred fertility charm, and widely believed to have healing and regenerative powers. The shell was pierced and worn as a sacred amulet by the Romans, and was often placed in graves to accompany the dead on their way to a New Cycle.

Fish

A worldwide ancient symbol of the vulva (yoni), and in turn the Great Mother, was the pointed oval sign known as *vesica piscis,*

"vessel of the fish" (also symbolized by joining the thumb and forefinger together). According to the *Women's Encyclopedia of Myths and Secrets,* the ancients insisted that women's sexual secretions smelled like fish, which is why the sign of the yoni came to be called *vesica piscis.* The fish symbol of the yonic goddess was so revered throughout the Roman Empire that

Christian authorities insisted on taking it over, along with extensive revision of classic goddess myths to deny its earlier female genital meanings.

Beans

Yes, *beans*. Believe it or not, the Romans considered beans to be female-genital symbols . . . symbolism that lives on to this day. The Italian slang term for female genitals is *fava,* or "bean." Those living in early Roman times believed that beans housed "ancestral spirits," and had the magical power to impregnate. In fact, eating beans was taboo among the Pythagoreans due to their spiritual possession. Indeed, legend has it that ten disciples of Pythagoras, a devout champion of virginity, were under assault with no place to flee but a bean field. They died rather than trample the genitally inclined mystical fruit. By the way, fava beans also have a rich historical reputation as an aphrodisiac, and in particular, as an erection booster. These legumes are alleged to have incited the ancient Roman poet Cicero to passion.

THE HILLS WERE ALIVE, BUT WAS THE SOUND . . . MUSIC?

The flute is good that's made of wood,
And is, I own, the neatest;
Yet none the less, I must confess
the silent flute's the sweetest.
—"THE CUPID" (1736)

Many kinds of musical instruments have their origins as representations of the genitalia. To primitive man, one of the principle uses of musical instruments, if not the chief use, was to celebrate life's primal functions: sex and/or fertility.

The flute has a long association with sex and genitalia, born of primitive logic. Quite simply, it began when ancient man first noticed the keen resemblance between a pierced straight instrument and the penis. According to Curt Sachs's *The History of Musical Instruments,* early civilizations, governed as they were by masculine impulses, soon connected the following ideas together: Flute-Phallus-Fertility-Life-Rebirth. These ancient people came to associate flute playing with innumerable phallic ceremonies and with fertility in general. In ancient cemeteries, a flute found buried with the remains does not mean the person was a musician. As a life charm, flutes were placed with the dead in the hopes of a good rebirth.

This melodic instrument has spawned numerous expressions for the penis, including the living flute, the one-eyed flute, the silent flute, and of course, my favorite, the skin flute.

• In New Guinea, natives pounded out a melodic beat using a trough of stone, representing the vulva, which they pounded with a pestle, representing the spirit of a penis.
• The split drum, considered one of the most important of the early instruments, is a symbol of the vulva. Found in the Pacific Islands, Africa, and parts of Asia, this instrument generally was made from a large tree trunk with a slit in the middle and was played by ramming it with a stick.
• The conch shell, long considered to be a common symbol of the feminine spirit, and specifically the vagina, is

also often used as a musical instrument (particularly in India) where the emerging sound is considered to be one of "eternity" and "pure space."

SEASON'S GREETINGS

You might be surprised to discover that many of the traditions celebrated during favorite holidays actually have pagan origins and (what else?) genital symbolism. Among these are certain Christmas festivities. . . .

Mistletoe

Also known as the "golden bough" (given the golden color of dry mistletoe) mistletoe was, according to classical legend, sacred to the Celtic druids, and carried rich phallic symbolism. The druids considered mistletoe to be the genitalia of the oak god (Zeus or Jupiter) and the plant's poisonous white berries to be drops of his semen (in the same way as the red berries of holly were seen as menstrual blood of the goddess Hel [Holle]). Druid priests would ceremonially "castrate" the oak god at the winter solstice fertility festivals (the season of sacrifice) with a golden sickle. As with many pagan rituals, the rites of the oak god were generally accompanied by frenzied nights of drunken debauchery. What remains today—our present Christmastime custom of kissing under the mistletoe—is a pale shadow remnant of the sexual orgies held in honor of the Earth and hopes of a fertile season!

Yule Log

In France, the greatest heathen festival of the north was Yule, celebrated during the season of the sun's rebirth (Yule was assimilated to Christmas in the Middle Ages). This time of revelry was observed with a large festive log known as the noel log, which represented the phallus of a god (said to be the phallic god Cernunnos). In Scandinavia, the Yule festival was a twelve-day December celebration in honor of the pagan sex and fertility god Jul (pronounced "yule"). A large single log, the yule log—representing Jul's phallus—was kept with a fire against it for twelve days. On each of those days, a sacrifice was offered to Jul.

The Christmas Tree

Yes, like it or not, the beloved Christmas tree was also purely pagan in origin, having nothing to do with Jesus, His birth, or His life. Our earliest beginnings feature the lovely evergreen, worshipped as a symbol of life, fertility, sexual potency, and reproduction. And all of that, of course, spells phallic symbol. As such, evergreen trees were often brought into the home and displayed as idols, and later, decorated and presented with gifts.

SPRING FEVER

Hooray! Hooray! The First of May;
Outdoor Screwing Begins Today!
—AMERICAN FOLK RHYME

May Days

In Northern Europe, up until about the sixteenth century, the month of May was known as the time to "wear the green" to honor the Earth Mother's "new clothes." May was also the time of sexual freedom for couples—regardless of martial status—to have sex in newly plowed fields to encourage the growth of the crops.

The maypole was originally a symbol for the May King's phallus, and was traditionally set up and decorated with ribbons and flowers for festivities initiating a new season of growth and fertility. While the pole itself was a phallic symbol, the round dance and the wheel hung from the top added the female element. After dancing around the merrily adorned mast, couples would head for the woods to continue their own private celebration. The god's Phallus—in the guise of the maypole—was later planted in the Earth's womb. (Makes you wonder if parents, watching their little ones gaily prancing about the brightly decorated maypole, have a clue . . .)

Principal Symbols Commonly Used Throughout History to Evoke FEMALE GENITALIA:

Shells
Flowers:
   Lotus, Rose, Lily
Fruit:
   Apricot, Fig, Plum, Peach
Myrtle
Coco-de-Mer,
Cardamom Seeds

Leaves of the Willow Tree
Almond
Oyster

Principal Symbols Commonly Used Throughout History to Evoke THE PHALLUS:

Axe
Plow
Dagger
Sword
Rain
Sun
Fish
Bird
Serpent
Bull
Horn
Moon
Foot
Thumb
Standing Stone
Column
Tree

YIKES! YOU WANT TO DO *WHAT* TO IT?

"*Man is wrong to be ashamed of mentioning and displaying it, always covering and hiding it. He should, on the contrary, decorate and display it with the proper gravity, as if it were an envoy.*"

—LEONARDO DA VINCI

SITTING ON PINS AND NEEDLES

There was a time when getting pierced was benignly limited to one's earlobes. Later, however, piercing emerged as a form of artistic expression as folks began to impale and accessorize eyebrows, nostrils, tongues, and navals (usually "innies"). But what of the human pincushion who ventured below the belt—into areas normally covered by underwear? Well, in the past, that involved only the few, the bold, the extreme. Not so anymore. To the uninitiated, genital piercing may appear to be the sole privy of S/M (sadomasochism) devotees and societal outsiders, but the fact is, soccer moms and young urban professionals are increasingly apt to sport genital jewelry.

The Paternity of Piercing

In spite of popular belief, genital piercing is not a recent fad engineered by the sexual underground or even the MTV generation. Bodily adornments of the genital sort are in fact an ancient and highly revered art. *The Kama Sutra* (which chronicles erotic Hindu customs dating back to the fourth century B.C.) provides detailed instructions for piercing of the lingam—an activity endured by thousands for the purpose of providing supreme pleasure during intercourse. That is not to say that enhanced erotica was the sole driving force behind early man's use of piercing implements. At the other end of the spectrum, ancient Greeks and Romans commonly pierced the foreskins of male slaves to *prevent* intercourse, and bound together the labia of females to keep them similarly celibate. Victorian aristocrats were known to pierce the penis for practical as well as decorative purposes, while still other cultures employed genital piercings in their rites of pubertal passage (the types of which would likely be met with a collective shiver when compared to those favored by today's skin enthusiasts).

So Why'd You Do that, Anyway?

Eighty or 90 percent of modern genital piercings are done for sexual gratification purposes, by folks wanting to spice up their sex lives, although increasing numbers of contemporary piercees indicate their needle in the intimate flesh experience was about empowerment, personal awakening, heightened body consciousness, or even a test of endurance. There are also those who blithely submit to risqué body adornment as a unique way to celebrate milestones or rites of passage (when a pen and pencil set won't do). And on the romantic front: a current trend among European couples finds many lovebirds opting for genital piercing as a symbol of the marital bond in lieu of the conventional finger ring. It seems many find piercing the genitals—including the mutual pain experienced—intones a more intense sexual commitment than a gold band easily slipped on and off the traditional digit. What price love.

A Rivet Runs Through It

Numerous varieties and styles of jewelry abound in today's savvy body piercing establishments. For a thorough and entertaining read on body piercings and fanciers, the reader is directed to V. Vale's *Modern Primitives*. (**Note to the kids:** In case you were thinking of trying this at home, don't. All piercings should be done by professional piercers on age-appropriate bodies.)

Male Piercings

The Prince Albert—said to have been named after Queen Victoria's husband, this piercing is a ring placed through the urethra at the base of the penis head. Called a "dressing ring" by Victorian haberdashers, the device was originally used to secure the male genitalia in either the right or left pant leg during that era's craze for extremely tight, crotch binding trousers, and thus minimize those

Prince Albert

unsightly bulges (the men slipped a sash through the ring and anchored it along their inseam). Legend has it that Prince Albert wore such a ring to retract his foreskin (preventing the buildup of smegma) to keep his member "sweet smelling." The hygienically considerate Albert did not wish to offend Her Majesty.

The Ampallang—a style indigenous to the areas surrounding the Indian Ocean, the ampallang is a piercing device placed horizontally through the center of the head of the penis just above the urethra (as one might imagine, trust in one's piercer is essential). Recommended as a preferred form of male adornment in the *Kama Sutra,* this piercing is still often done as part of puberty rites—usually performed by an old woman—and is said to greatly enhance the sensual pleasure of both partners. In an extreme case of you would if you loved me, some women may deny intercourse to a man not pierced in this fashion.

Apadravya—also recommended in the *Kama Sutra* (in which the term *apadravya* refers to any form of vaginal stim-

Apradravya

ulating device) as a sexual enhancement aid. This piercing—uncommon among today's modern enthusiasts—is generally a vertical placement through the penis shaft behind the head, and sometimes in the head itself.

Frenum—involves piercing the oh-so-sensitive loose piece of flesh beneath the penis head. This style is of European origin, and has served the extremes of both chastity and erotic stimulation.

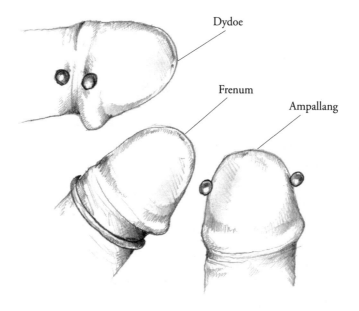

Dydoe

Frenum

Ampallang

Dydoe—this piercing reportedly originated in the Jewish community, and is said to return some of the sensation lost with the removal of the foreskin during circumcision. Partners of wearers also frequently report increased vaginal sensation during intercourse. Placement of the device is through the upper and lower edge of the corona on the penis head.

Foreskin—piercing the foreskin with single or multiple rings, buttons or bones was historically done among many cultures for the purposes of forced chastity. By sealing the foreskin over the glans, erections were impossible to achieve and painful to even attempt. The ancient Romans frequently pierced their male slaves in this manner, as were the Nubian slaves in pioneering America. By making intercourse, as well as masturbation unavailable, slave owners hoped to redirect sexual energy into harder work. Also, during the Victorian era, fathers often had sons pierced in this fashion prior to sending them off to study away from the family home.

Hafada—this piercing is done in the scrotum, and originated as a rite of puberty practiced in the Arabian communities. In this sense, the ceremonial piercing is inserted through the left side of the scrotum between the testicle and the base of the penis. Proving that the youth is "now and forever more a man," the ring is believed to prevent the testes from ever returning to the groin. This style of genital adornment spread among the military community when the revered French Foreign Legionaires, after spending time in the Arab countries, adopted the practice themselves.

Convicted American mass murderer/cannibal Albert Fish (1870–1936) reportedly had so many needles inserted into his genital region that they were thought to have short circuited the voltage from his electric chair.

Female Piercings

The Clitoral Hood—The tender tissue enfolding the clitoris glans can be pierced either vertically or horizontally. Vertical piercing (the most popular) stimulates the clitoris directly, although it may cause irritation and clitoral desensitization in some women, while horizontal piercing (the most orgasmically effective) stimulates the clitoris indirectly.

Labia Minora—The inner labia are the most popular site for female genital piercings because they are relatively thin, and tend to heal more quickly than any other body piercing.

Labia Majora—Women who choose to adorn their outer lips may opt for single piercings or multiple placement of a variety of rings, beads, barbells, and personal charms. Ladies involved in S/M activity often attach chains, weights and padlocks to their labia piercings (which may cause considerable stretching of the tissues).

Clitoris—For a successful piercing of this exquisitely sensitive organ, the glans should be at least a quarter inch wide and loosely hooded (a tight hood may cause the piercing to migrate out). Studs may be punched directly into the top of the glans, or placed through the sides of the shaft (barbell type or rings). You *really* want to have a piercer who knows what they're doing here.

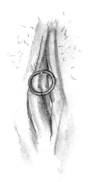

The Fourchette—this is a piercing made through the web of tissue on the bottom wall of the vagina over the perineum and is not recommended for a woman who enjoys vaginal penetration on a regular basis.

The Isabella—piercing made by entering beneath the clitoris and exiting above the hood. Experienced piercers caution that the possibility of severing the dorsal nerve and artery of the clitoris—leading to a complete loss of sensation—is quite high. Something to think about.

The Princess Albertina—this relatively new and experimental piercing is considered by those in the piercing-know to have a questionable safety factor. The Albertina forces a ring into the tiny, extremely sensitive female urethra and out through the hymen. The urethral area is not sturdy enough to withstand minor infections or the weight and friction of an attached ring. This piercing sounds uncomfortable and dangerous because it is.

Clip-ons

Those women who wish to decoratively adorn their genitalia—but find permanent piercing a bit much—may opt for temporary jewelry such as the "clit clip," a device which slips over the labia and clitoris much like a paper clip. Decorated with crystals or bells that hang from small chains, it holds the clitoris out and cuts off enough circulation to keep it "sensually" engorged (similar to the way a "cock ring" does to the penis).

Peculiar Practices in Other Places

God Lives *Where?*

The Sadhus, a tribe living up and down the Ganges of India, believe that the spirit of god resides inside the penis, and thus practice various rituals to modify the organ in order to establish a spiritual connection. In one such ritual, progressively heavier weights are hung (and worn continuously) on the penis of a select number of very young males in order to stretch and elongate the organ. By adulthood, these young men's penises are said to approach eighteen inches in length, and are carried by the owner coiled up in little baskets. It should also be noted the Sadhu men—along with their lengthy penises—are considered sacred. In this respect, the penis is often touched and kissed by women wishing the gift of fertility (although it should also be noted that the lengthy lingam is effectively rendered limp and thus useless as a fertility instrument in its own right).

Pearly Penises

A common penile modification practice of the Yakuza (Japanese mafia) involves inserting pearls into the area between the outer skin that slides freely over the inner core of the penis. To achieve this penis d' art, a chopstick or toothbrush is carved down to a sharp point to split the skin open (just below the head or just above the base of the penis), the skin flap is lifted up, the pearl is inserted, and the area bandaged until the wound heals. According to Vale's *Modern Primitives,* the men perform this "surgery" as part of a tradition, adding one pearl to the penis for each year they spend in jail (they claim the pearls make the penis larger and give it a different sensation). Once the pearl is inserted, the finished product is said (by observers) to resemble a large wart.

Tinkling Penises

In a similar ritual, Burmese males insert tiny gold, silver, or bronze bells under the skin of the penis to heighten sensitivity, increase endurance, and, more important, to make themselves more attractive to females. The practice, first noted by European traders in the fifteenth century, may involve the insertion of a dozen or more bells into the virile member. These men are said to feel especially proud if the tinkling of the bells can be heard as they walk about.

BOYS WILL BE BOYS

In the Some-Men-Just-Want-Everything-Bigger Category

In an activity designed to enlarge the meatus (A.K.A. the urethral opening, located at the tip of the penis) eager participants systematically cut or tear the meatus by placing increasingly larger instruments into the opening. The practice is referred to as a meatotomy, and, in an accomplishment befitting an entry in *Ripley's Believe It or Not,* a few men have succeeded in enlarging the opening enough to insert the glans of another man into the tip of their own penis (all together now: YEOWIEEE!!!).

This Bud's For You

Some men are unhappy with the size of their penis. Others, the shape. For those gents unhappy with *both,* a not-so-safe sex practice known as "scrotal infusion" may be the answer. In this process, a saline solution is injected into the scrotal sac (causing it to briefly resemble a water balloon) and by the next morning, the solution will have filtered into the penis. And now, without even mumbling any magic words, they have a member which resembles a beer can (brand unknown).

"Beeg" Penis

Other men wishing to experience the joys of a larger lingum, albeit temporary, are fond of using bees—that's right, bees—to increase the size of their organ, while simultaneously basking in the insect's piercing stings to enhance their erotic sensations. This practice dates back to nineteenth-century rites of select masochistic Hindus, who utilized bees to increase penile turgidity, and were said to revel in the pleasurable pain of a sting prior to engaging in intercourse. The procedure involves holding the bee by the wings and pushing the irritated insect on the glans penis, encouraging it to sting. When it does, the penis becomes painfully tender, and swells. Considerably. Some bee-men like to tie a piece of twine around the base to prolong the swelling effect, which generally is greatest on the second day.

From the Office Supply Room

Another type of erotic play activity enjoyed by some sexual enthusiasts—generally those involved in the S/M scene—involves genital stapling, with options that include: stapling the edges of the scrotal skin to the thighs; stapling the outer skin of the penis to the abdomen; and among women, stapling the outer labia together. Aficionados of this practice use either a surgical skin stapler—preferred—or a standard office type—unsterile and thus risky. Considered by practitioners to be either a form of bondage or a chastity device, be advised it also requires a special surgical-staple remover.

Extra Crispy . . . or Original?

Some folks enjoy the sense of danger and excitement generated by fire, and feel empowered when they're able to withstand its pain. To this end, according to Love's *Encyclopedia of Unusual Sexual Practices,* some men enjoy symbolically frying their genitals in hot oil. This sexual "game" involves placing hot oil in a large cup into which the genitals are lowered for a few seconds. The remaining oil cools—and is used as a lubricant for sexual acts to follow. Be aware that this activity is not suitable for men with piercings since metal absorbs heat and can therefore result in burnt flesh.

GIRLS JUST WANNA HAVE FUN

New Meaning for "Hand-Me-Down"

Women intent on exploring the outer limits of their inner vagina are rarely satisfied with items as mundane as dildoes. For optimal "fulfillment" these ladies often choose . . . the fist. Vaginal fisting (also known as "fist-fucking" or "hand-balling") is enjoyed by heterosexuals and gays alike, and is not necessarily limited to the realm of sado-masochism. As described by Deborah Addington in *A Hand in the Bush,* this activity involves gradually inserting the entire hand (previously prepped with copious amounts of water-based lubricant and a good manicure) up into the inner cavity of the vagina, and then curling it into a fist. Women wanting even more may find the answer in double-fisting where the fister inserts (or, to use Addington's phrase, "dives in" with) *both* hands.

TAKE IT OFF, TAKE IT ALL OFF

And finally, from the extreme files (like none of the above fit): some men, in search of the final frontier of body modification procedures, travel precariously down the narrow path of extreme surgery. To obtain the ultimate level of sexual gratification, these folks submit their genitals to a knife wielding cutter, who will either castrate (remove the testicles, resulting in a eunuch), truncate the penis, or completely remove the organ (body nullification), performed as per individual request.

The most common of these sexually driven fetishes is castration, with an estimated one hundred to three hundred folks voluntarily joining in the Eunuch Club each year. In addition to conventional surgical removal, castrations may be performed via the elastrator method (tying off the testicles at the base of the scrotum which causes them to die from lack of blood). After about twelve hours of agonizing pain, the feeling dulls and the balls are then cut off. This method is popular among S/M practitioners, who are likely to finish up with a bit of testicular cuisine: lightly cooked balls with a tasty mushroom sauce (really). Still other eunuch wannabes opt for the burdizzo, a farm tool that destroys the testicular blood vessels with one quick crush. Afterward, the testicles shrink up and are eventually absorbed into the body. Two words: "intense pain."

In February of 1999, Indiana police briefly infiltrated this shadowy underground world when they arrested Edward Botkin for practicing medicine without a license (specifically, performing castrations on men). Mr. Botkin, described as a quiet friendly man, kept numerous videotapes of his "surgeries," along with numerous jars of preserved testicles on the kitchen counter (some castrators—and eunuchs—are trophy hunters with vast testicle collections who also frequently tan the scrotums to keep as leather satchels). Police also found hundreds of letters from men around the country all requesting, even pleading for, surgical castration.

I'M NOT MAKING THIS UP!

•

"If the world were a logical place,
men would ride side saddle."

—RITA MAE BROWN

Here we find an eclectic array of genital oddities and anecdotes. Uncommonly interesting stuff, much like Forrest Gump's box of "you never know what you're gonna get" chocolates. No Rhyme. No Reason. No Particular Order.

GENITAL EDIBLES

Middle Age Betty Crockers

• European women living in the Middle Ages turned to their baking skills when it came to arousing sexual desire in their men. A seduction-minded wife would coat her naked body with honey, roll in a pile of wheat, carefully remove the grains from the skin, and then mill them counterclockwise. The bread dough prepared from this flour was then carefully kneaded between the upper thighs. After consuming this lovingly prepared bread, a man would have no need of today's little blue wonder pill to enhance his sexual prowess or his libido. On the other hand, a woman wishing to render her husband *less* amorous (read: make him impotent) followed the same procedure, with one exception: she milled the grain *clockwise*.

• Medieval German women also believed that the way to a man's heart was through his stomach, after a brief pit stop in the vagina. One of the favored aphrodisiacs of these gals involved placing an apple or a biscuit into the vagina just before bedtime. The following day the lass served up the marinated cuisine to her would-be paramour, who, after eating it, would hopefully fall "truly, madly, deeply" in love.

• Those Germans living in the Middle Ages apparently spent a lot of time in the kitchen whipping up sex remedies. Barren couples hoping to be blessed with children often found their fertility prescription in a palate-pleasing concoction called the *liebesknochen,* "bone of love," a thick, phallic shaped pastry filled with vanilla cream, known to pastry aficionados today as . . . the éclair.

Vagina Almondine

A medieval woman hoping to increase sexual desire in her man would place a live fish into her vagina (presumably a small one) and after it died, cooked it and fed it to her lover or husband.

On a related fish note, as a type of erotic—and certainly creative—foreplay, a male from Ponape (a Micronesian Island) is reported to sometimes place a small fish in his loved one's vagina, and then gently licks it out prior to coitus.

BUT DID THE BRIDE WEAR WHITE?

Let Them Eat Cake

In *The Complete Book of Sexual Trivia,* Leslee Welch writes that an Italian Renaissance woman hoping to seduce a potential lover would feed him *confarreatio* cake, a confection thought to have magical qualities. The cake was put in a small oven that was placed over the woman's naked vulva and baked by the "heat of passion" the individual possessed for her intended amour (makes you wonder if there wasn't a lot of gooey cake served up). In fact, the custom of serving wedding cake following the ceremony has its origin in the *confarreatio* cakes (small wheat cakes) eaten by newlywed couples of ancient Rome to ensure fertility. This ritual was of such importance that the marriage ceremony was referred to as a "confarreation" (wheat-wedding or ceremony of eating wheat together).

Fertile Toss

Many a wedding guest has participated in the age-old tradition of throwing rice at the blushing newly married couple—a custom that actually originated thousands of years ago. The symbolism? The thrown rice represented semen/ejaculation; sort of a here's-to-your-fertility gesture by the community.

Speaking of Rice . . .

There was at one time a belief among the Japanese that the penis was a key ingredient in the cooking process of rice. By exposing the erect penis before the boiling pot, they believed the steaming of the rice would be improved and hastened.

But Do You Still Need a License?

As told in *The Cradle of Erotica,* according to old Muslim and Jewish law, a female becomes the wife of a male the very moment his penis enters her vagina—with one caveat—there must be proof of consummation from four credible witnesses. The law stipulates that she remains his lawful spouse until such a time as another penis, called *El-ihhlil,** (liberator) penetrates her parts. At this point, consummation now constitutes divorce (where before it begat the marriage). Thus, adultery and fornication were considered legitimate ways to make or break a marital contract.

Dangerous Liaisons

In ancient Greece, adulterous men were occasionally punished by having their pubic hair shaved, followed by the insertion of a large

*El-ihhlil (the Legalizer or Liberator) was a common nickname for the penis because, by virtue of penetrating the vagina, it freed a woman from her former husband or lover and/or made her the lawful wife of her new paramour.

radish up their rectum. Among some Zulu groups, an adulterous wife was sometimes punished by having a cacti thrust into her vagina. But when it comes to punishing adulterers and adulteresses, few can match the cruelty of the primitive Pathan people of eastern Afghanistan. For the straying male: after being staked out in the hot sun, the Pathans shoved hot peppers up the man's anus, and then pushed sharp knobby thorns into his penis. After he was suitably attired, he was repeatedly kicked in the balls until he died. For her part: the sexually adventuresome wife was tied to a stake, her legs spread wide apart around a quickly growing plant, which grew inside her vagina until it painfully killed her.

In early times, flogging was a common punishment for a variety of crimes, and was most often carried out using a "pizzle," a whip made of a bull's penis.

Political Déjà Vu?

During the great European Witch Hunt of the sixteenth and seventeenth centuries, it's been estimated that more than 200,000 innocent women were sadistically tortured and burned to death as witches. The accused were investigated by Church Courts or by roving Inquisitors charged with probing the specific accusations of spell-casting. Invariably, however, prosecutors zeroed in on a favorite topic: sex with the devil. A well-documented aspect of the era's witch mania was the obsessive curiosity on the part of the prosecutors to hear these witches reveal all aspects of their sexual relations with the devil, including detailed descriptions of the devil's legendary "endowment." Indeed, page after page of court testimony revolves around the Devil's penis, said to be an enormous organ. Many of these accounts are presented in Nicholas Rémy's book, *Demonolatry*, which is based on trial records of hundreds of executed women. According to one accused witch, the devil's penis "was as long and thick as an arm" with seminal fluid "as cold as ice," while another testified it was

> *so thick that I experienced considerable pain when he copulated with me, because the said membre was as hard as flint and extremely cold. As [he] was leaving me, he kissed me repeatedly and fondled my breasts.*

No word on whether said devil offered her a job to keep quiet.

Grrrl Power

Empress Wu Hu, who reigned during the great T'ang Dynasty (700–900 A.D.), believed that a woman fellating a man represented male supremacy over the female, an image which did not please the Royal Ruler. In an act designed to "humble" men, she required—by royal decree—that all male governmental officials and visiting dignitaries pay homage to Her Imperial Highness by performing cunnilingus upon her. The Empress would simply throw open her robe, and the man would kneel before her to kiss her royal genitalia.

Lips and Genitals and Lips *as* Genitals

Ancient Phoenician and Egyptian male prostitutes were the first to wear lipstick, which was used to advertise their specialized talents of fellatio and cunnilingus. A few thousand years later, *The Naked Ape* author Desmond Morris suggested that the female custom of wearing red lipstick is an unconscious desire to attract the opposite sex by mimicking the redness of the genital labia.

Although the island of Lesbos is traditionally associated with lesbianism, the ancient Greeks associated the notorious isle with another activity. The Greek verbs *lesbiazo* and *lesbizo* actually refer to a decidedly non-lesbian activity: fellatio.

Destined for the Hard Rock Cafe?

In Chicago, during the mid-1960s, a chubby teenaged rock 'n' roll groupie named Cynthia (known as Cynthia Plaster Caster) along with a crew of assistants made plaster molds—followed by true-to-life reproductions—of numerous rock stars' penises. Calling themselves the "Plaster Casters," the girls reportedly devised the scheme in order to make themselves special in the competitive groupie market. One of Cynthia's friends would perform fellatio (or, as they called it, "plating," which is Cockney slang for a blow job) prior to the casting to prepare the artist's penis for the process (although it was often difficult for the stars to sustain their erections in the wet plaster). Penises preserved in the collection include those of superstars Jimi Hendrix, Led Zeppelin, Noel Redding of the Lovin' Spoonful, and Clint Poppie of the Dead Kennedys.

Speaking of Plaster . . .

A strong belief in the mystical power of the male organ inspired the ancient Japanese to utilize a practice known as the *hiobbashira* or "man pillar" when constructing a new monument. This involved entombing a living man in a standing position, penis erect (for awhile, anyway) within the walls of the structure in order to fortify the building and drive away evil spirits.

Be Careful on
the Pommel Horse

Young men of ancient Greece had no immodesty about openly or publicly displaying their genitals. The word "gymnastics" comes from the Greek *gymnos,* meaning "naked." When exercising nude at the gymnasium, young Greek men would often tie the foreskin (the early Greeks had a horror of circumcision) over the glans of the penis with a ribbon to prevent injury. The resulting bundle was known in Greek as *kynodesme,* literally "dog tie," and was the ancient equivalent of the modern jockstrap.

In spite of their penchant for flaunting the male nude body, the Greeks did have their limits. As mentioned above, in early times, all Greek men were uncircumcised, and considered the flaccid penis inoffensive and natural. An erection in public, however, or even a peeling back of the foreskin to reveal the glans of the penis was a different story; a vulgar one, which constituted a crime of indecent exposure.

Is This Where the Term "Woody" Comes From?

Prior to constructing a new harpoon, a hunter of the Kiwai tribe in New Guinea will press his penis firmly into the trunk of the tree he has selected to make the weapon's shaft. The purpose? In wanting his new weapon to be straight, strong, and capable of deep penetration, he performs this ritual in an attempt to instill these qualities *into the tree*.

"Mentoring" Members

Trees weren't the only things thought to be capable of receiving character traits from the penis. In parts of Greece during the seventh century B.C., a grown man's valuable qualities were thought to be incorporated in his phallus (those being his noble virtues of strength, a sense of duty, eloquence, generosity, courage). In turn, noblemen of the times believed the phallus could effectively transfer their best qualities to young impressionable boys, and thus, sexual relations between the two were fairly common.

That's My Story and I'm Stickin' to It

In Andalusia, a rural community in southeastern Spain, masculine identity is firmly ensconced in the male genitals, within which, they devoutly believe, lies the locus of male power, emotions, will, and strength. Men in this community speak as if compelled to act according to the desires of the penis or testicles.

For example, if a man impulsively decides to miss a day's work, and is asked to justify it, he will likely say *"Porque me sale de los cojones,"* literally, "Because it comes to me from the balls." If a wife should ask her tardy husband why he did not come home earlier, his stock answer is *"Porque no me salio de la chorra,"* translation: "Because it didn't come out of my prick."

I swear to Tell the Truth, the Whole Truth, and Nothing but Truth, So Help My Penis

The penis, honorable organ that it was, played a central role in securing the truthfulness of one's word. For example, among the ancient Hebrews, men swore an oath while holding the penis of the man the oath was made to. Early Egyptians on the other hand, often swore an oath while holding *each others'* genitals. And Arabs living in nineteenth-century Sudan asked that their organs fall off if they should break their solemn oath.

Well *This* Explains Everything

Over the last several decades, various theories have been proffered to explain the evilness of Adolph Hitler. One of the more colorful was floated in a 1981 book published in Germany. The tome suggested (in all seriousness) that when Hitler was a youth, a billy goat took a bite from his penis, an event which triggered his deranged career.

Before the Lap Dance

Empress Theodora, prostitute turned royal wife of sixth-century Byzantine emperor Justinian I (527–565 B.C.) was reported to have enjoyed performing as a striptease dancer, and entertained thousands of spectators with a rather unusual (o.k. bizarre) antic that involved allowing geese to peck grain from her genitals.

Golly, Toto, I Guess We're
Not in Kansas Anymore

• When the husband of a Tasmanian woman dies, the law requires that she wear her dead husband's penis around her neck. The Aboriginal women of Gippsland, Australia are required to do the same.

• When males of the Aboriginal Walibri tribe of central Australia greet each other, they customarily grab penises (of the other) instead of shaking hands.

GENITAL FASHIONS

The African Hottentots prize the female who has large labia minora (inner lips). In order to achieve the desired status, beginning at an early age girls routinely stretch, pull, and massage these tissues. This genital fashion statement reportedly originated from girls who masturbated so often that their labia became extended. The Hottentot men, preferring a wife with a healthy sex drive, apparently chose these women first, and later discovered they also enjoyed the sensations provided by the labia engulfing their penis, a discovery which eventually resulted in men refusing to marry women with unstretched labia. Thus began the labia stretching competition. Today, there is a medical condition named for this phenomenon: the Hottentot apron (elongated labia minora).

The Ponapeans of the Eastern Caroline Islands also find the woman with an enlarged, pendulous labia and clitoris sexually attractive. Beginning in early childhood, and continuing through puberty, they employ elderly impotent men to beat, suck, and pull on the genitals to produce the desired results. The same kind of sucking and pulling activity may also be directed to the girl's clitoris, along with the application of large black ants, whose stinging bites result in a swelling of the genitals.

The ancient Chinese and Japanese had a different means to achieve aesthetically appealing genitalia which included, curiously enough, the "art" of foot-binding. This barbaric and tortuous practice, common for hundreds of years among both cultures, had a twofold purpose. Not only were bound feet seen as more attractive by presenting a petite appearance, they were also believed to enhance a woman's sexual desirability. How so? It was believed that footbinding also made the female's thighs and mons veneris smaller. And thus, claimed the men, the pubic area, including the outer vagina, was made smaller, and, more important, tighter (and more suitable and pleasing for sexual intercourse).

The native women of New Ireland lived a blissfully naked life until missionaries showed up on the island. Appalled at the exposed female body, the missionaries provided the island women with petticoats to cover their vaginas, a gift the women gleefully accepted. In making a resolute fashion statement, however, the women wore the petticoats on their heads.

Costume Party

Eighth-century Japanese aristocrats practiced the ancient art of *Tsutsumi,* or "packaging." This activity involved wrapping their sexual organs with silk and ribbons in complex and intricate designs, and then offering them as gifts to their lovers.

The erotically minded Japanese also practiced the art of wrapping the penis in paper "costumes" (usual disguises include geese, fish, squids, and dragons), which they referred to as *Kokigami.* In their book *Kokigami: The Intimate Art of the Little Paper Costume,* authors Heather Busch and Burton Silver offer the following dialogue and role-play for those utilizing the dragon *Kokigami*:

> *The crafty Dragon likes to breathe his fire into the dark jeweled cave. Ravaging, vengeful, sly . . .* "Where are my precious jewels? My treasures? My trophies? Are they hidden there in your dark cave?" *The reply:* "Come on hot stuff! Careful the iron gates don't snap shut and sever your burning tongue!" *. . . With arms outstretched and fingers curled like claws, move forward warily with the knees bent. The hips may be flicked about spasmodically, accompanied by the low seductive roar of a raging furnace.*

Disappearing Act

In many Oceanic and Asian cultures, some young men suffer from a psychological phenomenon known as "Koro" (also called *suk-yeong* among the Southern Chinese)—an irrational fear that their penis is shrinking and disappearing into the abdomen, and, when it shrinks all the way in, the man dies. The anxiety and fear becomes so intense in some patients that they are forced to hold on to their penises at all times, either with their hands or with instrumental aids such as rubber bands, strings, clamps, chopsticks, clothes pegs, etc. (which themselves sometimes cause severe injury to the penis).

Penis Voodoo

Belief in black magic and evil spells runs strong in west Africa, where many inhabitants believe that foreign sorcerers can cause a man's genitalia to shrink with a mere handshake. In the summer of 1998 alone, vigilante mobs in Senegal attacked and killed over a dozen victims by beating, stabbing, or burning them following the innocent contact of a hand-to-hand greeting. In each case, the instigator of such attacks claimed his penis was "disappearing."

DICKTIONARY

It Pays to Improve Your Genital Vocabulary

"VA-GI-NA (Va·ji·na),
n. 1. the box a penis comes in."

—GRAFFITI, UNIVERSITY BATHROOM WALL

WORD POWER:

The following terms* are used, albeit infrequently, by sexologists and other professionals to reference specific activities, preferences, and deviations related to genitalia—illustrating a world few are aware even exists.

   Acomoclitic—refers to those suffering from pubic hair phobia and thus preferring a sexual partner with a hairless vulva.
   Acucullophilic—refers to women or men who are only sexually aroused by circumcised males.

*Primary Source—Schmidt's *Cyclopedic Lexicon of Sex*

Amatripsis—masturbation technique that involves rubbing the labia together.

Amphimixis—refers to the direction of one's early energies and interests toward the sexual organs.

Atelophallia—a state of incomplete development of the penis, especially in terms of size.

Atelotremia—having an imperfectly developed vulva.

Autagonistophilia—a condition in which a person's sexual arousal and gratification (orgasm) requires the viewing of their sexual organs (and/or sexual acts) by other individuals. In other words, these are people who need people to look at them.

Anthropophagy—describes a form of cannibalism in which the practitioner derives sexual pleasure from eating the cooked genital parts of (usually) a member of the opposite sex.

Autocunnilingus—a woman who masturbates by sucking or tonguing her (own) vulval area.

Autofellatio—a man who masturbates by performing fellatio on himself.

Autopederasty—refers to a man inserting his penis into his own anus. While not physically possible for all men, those who can achieve it claim the practice can be highly pleasurable. The anus is lubricated, the testicles are pushed to one side and the semierect glans penis is pushed into the anus. Ejaculation is not considered possible due to the position and detumescence of the penis.

Autoscophilia—a condition in which a man's sexual arousal and orgasm is dependent upon looking at his own penis; or in the case of a woman, in looking at her own vulva.

Automonosexualism—is a syndrome in which a man is so self-centered and narcissistic he can achieve sexual satisfaction only through masturbation, or preferably—if he is limber enough—autofellatio.

Aulophobia—a morbid, obsessive fear of any musical instrument resembling the penis.

Baculophallia—technically, the condition of a rigid penis; however, the term is usually applied to an organ having a rather small diameter but remarkable rigidity.

Balanotage—refers to playful and erotic manipulations of the glans, or head of the penis.

Brachycolpia—having a short vagina or vaginal canal.

Brachyphallia—having a short penis.

Bugfucker—a man with a ridiculously small penis; hence a contemptible person.

Cacophallic—the unfortunate condition of having an inadequate penis, either one lacking in size or one unable to attain a suitable erect state.

Calliphallus—a term used to describe a handsome, elegant, or intriguing male sex organ.

Callitramata—refers to having a beautiful vulva, along with the possessors of such. Also may be called "callicunnate."

Cheilocunnidipity—refers to the act of visualizing the mouth or lips of a woman as the counterpart of the vulva.

Colobosis—refers to mutilation or castration of the penis as an act of jealous retaliation.

Colpalgia—feelings of discomfort or pain in the vagina, generally caused by too frequent intercourse or by excessive stretching due to intercourse with a large penis.

Colpophronate—an individual who thinks obsessively about the vagina and its pleasures.

Cunniknismos—the practice of tickling the vulva, using either the tongue or fingers.

Cunnilingus—the licking of the female genitalia. From *cunnus* (vulva) and *linguere* (to lick).

Cunnilalia—refers to those individuals who are sexually aroused by talking in a sexually explicit way about female genitals (whether in sexual stories, jokes, poems, or novels).

Cunniphrenia—a preoccupation with thoughts about oral activities involving the vulva.

Cunnotage—a playful and erotic rubbing of the female genitalia, generally during precoital sex play.

Dulcicunnia—having a sweet-smelling vulva or vagina.

Edeology—the study of genital organs. From *aidoia* (sex or genital organs).

Edeormia—arousal or stimulation of sexual desire at the mere sight of the sex organs.

Ederacinism—refers to the tearing out of one's sexual organs. This practice may be the result of sexual frenzy or from the desire to punish oneself for having erotic cravings.

Elytrostomia—refers to the nebulous belief that the size of a female's vagina can be estimated from the size of her mouth.

Eurotophobia—a morbid fear of the female sexual organs.

Formicophilia—a condition whereby a person's sexual arousal and gratification depends on the sensations produced by small creatures, ants (and other insects), snails or frogs, creeping, crawling, and nibbling the genitals.

Genitorture—sexual stimulation of male and/or female genitals by hitting, striking, squeezing, clamping, binding, etc.

Gymnophallus—a.k.a, the naked penis; more specifically, the word refers to a condomless sex organ.

Gynelophilous—refers to sexual arousal stemming primarily from one's lust for pubic hair, and/or their desire to collect pubic hair as a focus of erotic interest (especially of women). May also be called "pubephilia."

Gynelophism—a paraphilic act perpetrated by a sexual fetishist, in which the pubic tuft of the female is "scalped," or excised, often with the underlying tissue, as a trophy.

Harmataphobia—a paralyzing fear of sexual inadequacy, either in the size department, or in the performance department. Many experts contend that the proliferation of X-rated videos featuring well hung (very well hung) men with rock hard erections are at least partly to blame. Phobic fears develop when real men (and their real penises) watching these videos invariably compare themselves and come up "short."

Hypogenitalism—underdevelopment of the sexual organs.

Knismophallia—the practice of tickling the penis in order to obtain sexual gratification.

Kolpeuryntomania—a paraphilic activity in which the perpetrator derives sexual pleasure from the sadistic desire to stretch and mutilate the female sexual organs. Various assortments of artificial phalluses are generally used to accomplish the desired goal (such devices are referred to as "kolpeurynters").

Lecheur—a male who derives sexual pleasure from licking female genitalia.

Macrogenitosomia—the early development of genitalia in either boys or girls.

Medectasia—the bulge apparent in a man's pants from an erect penis.

Medocure—the cosmetic care of the male sex organ and surrounding genital area, (and) generally includes clipping and styling the hair, applying aromatic fragrances, creaming the skin, massaging, etc. One who practices the art of medocure is referred to as a "medocurix." In the *Cyclopedic Lexicon of Sex,* author J. E. Schmidt writes that the practice of medocures dates back to ancient times, when concubines and slave girls applied fragrant concoctions to the genitalia of their masters. Articles used by these women in performing their art—including genital aprons, brushes and oil dispensers—are on display in various European museums, including the British Museum.

Medothorpia—an aversion to or fear of the erect male penis.

Mentulate—having an unusually large penis.

Mentulhedonia—a sense of pride or supreme satisfaction in being a man . . . and having a penis.

Mentulamania—constant preoccupation with one's own penis, whether in thought or action (i.e. excessive masturbation).

Mentulaphrenia—preoccupation with thoughts of the male sex organ, usually by a female.

Microedea—a peculiar delusion in which the victim believes his sex organs are getting smaller.

Microgenitalia—term used to describe a female with exceptionally small genitalia.

Micropenis/Microphallus—term(s) used to describe a congenital condition in which the penis is exceptionally small . . . a stretched adult micropenis measures less than 2.68 inches.

Muliebraphphrenia—a condition characterized by constant preoccupation with thoughts and fantasies of the female sex organs.

Nasophilia—while the term nasophilia refers to sexual arousal from the sight, touch, act of licking, or sucking a partner's nose, people sometimes use nasolingus (licking or sucking the nose) as a substitute penis during intercourse, occasionally asking their partner to blow their nose in simulation of an ejaculation.

Osmolagnia—refers to sexual arousal caused by smells and odors emanating from the sexual areas of the body, (and) widely thought to be the primary motivating factor in the enjoyment of or preference for fellatio or cunnilingus.

Pedomentia—term for the omnipresent yet groundless belief that the size of a man's penis can be estimated from the size of his feet.

Penoclitoris—a medical term used to describe the sexually ambiguous phallus of a newborn.

Peodeiktophilia—used to describe paraphilic exhibitionism, in which a man's sexual arousal and attainment of orgasm depends on evoking surprise, dismay, shock, panic, or embarrassment from a stranger (usually a woman) by exhibiting his flaccid or erect penis. It is interesting to note that no similar term exists for the paraphilic act of a female's exposing her genitalia.

Phallophilia—sexual attraction that one has for an erect penis of either extraordinary dimensions or endurance.

Phallocrypsis—used to describe the retraction of the penis to the point where it is hardly visible.

Phallodynia—used by physicians to describe pain in the penis.

Phalloplasty—what doctors call plastic surgery to construct (or reconstruct) a penis. This procedure is done: (a) to remedy birth defects, (b) on men who have had an accident resulting in amputation of the penis, and (c) on people who feel they were born accidents (i.e., as part of a female-to-male sex change procedure).

Phallanastrophe—an abnormal condition in which the penis is permanently bent upward.

Phallesthesia—the feeling or illusion that one has a penis as experienced by (some) women. She may occasionally feel that her "missing" penis was in fact taken from her.

Phallocacosis—the belief held by a man that his sexual

organs are repulsive to a woman (a belief that often leads to impotence).

Phallohapsis—caressing or fondling, usually by a female, of the male genitalia.

Phallolalia—refers to sexual arousal which occurs as a result of explicit sexual *talk* (whether in jokes, stories, poems, or novels) involving the penis.

Phallomanic—a woman who is excessively fond of the penis.

Phallomeiosis—refers to irrational thoughts by a man that his penis is *too small* to effectively engage in sexual intercourse.

Phallomecism—having an unusually long penis.

Phallophobia—used to describe a morbid fear of the penis, especially when it is erect.

Phallopleiosis—a condition in which a man thinks his penis is *too large,* and therefore abstains from sexual intercourse fearing he will injure his partner.

Phallorhiknosis—refers to the dreaded penis shriveling that naturally occurs as a man ages.

Pudendacure—antiquated term referring to the cosmetic care of female genitalia. Usually involves washing and shaping pubic hair, cleansing and application of aromatic fragrance to the vulva, soothing creams, etc. While many women perform their own ritual, professionals may also be used. Contemporary care of the vulval area generally involves bikini waxing along with the application of soothing creams and aromatherapy.

Spanish Collar—a colloquial term for a foreskin that is so tight it irritates the penis, causing frequent erection and painful swelling.

Scoptolagnia—used to describe sexual arousal occurring simply from looking at the genitals of the opposite sex.

Spelacratia—an unusual and peculiar unwillingness of the male to insert his penis in the vagina, based on a primitive dislike of cracks, chinks, fissures, caverns, and the like.

Stigmatophilia—a condition in which a person's sexual arousal and orgasm is dependent on one's partner (or one's self) being tattooed, scarified, or pierced for jewelry in the genitals.

Teratophallia—used to describe either: (1) a marked deformity of the penis; or (2) a penis of monstrous size.

Turpicunnia—a condition whereby a woman has an unattractive Vulva.

Vaginoplasty—a medical term used to refer to the construction of an artificial vagina, done in the case of a female born without one, or for those undergoing male-to-female sex reassignment surgery.

Vulvolimia—an insatiable sexual craving for the female vulva, and subsequent contact with the area.

SOURCES

Addington, Deborah. *A Hand in the Bush*. San Francisco: Greenery Press, 1997.

Agonito, Rosemary. *History of Ideas on Woman*. New York: G.P. Putnam's Sons, 1977.

Allegro, John M. *The End of a Road*. New York: Dial Press, 1971.

———. *The Sacred Mushroom and the Cross*. New York: Doubleday, 1970.

Allende, Isabel. *Aphrodite: A Memoir of the Senses*. New York: HarperCollins, 1998.

Aman, Reinhold. "Terms of Abuse, Terms of Endearment, and Pet Names for Breasts and Other Naughty Body Parts." *Maledicta*, Vol. 10, (1988–1989), pp. 49–65.

———. "What Is This Thing Called, Love? More Genital Pet Names." *Maledicta*, Vol. 5, 1981, pp. 41–44.

———. *Talking Dirty: A Bawdy Compendium of Colorful Language, Humorous Insults and Wicked Jokes*. New York: Carroll & Graf, 1993.

Angier, Natalie. *Woman: An Intimate Geography.* New York: Houghton Mifflin, 1999.

Anonymous. *My Secret Life.* New York: Blue Moon Books, 1988.

Aristotle. *On the Parts of the Animals* (trans. by W. Ogle). London: Kegan Paul, Trench, Truenberg and Co., 1882.

Ayto, John. *Dictionary of Word Origins.* New York: Little, Brown, 1990.

Baldwin, Dorothy. *Understanding Female Sexual Health.* New York: Hippocrene Books, 1993.

———. *Understanding Male Sexual Health.* New York: Hippocrene Books, 1993.

Barbach, Lonnie. *For Yourself: The Fulfillment of Female Sexuality.* New York: Doubleday, 1975.

———. *50 Ways to Please Your Lover.* New York: Penguin, 1997.

Barker-Benefield, G. J. "A Historical Perspective on Women's Health Care—Female Circumcision." *Women and Health: Issues on Women's Health Care,* Vol. 1, No. 1, Jan/Feb 1976.

Beeman, William O. "What are you? Male, Merm, Herm, Ferm or Female?" *Baltimore Morning Sun,* March 17, 1996.

Betsky, Aaron. *Building Sex: Men, Women, Architecture and the Construction of Sexuality.* New York: William Morrow, 1995.

Bettelheim, Bruno. *Symbolic Wounds: Puberty Rites and the Envious Male.* Glencoe, Illinois: Free Press, 1954.

Bechtel, Stefan, and Laurence Roy Stains. *Sex: A Man's Guide.* Emmaus, PA: Rodale Press, 1996.

Berle, Milton, with Haskell Frankel. *Milton Berle: An Autobiography.* New York: Delacorte Press, 1974.

Bigelow, Jim. *The Joy of Uncircumcising!* Aptos, CA: Hourglass, 1998.

Bogaert, Anthony F., and Scott Hershberger. "The Relation Between Sexual Orientation and Penile Size." *Archives of Sexual Behavior.* June, 1999; 28(3): 213–21.

Boston Women's Health Book Collective. *The New Our Bodies, Our Selves.* New York: Simon & Schuster, 1992.

Botting, Kate and Douglas Botting. *Sex Appeal: The Art and Science of Sexual Attraction.* New York: St. Martin's Press, 1995.

Brame, Gloria, William D. Brame and Jon Jacobs. *Different Loving: The World of Sexual Dominance and Submission.* New York: Villard Books, 1993.

Brent, Harrison. *Pauline Bonaparte: A Woman of Affairs.* New York: Rinehart and Co., 1946.

Brown, Sanger, II. *Sex Worship and Symbolism.* Boston: Gorham Press, 1922.

Bryk, Felix. *Circumcision in Man and Woman: It's History, Psychology and Ethnology.* New York: American Ethnological Press, 1934.

Buck, Mitchell, trans. *The Priapeia: An Anthology of Poems on Priapus.* Privately printed: 1937.

Bullough, Vern L., and Bonnie Bullough. *Cross Dressing, Sex and Gender.* Philadelphia: University of Pennsylvania Press, 1993.

Bullough, Vern L. *Sexual Variance in Society and History.* New York: John Wiley & Sons, 1976.

Burton, Sir Richard, trans. *Book of the Thousand Nights and a Night.* New York: Heritage Press, 1934.

————. *The Hindu Art of Love (Ananga Ranga).* London: Castle Books, 1969.

Burton, Sir Richard and F. F. Arbuthnot, trans. *The Kama Sutra of Vatsyayana.* London: George Allen and Unwin, 1963.

Burton, Sir Richard, trans. *The Perfumed Garden of the Shaykh Nefzawi.* Cleveland: Classics Library, 1886.

Busch, Heather, and Burton Silver. *Kokigami: The Intimate Art of the Little Paper Costume.* Berkeley, CA: Ten Speed Press, 1990.

Busenbark, Ernest. *Symbols, Sex and the Stars.* Escondido: Book Tree, 1949.

Campbell, Joseph. *Masks of God: Creative Mythology.* New York: Viking, 1970.

Camphausen, Rufus C. *The Yoni: Sacred Symbol of Female Creative Power.* Rochester, VT: Inner Traditions International, 1996.

————. *The Encyclopedia of Erotic Wisdom.* Rochester: Inner Traditions International, 1991.

Casanova, Giacomo. *History of My Life,* trans. Willard R. Trask. Baltimore: Johns Hopkins University Press, 1997.

Chang, Stephen T. *The Tao of Sexology.* San Francisco: Tao Publishing, 1986.

Chichester, Brian and Kenton Robinson. *Sex Secrets: Ways to Satisfy Your Partner Every Time.* Emmaus, PA: Rodale Press, 1996.

Czaja, Michael. *Gods of Myth and Stone: Phallicism in Japanese Folk Religion.* New York; John Weatherhill, 1974.

Cooper, Wendy. *Hair: Sex, Society, Symbolism.* New York: Stein & Day, 1971.

Cornog, Martha. "Tom, Dick and Hairy: Notes on Genital Pet Names." *Maledicta,* Vol. 5 (1&2) 1981, pp. 31–40.

Crooks, Robert and Karla Baur. *Our Sexuality* (seventh ed.). Pacific Grove: Brooks/Cole, 1999.

Cutner, Herbert. *A Short History of Sex-Worship.* London: Watts, 1950.

Danielou, Alain, trans. *The Complete Kama Sutra.* Rochester: Park Street Press, 1994.

Danielou, Alain. *The Phallus: Sacred Symbol of Male Creative Power.* Rochester: Inner Traditions, 1993.

Daraul, Arkon. *A History of Secret Societies.* New York: Citadel Press, 1961.

Dening, Sarah. *The Mythology of Sex.* New York: Macmillan, 1996.

DeMoya, Armando, Dorothy DeMoya, Martha E. Lewis, and Howard R. Lewis. *Sex and Health: A Practical Guide to Sexual Medicine.* New York: Stein and Day, 1983.

Dorkenoo, Efua. *Cutting the Rose.* London: Minority Rights Publications, 1994.

Douglas, Nik and Penny Slinger. *Sexual Secrets.* Rochester: Destiny Books, 1979.

Dreifus, Claudia, ed. *Seizing Our Bodies: The Politics of Women's Health.* New York: Random House, 1977.

Dulaure, Jacques-Antoine. *The Gods of Generation: A History of Phallic Cults Among Ancients and Moderns.* New York: Panurge Press, 1934.

Dunas, Felice, with Philip Goldberg. *Passion Play.* New York: Riverhead Books, 1997.

Edwardes, Allen. *The Jewel in the Lotus.* New York: Julian Press, 1959.

Edwardes, Allen, and R.E.L. Masters. *The Cradle of Erotica.* New York: Julian Press, 1963.

Eilberg-Schwartz, Howard, and Wendy Doniger, eds. *Off With Her Head! The Denial of Women's Identity in Myth, Religion, and Culture.* Berkeley: University of California Press, 1995.

Elliot, Carl. "Why Can't We Go on as Three? Intersexuality as a Third Sex Category." *The Hastings Center Report.* Vol. 28, No. 3, May 15, 1998, p. 36.

Ellis, Albert, and Albert Abarbanel, eds. *The Encyclopedia of Sexual Behavior.* New York: Jason Aronson, 1973.

Ensler, Eve. *The Vagina Monologues.* New York: Villard Books, 1998.

Ehrenreich, Barbara, and Deidre English. *For Her Own Good.* New York: Anchor/Doubleday, 1978.

Fallopio, Gabriel. *Observationes Anatomicae.* Venice: M.A. Ulman, 1561.

Fausto-Sterling, Anne. *Sexing the Body: Gender Politics and the Construction of Sexuality.* New York: Basic Books, 2000.

Fisher, Helen. *The Sex Contract: The Evolution of Human Behavior.* New York: William Morrow, 1982.

———. *Anatomy of Love.* New York: Random House, 1992.

Fleiss, Paul. "The Case Against Circumcision." *Mothering: The Magazine of Natural Family Living,* Winter 1997.

Fleugal, J. C. *The Psychology of Clothes.* London: Hogarth Press, 1950.

Francoeur, Robert T., ed. *The Complete Dictionary of Sexology.* New York: Continuum Publishing, 1995.

Francoeur, Robert T. *Becoming a Sexual Person.* (second ed.) New York: Macmillan, 1991.

Freedman, Hy. *Sex Link.* New York: M. Evans and Company, 1977.

Freud, Sigmund. *New Introductory Lectures on Psychoanalysis,* trans. and ed. James Stanchey. New York: W.W. Norton, 1965.

———. "Fragment of an Analysis of a Case of Hysteria," trans. and ed. James Stanchey. *The Standard Edition for the Complete Psychological Works by Sigmund Freud,* Vol. VII. London: Hogarth Press, 1953.

————. *A General Introduction to Psychoanalysis.* New York: Boni and Liveright, 1920.

————. *The Future of an Illusion.* New York: Boni and Liveright, 1920.

Funk, Wilfred. *Word Origins and Their Romantic Stories.* New York: Bell Publishing Co., 1978.

Galen. *On the Usefulness of the Parts of the Body,* Vol. II. trans. Margaret Tallmadge May. Ithaca, New York: Cornell University Press, 1968.

Gilbert, Harriet, ed. *Fetishes, Florentine Girdles, and Other Explorations Into the Sexual Imagination.* New York: HarperCollins, 1993.

Goldberg, Ben Zion. *The Sacred Fire: The Story of Sex in Religion.* New York: University Books, 1958.

Gornick, Vivian, and Barbara K. Moran, eds. *Woman in Sexist Society.* New York: New American Library, 1972.

Grafenberg, Ernst. "The Role of the Urethra in Female Orgasm." *International Journal of Sexology.* 1950; 3:145–148.

Granzig, William. *Leather Language: A Clinician's Guide to S/M Terminology,* Clinical Monograph Number 2. New York: American Academy of Clinical Sexologists, 1994.

Graves, Robert. *The Greek Myths,* Vol. I. New York: Penguin Books, Inc., 1960.

Gregerson, Edgar. *Sexual Practices: The Story of Human Sexuality.* New York: FranklinWatts, 1983.

Griffin, Gary. *Penis Size and Enlargement: Facts, Fallacies, and Proven Methods.* Aptos, CA: Hourglass, 1995.

Gross, Samuel W. "On Sexual Debility and Impotence." *Medical and Surgical Reporter,* Philadelphia. May 5, 1877, p. 391.

Hartwich, Alexander, ed. *Aberrations of Sexual Life.* New York: Capricorn Books, 1960.

Hays, H. R. *In The Beginnings: Early Man and His Gods.* New York: G.P. Putnam's Sons, 1963.

Hendrickson, Robert. *The Facts on File Encyclopedia of Word and Phrase Origins.* New York: Facts on File Publications, 1987.

Herodotus, *The Histories*. trans. Henry Cary, New York: D. Appleton & Co. 1899.

Hinsie, Leland E. and Robert J. Campbell. *Psychiatric Dictionary,* fourth ed. New York: Oxford University Press, 1970.

Hosken, Fran. *The Hosken Report: Genital and Sexual Mutilation of Females.* Lexington: Women's International Network News, 1982.

Humana, Charles. *The Keeper of the Bed: A Study of the Eunuch.* London: Arlington Books, 1973.

Jenkins, Mark. "Separated at Birth." *Men's Health,* No. 6, Vol. 13, July 1998.

Joannides, Paul. *The Guide to Getting It On.* West Hollywood, CA: Goofy Foot Press, 1999.

Johnson, Sterling. *English as a Second F*cking Language.* New York: St. Martin's Press, 1995.

Jung, Carl G. *Man and His Symbols.* New York: Dell Publishing, 1964.

――――. *Memories, Dreams, Reflections.* ed. Aniela Jaffe and trans. Richard and Clara Winston. New York: Vintage Books, 1965.

Katchadourian, Herant A. *The Biological Aspects of Human Sexuality,* fourth ed. Fort Worth: Holt, Rinehart and Winston, 1990.

Kearns, Doris. *Lyndon Johnson and the American Dream.* New York: Harper and Row, 1976.

Kellogg, John Harvey. *Ladies Guide in Health and Disease.* Battle Creek, MI: Health Publishing Company, 1883.

Kern, Stephen. *Anatomy and Destiny.* Indianapolis: Bobbs-Merrill Company, 1975.

Keuls, Eva C. *The Reign of the Phallus: Sexual Politics in Ancient Athens.* New York: Harper and Row, 1978.

Kiefer, Otto. *Sexual Life in Ancient Rome.* London: Abbey Library, 1934.

Kinsey, A. C., W. B. Pomeroy, C. E. Martin, and P. H. Gebhard. *Sexual Behavior in the Human Female.* New York: Simon & Schuster, 1953.

Kinsey, A. C., W. B. Pomeroy, and C. E. Martin. *Sexual Behavior in the Human Male.* Philadelphia: W. B. Saunders Co., 1948.

Klein, Randy Sue. "Penile Augmentation Surgery," *Electronic J. of Human Sexuality.* Vol. 2, March, 1999, http://www.ejhs.org/volume2/consent1.htm.

Knight, Richard Payne and Thomas Wright. *Sexual Symbolism: A History of Phallic Worship.* New York: Julian Press, 1962.

Kolodney, Robert C., William H. Masters, and Virginia E. Johnson. *Textbook of Sexual Medicine.* Boston: Little Brown and Company, 1979.

Ladas, Alice Kahn, Beverly Whipple and John D. Perry. *The G Spot and Other Recent Discoveries About Human Sexuality.* New York: Holt, Rinehart and Winston, 1982.

Laqueur, Thomas. *Making Sex: Body and Gender from the Greeks to Freud.* Cambridge, Mass: Harvard University Press, 1990.

Laumann, E. O., C. M. Masi, and E. W. Zuckerman. "Circumcision in the United States: Prevalence, Prophylactic Effects and Sexual Practice." *JAMA.* 1997; 27:1052–1057.

Levy, Howard S. and Akira Ishihara. *The Tao of Sex.* Lower Lake, CA: Integral Publishing, 1968.,

Levins, Hoag. *American Sex Machines: The Hidden History of Sex at the U.S. Patent Office,* Holbrook, MA: Adams Media Corporation, 1996.

Lewinsohn, Richard. *A History of Sexual Customs,* trans. Alexander Mayce. New York: Harper & Brothers, 1958.

Licht, Hans (pseudonym of Paul Brandt). *Sexual Life in Ancient Greece.* London: Routledge & Keegan Paul, 1932.

Lightfoot-Klein, Hanny. *Prisoners of Ritual: An Odyssey into Female Genital Circumcision in Africa.* New York: Haworth Press, 1989.

Love, Brenda. *Encyclopedia of Unusual Sex Practices.* New Jersey: Barricade Books, 1992.

Lowry, Thomas Power, ed. *The Classic Clitoris.* Chicago: Nelson-Hall, 1978.

Marr, G. Simpson. *Sex in Religion.* London: George Allen & Unwin, 1936.

Masters, William H., and Virginia E. Johnson. *Human Sexual Response.* Boston: Little, Brown and Company, 1966.

Masters, William H., Virginia E. Johnson, and Robert C. Kolodny. *Sex and Human Loving.* Boston: Little, Brown and Company, 1988.

McCammon, Susan, David Knox and Caroline Schacht. *Choices in Sexuality.* Minneapolis/St. Paul: West Publishing Company, 1993.

Mills, Jane. *Womanwords: A Dictionary of Words about Women.* New York: Macmillan, 1989.

Milsten, Richard. *Male Sexual Function: Myth, Fantasy and Reality.* New York: Avon Books, 1979.

Mitchell, Deborah. *Nature's Aphrodisiacs.* New York: Dell Publishing, 1999.

Nemecek, Ottokar. *Virginity: Prenuptial Rites and Rituals.* New York: Philosophical Library, 1958.

Nevid, Jeffrey S., Lois Fichner-Rathus, and Spencer A. Rathus. *Human Sexuality in a World of Diversity,* second ed. Boston: Allyn and Bacon, 1995.

Nickell, Nancy L. *Nature's Aphrodisiacs.* Freedom, CA: Crossing Press, 1999.

O'Connell, Helen E., et al. "Anatomical Relationship Between the Urethra and Clitoris." *Journal of Urology.* 1998;159:1892–1899.

Paola, Angelo S. *Under the Fig Leaf.* Los Angeles: Health Information Press, 1999.

Panati, Charles. *Extraordinary Endings of Practically Everything and Everybody.* New York: Harper & Row, 1989.

———. *Sexy Origins and Intimate Things.* New York: Penguin Books, 1998.

Parsons, Alexandra. *Facts and Phalluses: A Collection of Bizarre and Intriguing Truths, Legends, and Measurements.* New York: St. Martin's Press, 1989.

Platina, Bartolomeo. *The Lives of the Popes* [vol. 1] *from the life of our Savior to the accession of Gregory VII* [in 1073]. Edited by W. Benham. London: Griffith, Farran, 1888.

Ploss, Herman Heinreich, Max Bartels and Paul Bartels. *Femina Libido Sexualis.* New York: Medical Press, 1965.

Purvis, Kenneth. *The Male Sexual Machine.* New York: St. Martin's Press, 1992.

Ramsdale, David and Ellen Ramsdale. *Sexual Energy Ecstasy: A Practical Guide to Lovemaking Secrets of the East and West.* New York: Bantam Books, 1993.

Rancier, Lance. *The Sex Chronicles: Strange But True Tales From Around the World.* Los Angeles: General Publishing Group, 1997.

Rasputin, Maria and Patte Barham. *Rasputin: The Man Behind the Myth.* New Jersey: Prentice Hall, 1977.

Rawson, Hugh. *Wicked Words.* New York: Crown, 1989.

Reinisch, June, with Ruth Beasley. *The Kinsey Institute's New Report on Sex.* New York: St. Martin's Press, 1990.

Rémy, Nicholas. *Demonolatry.* (trans. by E. A. Ashwin). London: John Rodker, 1930.

Renshaw, Domeena. *Seven Weeks to Better Sex.* New York: Random House, 1995.

Reuben, David. *Everything You Always Wanted to Know About Sex.* New York: David McKay Company, 1969.

Richards, Brian. *The Penis.* New York: Valentine Press, 1977.

Rocco, Sha (pseudonym of Abisha S. Hudson). *The Masculine Cross and Ancient Sex Worship.* New York: Commonwealth Co., 1904.

Rodgers, Bruce. *The Queens' Vernacular: A Gay Lexicon.* San Francisco: Straight Arrow Books, 1972.

Rosen, Barbara. *Witchcraft.* New York: Taplinger Publishing Co., 1972.

Rossi, William A. *The Sex Life of the Foot and Shoe.* New York; E.P. Dutton & Co., 1976.

Ruan, Fang Fu. *Sex in China: Studies in Sexology in Chinese Culture.* New York: Plenum Press, 1991.

Rubin, Jerry and Mimi Leonard. *The War Between the Sheets.* New York: Richard Marek Publishers, 1980.

Rutledge, Leigh W. *The New Gay Book of Lists.* Los Angeles: Alyson Publications, 1996.

Ryan, George. *Reclaiming Male Sexuality.* New York: M. Evans and Company, Inc., 1997.

Sachs, Curt. *The History of Musical Instruments.* New York: W.W. Norton & Company, Inc., 1940.

Schiebinger, Londa. *Nature's Body: Gender in the Making of Modern Science.* Boston: Beacon Press, 1993.

Schmidt, J. E., *Cyclopedic Lexicon of Sex: Exotic Practices, Expressions, Variations of the Libido.* New York: Brussel & Brussel, Inc., 1967.

Schwartz, Kit. *The Male Member.* New York: St. Martin's Press, 1985.

———. *The Female Member.* New York: St. Martin's Press, 1988.

Scott, George Ryley. *Phallic Worship: A History of Sex and Sexual Rites.* London: Luxor Press, 1966.

Sevely, Josephine Lowndes. *Eve's Secrets: A New Theory of Female Sexuality.* New York: Random House, 1987.

Sheidlower, Jesse, ed. *The F Word.* New York: Random House, 1995.

Sherfey, Mary Jane. *The Nature and Evolution of Female Sexuality.* New York: Random House, 1972.

Simons, G. L. *The Book of Sexual Records.* London: Virgin Publishing, 1998.

———. *The Illustrated Book of Sexual Records.* New York: Delilah Communications, 1982.

———. *Sex and Superstition.* New York: Harper & Row, 1973.

Smith, Homer. *Man and His Gods.* Boston: Little, Brown and Co., 1952.

Spears, Richard A. *Slang and Euphemism.* New York: Penguin Books (Second Edition) 1991.

Spignesi, Stephen. *The Odd Index.* New York: Penguin Books, 1994.

Stein, Gertrude. *Tender Buttons.* New York: Claire Marie, 1914.

Stewart, F., Guest, F., Stewart, G., Hatcher, R. *My Body, My Health.* New York: John Wiley & Sons, 1981.

Strage, Mark. *The Durable Fig Leaf.* New York: Dorset Press, 1993.

Taylor, G. Rattay. *Sex in History.* New York: Vanguard Press, 1954.

Taylor, John. "The Long, Hard Days of Dr. Dick. (Penis Enlargement Specialist Dr. Melvyn Rosenstein and Other Physicians Who Perform Male Cosmetic Surgery)." *Esquire,* Vol. 24, September, 1995.

Taylor, J. R., A. P. Lockwood, and A. J. Taylor. "The prepuce: Specialized Mucosa of the Penis and Its Loss to Circumcision." *Br J Urol;* 1996; 77:291–275.

Tannahill, Reay. *Sex in History.* New York: Stein and Day, 1980.

Tavris, Carol, and Carol Offir. *The Longest War: Sex Differences in Perspective.* New York: Harcourt Brace Jovanovich, Inc. 1977.

Thomas, Julian, "The Mystery of the Missing Penis." *New Scientist,* March, 1997.

Thorn, Mark. *Taboo No More: The Phallus in Fact, Fiction and Fantasy.* New York: Shapolsky Publishers, 1990.

Tranquillus, Suetonius. *The Twelve Caesars* (trans. by Robert Graves). London: Penguin, 1957.

Twain, Mark. *The Mammoth Cod, and Address to the Stomach Club.* Milwaukee: Maledicta Press, 1976.

Vale, V. and Andrea Juno, eds. *Modern Primitives.* San Francisco: Re/Search, 1989.

Valensin, Georges. *The French Art of Sex Manners.* London: NEL, 1970.

Van de Velde, Theodore H. *Ideal marriage: Its Physiology and Technique,* trans. Stella Browne. New York: Random House, 1966.

Van Gulik, Robert H. *Sexual Life in Ancient China.* Leiden, the Netherlands: E. J. Brill, 1961.

Vanggaard, Thorkil. *Phallos: A Symbol and Its History in the Male World.* New York: International Universities Press, Inc., 1972.

Vardy, Peter. *The Puzzle of Sex.* Armonk, New York: M. E. Sharpe, 1997.

Venette, Nicholas. *The Mysteries of Conjugal Love reveal'd.* (The Eighth French Edition, done into English by a Gentleman). Paris: Charles Carrington, 1906.

Verrier, Elwin. "The Vagina Dentata Legend." *British Journal of Medical Psychology,* 1941, Vol. 19.

Vinci da, Leonardo. *The Notebooks of Leonardo da Vinci,* ed. Edward MacCurdy. New York: Reynal & Hitchcock, 1939.

Walker, Barbara, G. *The Woman's Encyclopedia of Myths and Secrets.* New York: HarperCollins, 1983.

————. *The Woman's Dictionary of Symbols and Sacred Objects.* New York: HarperCollins, 1988.

Walker, Benjamin. *The Hindu World.* New York: Praeger Publishers, 1968.

Wallace, I., A. Wallace, D. Wallechinsky, and S. Wallace. *The Intimate Sex Lives of Famous People.* New York: Delacorte Press, 1981.

Wallace, Robert A. *How They Do It.* New York: William Morrow, 1980.

Wallerstein, Edward. *Circumcision: An American Health Fallacy.* New York: Springer, 1980.

Welch, Leslee. *The Complete Book of Sexual Trivia.* New York: Carol Publishing Group, 1992.

Westropp, Hodder M. and C. Staniland Wake. *Ancient Symbol Worship: Influence of the Phallic Idea in the Religions of Antiquity.* New York: Humanities Press, 1972.

Wilcox, R. Turner. *The Mode in Footwear.* New York: Charles Scribner's Sons, 1948.

Winks, Cathy. *The Good Vibrations Guide: The G-Spot.* San Francisco: Down There Press, 1998.

X, Dr. Jacobus (pseudonym of Louis Jacolliot). *Wanderings in Untrodden Fields of Anthropology.* Paris: 1898.

Zacks, Richard. *An Underground Education.* New York: Doubleday, 1997.

———. *History Laid Bare: Love, Sex and Perversity from the Ancient Etruscans to Warren G. Harding.* New York: HarperCollins, 1994.

Zilbergeld, Bernie. *Male Sexuality.* Boston: Little, Brown and Company, 1978.